THE PHONETICS OF ENGLISH

THE PHONETICS OF ENGLISH

BY

IDA C. WARD, D.Lit.

Late Professor of West African Languages
School of Oriental and African Studies
University of London

WITH A FOREWORD BY

A. C. GIMSON

Professor of Phonetics
University College London

FIFTH EDITION

/ard, The Phonetics of English

Now published by Cambridge University Press
he Pitt Building, Trumpington Street, Cambridge CB2 1RP
entley House, 200 Euston Road, London NW1 2DB
2 East 57th Street, New York, NY 10022, USA
96 Beaconsfield Parade, Middle Park, Melbourne 3206,
                                        Australia

5BN 0 521 21096 8

Published by

W. HEFFER AND SONS LTD

20 Trinity Street, Cambridge, England

ISBN 0 85270 072 5

First published 1929
Second edition 1931
Third edition (entirely revised with additional chapter) 1939
Fourth edition 1945
Reprinted with minor corrections 1948
Reprinted 1950, 1952, 1956, 1958, 1960, 1962, 1968
Fifth edition 1972

Printed in Great Britain by W. Heffer and Sons Ltd Cambridge

FOREWORD

SINCE the sixteenth century the pronunciation of English has been described in hundreds of books, most of which displayed until the last century strongly prescriptive and normative attitudes. In the last hundred years, during which time description began to aim at a greater degree of scientific objectivity, two names have dominated the scene of phonetic analysis applied to English—those of Henry Sweet and Daniel Jones. It was Daniel Jones who founded the Department of Phonetics at University College London in 1907 and appointed Ida Ward to his staff in 1919, after she had had some years of experience in school teaching. It proved to be a most fruitful appointment, both because of her powers of shrewd and detached observation and because of her practical knowledge of what was relevant in language teaching. Later she was to carry out pioneer work in the linguistic analysis of African languages, notably Efik, Ibo, Twi and Yoruba, and at the time of her death in 1949 she was Professor of West African Languages at the London School of Oriental and African Studies.

But, despite her high reputation as an Africanist, many English and foreign students of English have reason to be grateful for her work on her mother tongue, both in her writing and her teaching. Although Daniel Jones's influence is apparent in everything she wrote on English, she was not overshadowed by his international eminence. The *Handbook of English Intonation*, written with L. E. Armstrong and first published in 1926, proved to be a most successful practical guide for foreign learners of English which is still used with profit today. The present

Phonetics of English, first published in 1929, appeared in revised forms up to the time of her death. It, too, continues to be used widely in this country and abroad.

It is natural that the publishers should feel that, more than forty years after the first publication and twenty-two years after Professor Ward's death, there may be a case for a complete revision of the book. Many works on English pronunciation have been written since the war; phonetic and phonological theory has evolved; the relationship of society and pronunciation is different from what it was forty years ago; the very concept of Received Pronunciation is in question; the BBC no longer has an Advisory Committee on Pronunciation, and indeed no longer sets out to provide a model of pronunciation; there is now a more realistic approach to the teaching of spoken English in our schools. Most books on English pronunciation written between the two wars date so seriously in the attitudes they adopt and in the information they impart that there can be no question of prolonging their life. But Ward's *Phonetics of English* is still in demand because her approach remains remarkably pertinent to the present situation. It is interesting to note that many of her observations concerning new developments in pronunciation have been borne out by present-day common usage; the advice which she gives to those concerned with language teaching remains as valid today as it was forty years ago.

It seems important, therefore, that this book should continue to appear largely in its original form, since it contains information both of historical interest and of contemporary relevance. (The speeches of King George V and President Roosevelt, for instance, may not be typical of present-day British or American usage, but the phonetic transcriptions made of them by Professor Ward are full of interest for any student of English.) Again, until we have available a comprehensive survey of the pronunciation of contemporary English dialects, Ward's observations on these matters remain as true and valuable as they ever were. Finally, not the least of the virtues of this book is the simplicity of its style, which renders it accessible to any kind of reader, at a time when so much current linguistic writing is abstruse and esoteric. Thus, the changes made by Mr. K. Laycock in this new reprint are of a minor kind, e.g. the adjustment of the references to the now defunct BBC Advisory Committee on Pronunciation and to what used to be known as 'Training Colleges'. The Bibliography has also been brought up to date, so many of the titles mentioned by Miss Ward no longer being easily available. The reader who consults the more recent books now included will find much new material in a different theoretical framework but also much that is merely a re-statement of evidence given in this book or a development of ideas already outlined or implicit here.

UNIVERSITY COLLEGE LONDON   A. C. GIMSON

May, 1971

PREFACE

THE aim of this book is to present the main facts of English pronunciation of to-day. The writer has had in mind the teacher who is expected to deal with indistinct or dialectal speech, and for this reason, she has made the book as practical as possible. It is hoped that the teacher or student may make his own observations on local and individual usages and develop for himself the hints given on correction. These suggestions are based on many years of practical experience in lecturing to teachers and teaching in school.

If dialectal speech is illustrated from Yorkshire and Cockney more than from other dialects, the writer's excuse is that she knows these dialects much better than any others; moreover, many of the peculiarities of Cockney speech which are discussed, can stand for those of other Southern dialects, and those of Yorkshire for many Northern dialects.

The writer wishes to acknowledge her indebtedness to Mr. A. K. Maxwell for the drawings of the open mouth and the vocal chords, and to Mr. T. L. Poulton for the remaining diagrams of tongue positions.

UNIVERSITY COLLEGE
LONDON

September, 1928

PREFACE TO SECOND EDITION

A FEW pages of phonetic transcription have been added to this edition. Since Cockney and Yorkshire have been used considerably as examples of dialect speech, extracts have been chosen which illustrate these two dialects.

I am very much indebted to Mr. Bernard Shaw for his permission to use a passage from *Pygmalion*, and to Mr. J. B. Priestley for allowing me to take an extract from *The Good Companions* for this purpose.

I. C. W.

PREFACE TO THIRD EDITION

THE book has been entirely revised and additional chapters have been added on Broadcasting and Spoken English, on British and American English and on Recent Developments in English Pronunciation. Two new phonetic texts are also included, one of the Christmas message to the Empire of His late Majesty, King George V, in 1935, which has been transcribed from a gramophone record made by H.M.V. Gramophone Co., and the other of President Roosevelt's broadcast speech on the occasion of the special convocation of Congress on October 13th, 1937, which has been transcribed from a recording made by the B.B.C.

I have to acknowledge with gratitude the gracious permission accorded by His Majesty the King to make use of the record of King George V's 1935 Christmas Broadcast, and to H.M.V. Gramophone Company for their consent.

I. C. W.

December, 1938

PREFACE TO FOURTH EDITION

THIS edition comes out in war-time. Corrections and slight additions only have been made, many of these in response to friendly suggestions and questions from readers of the book.

October, 1944

PUBLISHER'S NOTE TO
FIFTH EDITION 1972
Some minor notes called for
by the changes of time have been
inserted in square brackets [   ].

CONTENTS

FOREWORD - - - - - - - *page* v

PREFACE - - - - - - - - viii

PREFACE TO SECOND EDITION - - - - ix

PREFACE TO THIRD EDITION - - - - ix

PREFACE TO FOURTH EDITION - - - - x

ILLUSTRATIONS - - - - - - xiii

LIST OF SYMBOLS - - - - - - xv

I STANDARD PRONUNCIATION - - 1

II BROADCASTING AND SPOKEN ENGLISH - 11

III CORRECTION OF PRONUNCIATION - 23

IV QUALIFICATIONS OF THE TEACHER - 28

V PHONETIC TRANSCRIPTION - - - 32

VI USE OF PHONETICS IN THE TEACHING OF ENGLISH - - - - - 36

VII SPELLING PRONUNCIATIONS - - 38

VIII ORGANS OF SPEECH - - - - 48

IX VOWELS AND CONSONANTS: CLASSIFICATION OF VOWELS - - - 65

X PHONEMES - - - - - 74

XI ENGLISH VOWELS IN DETAIL - - 79

XII ENGLISH DIPHTHONGS - - - 111

XIII NASALISATION OF VOWELS - - 125

XIV CLASSIFICATION OF CONSONANTS: ENGLISH
CONSONANTS IN DETAIL - - 127

XV SOUND ATTRIBUTES: LENGTH, STRESS,
INTONATION - - - - 156

XVI SOUNDS IN CONNECTED SPEECH - - 180

XVII RECENT DEVELOPMENTS IN ENGLISH
PRONUNCIATION - - - - 199

XVIII BRITISH ENGLISH AND AMERICAN
ENGLISH - - - - - 206

XIX PHONETIC TRANSCRIPTIONS - - 220

APPENDIX I SUGGESTED COURSE FOR COLLEGES
OF EDUCATION - - - 241

" II EXERCISES IN EAR TRAINING - 243

BIBLIOGRAPHY - - - - - - - 246

INDEX - - - - - - - - 249

PHONETIC INDEX - - - - - - 254

ILLUSTRATIONS

FIG.		CHAP.	PAGE
1	Variant Pronunciations - - -	I	5
2	Organs of Speech - - - -	VIII	49
3	Open Mouth - - - - -	,,	51
4	Vocal Cords in Four Positions - -	,,	52
5	Soft Palate Raised and Lowered -	,,	57
6	Open Mouth with Palate Raised -	,,	58
7	Photograph of Tongue Spreading and Contraction - - - -	,,	60
8	Tongue Positions of Cardinal Vowels i, a, ɑ, u - - -	IX ,,	69
9	Tongue Positions of the Eight Primary Cardinal Vowels - - -	,,	70
10	Cardinal Vowel Diagram - - -	,,	70, 71
11	Photographs of Lip Positions -	,,	72
12	Illustrating Principles of Correction -	XI	80
13	English Vowels - - - -	,,	81
14	Varieties of i Vowel - - -	,,	82
15	,, ,, ɪ ,, - - -	,,	86
16	,, ,, ɛ ,, - - -	,,	88
17	,, ,, æ ,, - - -	,,	90
18	The u Phoneme - - - -	,,	100
19	Varieties of u Vowel - - -	,,	101
20	,, ,, ʌ ,, - - -	,,	104
21	Semi-weak Vowels - - -	,,	109

FIG.		CHAP.	PAGE.
22	English Diphthongs (*a*) - -	XII	112
23	,, ,, (*b*) - -	,,	112
24	Varieties of **ei** Diphthong - -	,,	113
25	,, ,, **ou** ,, - -	,,	115
26	,, ,, **ai** ,. · -	,,	117
27	,, ,, **au** ,, - -	,,	118
28	Triphthongs - - - - -	,,	123
29	English Plosive Consonants - -	XIV	130
30	Illustrating Nasal Plosion - -	,,	132
31	Illustrating the Starting Position for tθ, ts, tʃ, tᶇ - - - -	,,	137
32	Nasal Consonants - - - -	,,	139
33	Primary Articulation of *l* - -	,,	140
34	Clear and Dark *l* - - - -	,,	141
35	Over-dark *l* - - - - -	,,	143
36	Rolled *r* - - - - -	,,	144
37	Fricative *r* - - - - -	,,	145
38	Inverted *r* - - - - -	,,	145
39	Uvular Rolled *r* - - - -	,,	146
40	English Fricative Consonants - -	,,	148
41	Semi-Vowels - - - - -	,,	151
42	Illustrating Assimilation - -	XVI	191
43	American *versus* British Vowels -	XVIII	209

LIST OF SYMBOLS

THE alphabet used is that of the International Phonetic Association in its " narrow " form. For the benefit of those students who are used to the " broad " form, the differences between the two are here set out.

Narrow.	*Broad.*
i	iː
ɪ	i
u	uː
ʊ	u
ɑ	ɑː
ɔ	ɔː
ɒ	ɔ
ɜ	əː

ː placed after a vowel indicates full length.

ˑ ,, ,, ,, ,, ,, half ,,

◌ placed underneath a symbol indicates that the sound is syllabic: e.g. pɑ·sn̩ɪdʒ—three syllables (parsonage).

ˈ placed before a symbol shows that the syllable is stressed: e.g. təˈmɒroʊ.

Secondary stress is marked thus ˌ, e.g. pɪˌkjulɪˈærɪtɪ (*peculiarity*).

◌ placed underneath or over a symbol indicates that the sound is pronounced without voice: e.g. n̥, ŋ̊.

English Vowels.			*English Diphthongs.*		
i	as in	*see*	eɪ	as in	*play*
ɪ	,, ,,	*sit*	oʊ	,, ,,	*go*
ɛ	,, ,,	*set*	aɪ	,, ,,	*my*
æ	,, ,,	*sat*	aʊ	,, ,,	*now*
ɑ	,, ,,	*calm*	ɔɪ	,, ,,	*boy*

xvi LIST OF SYMBOLS

English Vowels.

ɒ	as in	*not*
ɔ	,, ,,	*bought*
ʊ	,, ,,	*put*
u	,, ,,	*soon*
ʌ	,, ,,	*but*
ɜ	,, ,,	*bird*
ə	,, ,,	*about*

English Diphthongs.

ɪə	as in	*here*
ɛə	,, ,,	*there*
ɔə	,, ,,	*more*
əʊ	,, ,,	*poor*

English Consonants.

p	as in	*put*
b	,, ,,	*but*
t	,, ,,	*ten*
d	,, ,,	*den*
k	,, ,,	*come*
g	,, ,,	*go*
tʃ	,, ,,	*church*
dʒ	,, ,,	*judge*
m	,, ,,	*make*
n	,, ,,	*not*
ŋ	,, ,,	*long*
l	,, ,,	*like*
ɫ	,, ,,	*well*

f	as in	*full*
v	,, ,,	*very*
θ	,, ,,	*thin*
ð	,, ,,	*then*
s	,, ,,	*some*
z	,, ,,	*zeal*
ʃ	,, ,,	*ship*
ʒ	,, ,,	*pleasure*
r (or ɹ)	,,	*run*
h	,, ,,	*hat*
w	,, ,,	*went*
ʍ	,, ,,	*white*
j	,, ,,	*yet*

OTHER SYMBOLS

Vowels.

ʏ Front close rounded vowel, similar to the French vowel in *rue* (see § 83).

ø Half-close front rounded vowel, similar to the French vowel in *peu* (see § 83).

œ Half-open front rounded vowel, similar to the French vowel in *sœur* (see § 83).

ɯ Close back unrounded vowel (see § 361 (v)).

ɤ Half-close   back   unrounded   vowel   (see   §§ 167,
        175 c).

ï Centralised **i** (see § 171).

ü   ,,   **u** ,,   § 171, 172).

ë   ,,   **e** ,,   § 200).

ö   ,,   **o** ,,   § 200).

        The symbols **i, e, ɛ, a, ɑ, ɔ, o, u** are used to denote
        the eight primary cardinal vowels (see § 99).

Consonants.

ɸ Bi-labial fricative, voiceless (see § 84 c).

β   ,,   ,,   voiced   ,,   § 84 c).

ɹ Fricative *r* (see § 271 iii).

ɾ One-tap *r* (see § 271 ii).

ʀ Uvular rolled *r* (see § 271 v).

ʁ   ,,   fricative *r* (see § 271 v).

ç Palatal fricative, voiceless (see §§ 282 c, 334).

x Velar fricative, voiceless (see § 242).

l̥ Voiceless l (see §§ 77 d, 266 c, 334).

m̥, n̥, ŋ̊ Voiceless **m, n, ŋ** respectively (see §§ 77 d, **334**).

ɱ Labio-dental nasal (see § 353).

ɦ Voiced h (see § 278 vi).

ʔ Glottal stop (see §§ 75 d, 250 e, 250 (e) (f), 251).

Note to reprint of the Fourth Edition.

   A simplified phonetic transcription is used in N. C. Scott's
"English Conversations" and Peter MacCarthy's "English
Pronunciation". The difference between this and the broad
transcription is that

a	is used instead of	æ		eə	is used instead of	ɛə
aː	,,	,,	ɑː	oə	,,	,,	ɔə
o	,,	,,	ɔ	oi	,,	,,	ɔi
oː	,,	,,	ɔː			

(See example on p. 35.)

CHAPTER 1
STANDARD PRONUNCIATION

1. It is necessary at the outset of a book such as this to discuss the vexed question of " standard pronunciation," since teachers are being told—in the daily press and elsewhere—that the English language is degenerating into mere unintelligible jargon, and that it is their responsibility to preserve a standard, and turn out their pupils able to express themselves in correct and vigorous English, spoken in a clear and pleasing manner.

2. What *is* Standard Pronunciation? No one can adequately define it, because such a thing does not exist; yet every one knows what is meant when one speaks of Standard English, and the Committee on the Teaching of English in England, without entering into the question in any detail, describes it as one free from vulgarisms and provincialisms.[1] The term " Standard English " implies one type of speech which is used by the educated population of the country, and which has received the approval of some authoritative body. But an examination of facts proves that no two people, even of the same district and upbringing, speak exactly alike. Different generations have not the same habits in speech sounds or in vocabulary. Nor is there at present any body of experts which has the authority to state what standard pronunciation is and to insist on its introduction into the schools.

3. There are many divergencies in the speech of educated people of different districts. The educated Northerner may use the sound a or æ in words like *dance, grass*, etc., where a Southerner would use ɑ; an

[1] See *Report on the Teaching of English in England*, 1921, p. 66.

educated Westerner may pronounce what is called a
retroflex " *r* " in words like *farm*, *port* (faɹm, pɔɹt), where
other people would use no *r* at all; not all educated
Londoners use the same diphthong in words like *go* and
cold; and the speech of educated Australians, Canadians,
South Africans, and Americans differs in many respects
from that of Englishmen. It may be argued, however,
that although these divergencies among educated
people exist, they are comparatively small, and can be
ignored. This is, to a certain extent, true; but before
any pronouncement is made on the subject, the state
of English pronunciation at the present day should be
thoroughly examined and understood, and all the
arguments for and against the establishment of a standard
speech in the country, and for the teaching of such a
pronunciation in the schools, should be plainly stated.

4. The type of speech used by an individual depends
chiefly on the region in which he is brought up and the
social class to which he belongs. These two factors
give rise to what may be called Local and Class Dialects,
dialects which have a long and interesting history. Is
there any argument to be used for the replacing of these
dialects by a standard pronunciation (which means, in
time, abolishing the dialects), or, while not discouraging
the use of the dialect, for advocating the acquirement
of a standard pronunciation as an auxiliary language?

5. The student should, first of all, disabuse his
mind of the idea, which is very common, that one
dialect—class or local—is intrinsically better, or more
beautiful, or more " historically correct " than another.
All the dialects are developments of English in different
directions, or at different rates and from different

starting points. Cockney is one form of English, as Yorkshire and Devonshire are other forms. One may have more sonorous sounds, a more varied intonation than another, and in this way, may strike the ear as more musical. But the general principle upon which people unconsciously judge a pronunciation is that of the associations which it calls up. If we are accustomed to hearing one type of pronunciation used by people of vulgar and uncouth habits, with harsh and discordant voices, we consider that dialect ugly. One often hears it said that the Cockney pronunciation of the word *paint* (paɪnt) is ugly because aɪ is an ugly diphthong; whereas the same diphthong is used in *pint* (paɪnt) by non-Cockney speakers, and is considered beautiful. In the same way a Northerner's pronunciation of *but* as bʊt is called " broad," while there is no question of criticising the same vowel in *put* (pʊt). Moreover the dialect of a distant part of the country may be thought " quaint " and romantic, while that nearest is looked on as a debased form of English. Country dialects are said to be good and pure, while town dialects are considered bad and slipshod English. Again, these judgments depend largely on association: the simpler country life appeals to the aesthetic sense, and the country speech is included in this appeal; while the speech of the town receives part of the condemnation which is directed against the rush and bustle of a more complex life. There is, however, one reason which has some justification behind it for considering town dialects bad and country dialects good. Owing to the influx into the towns of people from different parts of the country, the original local dialect has come under many and varying influences, and is, in consequence, not so pure as the country dialect. The kind of person, too, who uses a dialect is likely to influence our judgment of his speech; if he is slipshod in appearance and impolite in manners, we are inclined to think his speech is bad.   In so far as any speech is the result of continued lazy habits of articulation, it is to be deplored and condemned.   A slovenly pronunciation, however, which is lacking in precision and difficult to understand, is not confined to any one part of the country, nor to one class of people, but may be heard often enough from lecturers and preachers, as well as from loungers at the street corners of any town or of any country village. There is, indeed, a refinement of voice and manner and a precision of speech associated with good breeding, and often accompanying a " standard " pronunciation, which, of course, should be encouraged, since speech is a form of social behaviour, and like other kinds of social behaviour, e.g. table manners, dress, general behaviour in public places, it has its rules and customs.   The lack of this is often put down to " accent," under which general term all the factors which go to make up speech are judged.   In this book, however, we are concerned mainly with actual speech sounds and their use, and not with voice production or manners, but it should be remembered that pronunciation alone is not enough; idiom, usage and the social behaviour accompanying "good speech" are part and parcel of the whole.

6.   The preceding paragraph is not intended to support any and all kinds of dialectal speech, nor does the writer wish to put on one side the aesthetic point of view in the judgment of speech. It is merely an appeal

to the reader to consider carefully, before he condemns one type of speech and praises another, the true reasons which lie behind his dislikes and his preferences.

7. There are good reasons why it may be thought advisable to attempt to teach in the schools some kind of pronunciation which would be acceptable in any part of the country, and in any class of society. The chief argument is one of mutual intelligibility. It is obvious that in a country the size of the British Isles, any one speaker should be capable of understanding any other when he is talking English. At the present moment, such is not the case: a Cockney speaker would not be understood by a dialect speaker of Edinburgh or Leeds or Truro, and dialect speakers of much nearer districts than these would have difficulty in understanding each other. The following diagram, devised by Professor D. Jones, illustrates graphically the position of affairs as they actually are. The base of the cone represents a map of England, and the lines joining various points on its base to the apex, the different types of speech used at each place, the apex A representing a kind of pronunciation which bears no signs of any particular district. Thus the line joining L (London) and A (apex) would represent all the different kinds of pronunciation used by London speakers, from extreme Cockney at the base through varying degrees of Cockney up to the apex, when all distinctive signs of a

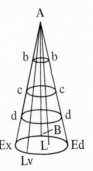

Fig. 1. Variant Pronunciations.

Ed = Edinburgh
Ex = Exeter
Lv = Liverpool

London dialect have been shed. The line joining B and A would show the same for Bradford (B) speakers, and so on for all parts of the country.[1]

8. If a section be taken across the cone at any point between the base and the apex, the differences at this point between the dialects of various places will be fewer than they are at the base, i.e. some of the most outstanding peculiarities will not be found: at a section further towards the apex, the differences will be still less and the types of pronunciation of the different localities will more nearly resemble each other; and as we near the apex, the divergencies which still exist have become so small as to be noticed only by a finely trained ear. These, for all practical purposes, may be neglected. Let us assume that at the section marked *d* such dissimilarities as would make for lack of understanding have dropped—i.e. a speaker from any part of the country using the type of speech represented here, would be understood by any other. This may be called the limit of intelligibility. For the sake of mutual understanding it can be argued that a pronunciation should be taught in the schools which lies above the line assumed at *d*. That would not necessarily, however, be a pronunciation used by educated speakers, and would contain many marked dialectal peculiarities; but it *would* be understandable, and thus

[1] The speech represented at the base of the cone is assumed to be that which would be used in reading English not containing dialect words and constructions, i.e. we are concerned with pronunciation, not grammar and vocabulary.

Note to Third Edition.—The cogency of this argument is greater now than when the book was first published. (See Chapter on Broadcasting.)

one object of pronunciation teaching would be secured. If the aim is to approach nearer to *one* type and to teach an *educated* pronunciation, we should have to choose a section nearer the apex of the cone. Let us assume such a section at *c*. This would represent a number of types of speech used by educated people from different parts of the country. It is still not *one* standard pronunciation, but it approaches thereto. At a section still nearer the apex (at *b*), the pronunciation will have lost all easily noticeable local differences. This type of speech may be considered as that most generally understood throughout the English-speaking world and may be called Received Pronunciation.

9. A second argument in favour of encouraging a more uniform type of pronunciation throughout the country lies in the prestige of the English language in other countries. English is the most universally used of all European languages, and from this point of view, it is desirable that something approaching a standard should be set up which would be recognised as the type to be recommended to foreigners.[1]

10. There is also the argument of convenience or expediency. The regional dialects may suffice for those people who have no need to move from their own districts; but few people nowadays remain all their lives in their native town or village without having occasion to leave it for one purpose or another. That language which serves for his own district will not easily serve for a more distant one, and the dialect speaker will find himself at a disadvantage in his travels, or in his ambition to improve his position, if he is unable

[1] See *Report on Teaching of English*, p. 67.

to use any other but his own local form of speech.[1]
Closely bound up with this point is the fact that certain
types of speech are considered as belonging to the lower
social classes, and if it is desired to break down class
barriers in this democratic age, an attempt at setting up a
more uniform pronunciation will lessen the feeling of
linguistic inferiority and will go far to overcome what
is at present one of the few remaining class distinctions.

11. In face of these arguments in favour of some
kind of standard pronunciation, we come to two practical
questions: first of all, what is it advisable to teach in
the schools, and secondly, how far is such a scheme of
pronunciation teaching possible? A consideration of
the wide divergencies in regional and class dialects and
even the pronunciation of educated speakers, leads us
to think that to aim at *one* standard speech—either
the apex of the cone or one chosen type, e.g. educated
London pronunciation,[2] or the speech of one man—
would be useless and unnecessary; useless, because it
would be impossible to carry out, and unnecessary
because several types of educated speech do exist
which would be acceptable anywhere. These recognised
types are not only mutually understandable, but vary
from each other only in slight details. A plan which
seems natural and feasible would be to teach the educated

[1] "Do you come from Yorkshire?" asked one College of Education student of another. "Yes," answered the other cheerfully,
"we're branded, aren't we?"

[2] Sir Mark Hunter put forward a plea for educated London
pronunciation to be considered as a standard, and based his
arguments on the history of English pronunciation. He would
allow, however, that a number of divergencies from this would
be found in educated provincial speech, and need not be dis-
couraged.

speech of the district in which the school is situated, a pronunciation represented by any part of the cone above the section we have assumed to be at (c). This plan has the advantage that the children have opportunities of hearing such a pronunciation, whereas if *one* type of speech were chosen, it would be familiar only to the children in the part of the country where that type was used; children in other parts of the country would *feel* this to be an affectation, and it would be looked on as such by their families, while the other might easily become natural. This would amount to setting up a number of modified received pronunciations, varying from Received Pronunciation in certain details in which they are influenced by the local dialects. There is likelihood of disagreement at first, as to what is to be accepted and what rejected in these local received pronunciations, but it should not be difficult in the long run to come to some agreement as to the limits beyond which speech is considered markedly vulgar or dialectal.

12. The second practical question, how far such a scheme is possible, depends partly on the importance which the head and staff of the schools attach to good speech, and partly on the skill of the teacher in tackling the difficulties of " curing " indistinct and slipshod speech and dialectal peculiarities. It is obvious that the teacher himself should use one of these local received pronunciations or one which lies above this section across the cone, and he should know the local received pronunciation of the district in which he is teaching. This is the first step towards establishing an educated speech throughout the country,[1] and it is in the Colleges

[1] *See Report*, p. 176.

of Education that this work must begin. The question of how these pronunciation difficulties are to be tackled is treated in the chapters "Correction of Pronunciation" and "Qualifications of the Teacher" and in App. I ("Suggested Course of Speech Training for Colleges of Education").

13. It should be possible to teach a pronunciation which is clear and distinct, which is free from slovenliness and from the outstanding peculiarities of the local dialect. It should be possible to encourage a pleasing voice and manner of speech. But teachers, in order to do anything at all, will have to think it worth while. The work will take time and much patience, besides skill and a rigorous training; some other part of school activity will probably have to be sacrificed and the results will be slow in showing themselves. The local speech will not disappear, but the children will gradually become bi-lingual, using their dialect with its familiar associations at home, and learning an auxiliary language which they will use in school, and which they will have at their command, if they wish to use it in after life.

14. *Note.*—The influence of broadcasting on the speech of the country is likely to make itself felt in the near future. Interest is taken in the Mother Tongue such as has probably not been known before, and broadcasting is a prominent factor in this interest. The B.B.C. has set up a committee on pronunciation, which decides on the pronunciation of doubtful words, and to whose rulings the announcers are expected to conform. It is a significant fact that, as the present writer has been informed, those announcers and speakers whose speech shows the influence of local dialect least are the most popular with the general public. [*See* page 22, note in brackets at foot.]

Chapter II

BROADCASTING AND SPOKEN ENGLISH

15. Since this book was first published in 1929, a new factor, at that time in its infancy, has taken an important place in the field of speech. That broadcasting would have considerable influence on the study and practice of English pronunciation was then predicted. It is now time to examine, in the light of the experience of the last nine years [to 1938], what that influence has been and how it is likely to develop. It will be necessary to examine the kinds of English which are acceptable in broadcasting, not only to the various social and regional groups of this country, but also to the millions of listeners in the [former] Dominions and Colonies and in America. Thus the question of standard pronunciation dealt with in Chapter I is in a very wide sense concerned in the matter. It will be necessary also to discuss the frequent objections to what is popularly called B.B.C. English, to analyse those characteristics which make for good broadcast speech—and conversely, what is bad—and to consider how all these affect the teaching of spoken English in schools and colleges.

16. It is obvious that only the fringe of the subject can be touched upon in this short chapter. The reader who wishes to pursue further the innumerable tracks which lead to interesting and diverse problems, is advised to read *The Broadcast Word*,[1] by Professor A. Lloyd James, and the booklets issued by the B.B.C. entitled *Broadcast English*:[1] he will be certain of good hunting. Here we must somewhat rigidly limit ourselves

[1] [Out of print.]

to the points enumerated in the preceding paragraph, after the examination of a few general principles.

17.   The British nation has become speech conscious—self-conscious in many cases—and comment and criticism are heard from all sides.   Much of this criticism is uninformed and without any basis of scientific knowledge; in the matter of speech, everyone who speaks, thinks that by this feat alone, he has the right, the power and the knowledge to criticise other people's performance in this art.   Since speech so intimately concerns each one of us, however, these personal reactions, due to the background of geographical and social life and education, even if they are illogical, must be allowed for and reckoned with.   It is, indeed, difficult to obtain an impartial and objective opinion from anyone, and we must stress once again the fact that in judging speech, the subjective is the point of view from which most people regard it.

18.   Perhaps the most outstanding general contribution which broadcast speech has made to the world is in directing attention to the spoken as opposed to the written word and in stressing the need for a definite conception of the differences between these two types of language.   Never since the period before the invention of printing has the spoken word played such an important role in the life of the world as it does to-day. The printing press had ruled our language for so many centuries that we had ceased to realise its tyranny and accepted its criteria unquestioningly.   The new means of communication in broadcasting, by which the spoken word takes an important place in the life of the community, causes us to examine with greater exactitude

what are the essential differences between spoken English and written English, what we can legitimately expect from each of these, and more important still, what each cannot provide.

19. If we examine the two forms of language, eye-language and ear-language,[1] we find they have little in common except intelligibility: the one conveys meaning through the eye, the other through the ear. Because of the work of the printing presses and the standardisation of spelling, the visual language is practically the same over the whole of the English-speaking world. Not so the spoken language. But because we have been conditioned to the written word by long tradition and by the processes of our education, we find it difficult to separate the two and are apt to think what is written in the black and white of the printed page is by some alchemy transformed exactly into the noises we make and recognise as the spoken language, and that *vice versa*, the ephemeral thing called speech is capable of accurate and standardised representation on paper. This confusion of sounds and letters is a frequent cause of the attitude of many to "standard" and "correct" pronunciation, viz. that it should conform in some way to the printed word. At the best, conventions must be made to show the relation of the auditory to the written language, and English is pre-eminently a language which defies all efforts at making such conventions. Moreover, it is impossible to record in an ordinary orthography those subtle elements of speech, such as degrees of stress

[1] *Note to 4th Edition.* Professor Wren in a recent paper read to the Philological Society speaks of English spelling as partially ideographic; he characterises it as " groups of letters representing groups of sounds."

and emphasis, relative length of syllables, pitch, the type of voice used, slight variations in pronunciation, all of which contribute to the general effect of the spoken word and to "accent" as a whole. It is necessary to remind ourselves of this frequently, as it is to remember that the spoken word is always changing while the written language remains static.[1]

20. The main criterion in judging speech is intelligibility. The requirements for intelligibility with our immediate neighbours are low, since context of situation, community of interests and surroundings supply much of the necessary material for understanding. A wider circle, however, is reached to-day through the greater mobility of all classes and especially through broadcasting.[2] The requirements for intelligibility in all forms of broadcast speech are therefore stricter; above all in radio transmission, where the eye gives no help as in television and the lack has to be supplied by the spoken word itself. But intelligibility is not all. Broadcast speech, to be acceptable to the majority of English speakers in the world, should be some form of speech which is not too far removed from the various standards of educated English in the different parts of the country and Commonwealth; indeed America may also be included. That is to say, it must not be too "precious" nor too vulgar, but a mean with no out-

[1] See Chapter XVII, p. 199.

[2] "So long as the oral language was restricted in its currency, nothing mattered, but when it was called upon to serve as a national and international medium of communication over the ether, there were bound to arise national and international questions of standard."—Prof. A. Lloyd James "The Art of Announcing."

standing pecularities in the way of vowel and consonant sound, of stress and intonation.

21. We should be reminded, however, and reminded frequently, that it would be impossible to please all listeners all the time. A "standard" acceptable to all could never be achieved, and indeed one of the criticisms hurled at the B.B.C. is that it is attempting to level, up or down according to the individual critic, the pronunciation of English and to impose on the country the speech of the men who form the body of its speaking officials. Such criticism is without foundation, since it is no part of the B.B.C or of its Advisory Committee on Spoken English to lay down principles for the speech of the general public.[1] How far the speech of announcers and other wireless talkers is likely to influence the speech of the country is discussed later in this chapter. But there is no doubt that certain characteristics of the type of pronunciation used by the majority of B.B.C. speaking officials rouse unfavourable reactions in many listeners, and it will be useful to investigate the reasons for this. The fundamental reason for this antagonism is the fact that these men, who belong to the younger generation of Englishmen educated mainly at the older universities, exhibit the "advance guard" of change in the speech of our time and therefore theirs is a minority speech; their speech habits, which to them are natural and not, as many critics say, "affected," are, like other habits of the younger generation, deplored by their elders.

22. The main characteristics of this type of speech are set out in Chapter XVII, where the changes which have been taking place in recent years are analysed. It

[1] See § 33 for the work of this Committee.

will be well to sum up here some of these which are not acceptable to many listeners. The chief ones are

(a) the flattening of diphthongs and triphthongs;

(b) the centralising of vowels, which makes all vowels nearer together in tongue position and in quality;

(c) the unrounding of vowels and diphthongs which have had lip-rounding; this removes some of the definite characteristics of such vowels.

(d) the "clipping" effect of weak vowels, where listeners expect strong ones;

(e) the non-pronunciation of *r* in post-vocalic positions. This is a characteristic of a large number of English people of all generations, and is not a recent tendency; note also, that this criticism is generally based upon spelling;

(f) the occasional use of intrusive "*r*".

23. The writer feels that she must make plain her own attitude to the question. While not one of the younger generation and not using many of their newer pronunciations, she feels that the announcers perform a difficult task with the utmost skill; their reading of news and announcing of items in the programmes is clear and business-like. When one realises the amount of material they get through in one news bulletin and how this would pall if the delivery were at all laboured, one must admit that these officials would be hard to beat at their somewhat thankless task.[1]

[1] See *The Broadcast Word*, p. 147, for what is expected of the announcer. See also the leading article in the *Listener* of Sept. 22nd, 1938, on " Reading the News," which stresses the weight of responsibility on the announcer who has news of a serious character to read.

24. The question of the use of dialect must again be touched on here.   Along with the accusation of imposing a dead level of uniformity of speech on the country, the B.B.C. is arraigned as the prime criminal in the death of dialect speech.   The dialects as general speech currency, were doomed before the advent of broadcasting, though probably the process has been hastened by the broadcast word.   Whether announcing in varieties of modified dialects would be more generally acceptable than the present régime is doubtful; in any case, only trial could prove this.   It should be noted that most of those who deplore the loss of our dialects are people who do not use them; nor do they bring up their children using them. Thus their wish to preserve dialect speech is from an aesthetic, historical or sentimental point of view.   This is a perfectly legitimate point of view and indeed there is no reason why local patriotism should not foster a feeling of pride in the dialect and its historical background, so long as this does not interfere with the acquirement of a more general type of speech by those who may need it.

25. One other factor in the dialect question is the use that is made of it for comic entertainment.   Such treatment is likely to militate against the natural use of dialect, while on the other hand, the bringing to the microphone of dialect speakers in different walks of life who have something of interest to say and whose speech rings true and sincere, gives dialect a pleasing dignity and reality.

26. We now come to an analysis of what makes good broadcast speech.   There is no doubt that new techniques for the microphone have had to be developed,

different from that of all other kinds of public speaking, from lecturing, preaching or declaiming. This is largely due to the intimate situation in which broadcast talk is received. It is inconceivable that we should sit in an easy chair by the fireside to be "preached at"; declamation is out of place and makes us feel uncomfortable, and the first reaction to pomposity is to switch off.

27. The best broadcast speech is natural; it is talk and not the recording of literary or journalistic prose. Here it will be seen that matter and its arrangement enters into the question as well as manner. It is manner, however, that concerns us most in this book, but no one can use a natural speaking manner if he has to read aloud material which has been written—probably unconsciously—for the eye and not for the ear, and which contains constructions or uses a word order such as would never in the ordinary course of affairs be *spoken*.[1] As far as speaking is concerned, however, by natural, we mean there must be no undue exaggeration of stress or intonation and no over-carefulness which makes itself observed. We are all familiar with the speaker who reads his script in the wooden fashion typical of a not too intelligent school-boy reading aloud; and even more unpleasant to listen to is the broadcaster, who, under the impression that he must be very distinct, uses "strong" forms of unimportant words and syllables, and in this way destroys the rhythm of the spoken language. For, if naturalness is the first virtue of broadcast-speech, it is evident that the rhythms and intonations of the ordinary spoken language must be preserved.

28. Since, however, the subject-matter of many broadcast talks is of such a nature that the speaker must

[1] See *The Tongues of Men*, by J. R. Firth, pp. 50–1

go slowly in order that the ideas should reach the minds of his hearers, he must in some way modify this natural technique. This is also true of a speaker in a big hall where his words have to reach the most distant member of a large audience. How can he preserve the naturalness which we consider essential? A slowing up of the whole speech is the most telling way of producing the desired effect, i.e. breaking the sentences into small sense-groups, making slightly longer pauses between the sense-groups than is usual in familiar speech, and taking each at a slower pace. But—and this is important—not destroying the natural rhythm by unnatural exaggeration of pronunciation or of stress, nor by giving undue prominence to unimportant words and syllables. It is, in fact, the slow motion picture translated into sound, i.e. no separate element is exaggerated and the normal proportion is not destroyed. One of the most successful exponents of this method of public speaking suitable for broadcasting, if perhaps too slow for normal occasions, was His late Majesty, King George V. A note on his excellent technique is added to the phonetic transcription of the record of his 1935 Christmas broadcast to the Empire in § 380.[1]

29. A further factor in the naturalness which is the main quality necessary in broadcast speech lies in the use of an ordinary voice and intonation. Until the advent of broadcasting, reading aloud or speaking for public purposes was confined to a few classes, the clergy, lawyers, the elocutionist and the political orator. Each had its own technique. Nowadays, the clerical voice

[1] Incidentally this method is recommended for the teaching of reading in school, in order to do away with the wooden word-by-word reading which is sometimes heard.

and manner, the oratorical devices of the public speaker and the tricks of the elocutionist move us no longer; and broadcasting is partly responsible for this. They are out of place at the microphone and a natural voice and intonation is demanded.

30.　How do these varied questions affect the teaching of spoken English in England? First of all, broadcasting gives a new prestige to the spoken word and should eventually range the oral at least on a level with the literary language in the work of schools and colleges. As far as standard pronunciation is concerned, it should reinforce the efforts of those who wish to give our school children the possibility of acquiring some form of "standard" speech, as an auxiliary language. The speed with which such a change may be anticipated should not be over-estimated, however. In the early days of broadcasting it was thought that reform would be rapid, but results of this kind are slow to show themselves. The teacher, however, can train the child to listen, to observe differences of pronunciation, to realise why he likes certain kinds more than others, to be tolerant of a type of speech which is other than that with which he is familiar. He can apply some of the principles of good broadcast speech to his own class-room work and that of his pupils, introducing naturalness, ease, good rhythm, pleasant manner into the work of all oral lessons, and thus do his share in the reinstatement of the spoken word to an honourable place in English education.

31.　The B.B.C. arranged for the broadcasting of speech-training lessons over a period of years. During this time an experiment was undertaken to test the value of the lessons. Gramophone records were made of the speech of a class of children in a Central School[1] in

[1] The designation is now obsolete: it was a middle school.

London before the course began and again at the end. A second class, not following the lessons, used as control, was also recorded. The results have been analysed and set out in a publication of the B.B.C. entitled *Evidence regarding Broadcast Speech Training*.[1] The second records showed evidence of change in pronunciation which was definitely better than that of the untaught class. But one could not expect that the whole speech habits of the children should be changed by a lesson a week over nine months. Broadcast speech-training lessons were given up in England in 1933, on a majority vote of the Central Council for School Broadcasting, mainly because of the objections which were raised to the imposition of a "standard" and to the lack of definition of what the "standard English" sounds are. It is interesting to note that a successful speech-training course was started in Scotland in 1935 definitely to teach "standard Scottish": in this case the "standard" was very carefully worked out by a special investigation committee formed on a national basis.[2]

32. Broadcasting gives to the student of English phonetics unlimited opportunity of hearing varieties of English pronunciation, and this should be a valuable adjunct to the ear-training which is so necessary a part of such work. This chapter is introduced here to encourage students to use the listening end of broadcasting and to bring an unbiased mind to the many still unsettled problems of spoken English.

[1] Enquiry Pamphlet No. 3: Central Council for School Broadcasting. [Out of print.]

[2] This information is from the report (in *Good Speech*, Jan., 1938) of a lecture by Miss Mary Somerville, B.B.C. Director of School Broadcasts, at the Speech Fellowship Conference in London, 1937.

33. *The B.B.C. Advisory Committee on Spoken English.*—The B.B.C. Advisory Committee on Spoken English as at present constituted, consists of a large and representative body of people, the chair of which is held in rotation, and goes up for election every two years; nobody may hold it three years in succession, but a man may be re-elected after he has been out of office for two years. The present chairman (1938) is Professor G. Gordon, of Magdalen College, Oxford. The research work is carried out by a sub-committee of four experts, Professor H. C. Wyld, of Merton College, Oxford; Professor Daniel Jones, of University College, London; Mr. H. Orton, of the University of Durham; and Professor A. Lloyd James, of the School of Oriental Studies, University of London (Hon. Sec.). This committee draws up the recommendations which are submitted to the big committee. Their work is varied and covers a wide field, as can be seen from the titles of the publications issued by the B.B.C. under the editorship of Professor Lloyd James [*Broadcast English*, out of print]. They deal with all the problems of pronunciation of doubtful words for announcing, of words with more than one accepted pronunciation; of personal and place names in England; of the "anglification" of Scottish and Welsh place names which is necessary for the understanding of English listeners; of the pronunciation of foreign terms in general use; of foreign personal and place names, etc. Some of their decisions, as is inevitable, meet with a certain opposition. It should be stated, however, that the committee does not attempt to set up a standard of general pronunciation either for the announcers or for the country. [The committee was disbanded during the Second World War. The B.B.C. now has a Pronunciation Unit which makes available to news-readers and others the most authentic pronunciation of difficult or uncertain words and names; and see Bibliography under Miller.]

Chapter III

CORRECTION OF PRONUNCIATION

34. Differences of speech fall into several clearly differentiated categories.

(1) A dialect speaker may use *words* which are not known in other parts of the country: e.g. in the West Riding of Yorkshire, the sentence *He's lakin at taws up a ginnel* [i z lɛːkɪn ət tɔːz ʊp ə gɪnɪl, He's playing at marbles in a passage] could not be understood, however it was pronounced, if the words *lakin*, *taws* and *ginnel* were not known.

(2) He may employ unusual constructions, ungrammatical or otherwise: e.g. *Wait while Monday* for *Wait till Monday* (Yorks.); *He come in the house and play with me every day* (East Anglia); *That belongs to I* (West Country).

(3) He may stress words differently: e.g. *mis-'chievous* instead of *'mischievous*.

(4) He may have an unusual rise and fall of the voice.

(5) He may use sounds in wrong places or sounds not found in educated speech: e.g. kʊm for kʌm (Yorks. and Lancs.); nʌʊ for nou (Cockney); lɑŋ for lɒŋ (East Anglia and West Country).

(6) He may insert or omit normal sounds or substitute one sound for another: e.g. mɪs'tʃiˑvɪəs for 'mɪstʃɪvəs, wɛst'mɪnɪstə for 'wɛstmɪnstə, 'gʌvəmənt for 'gʌvənmənt, etc.

35. A consideration of dialect speech in general would include a study of all these factors. In this book, however, we are concerned mainly with pronunciation, and for our purpose, the last two points must be discussed thoroughly. The question of stress and intonation (points 3 and 4) is touched on in a later chapter.

36. The two main mistakes, therefore, with which we are concerned are the use of sounds not found in educated speech—wrongly formed sounds—and the insertion, omission or substitution of sounds which do occur in educated speech. In the first class come such pronunciations as the Cockney tsïü ən tsïü ə fɔːwə for tu ən tu ə fɔː (or fɔə), nʌʊ or næʊ for noʊ, tsəi for tiː, kɛʔl for kɛtl (this last is not confined to Cockney); the Northern pronunciation kʊm, lʊv for kʌm, lʌv, mɔːtə for moʊtə, and the Midland pronunciation of sɪŋgɪŋg for sɪŋɪŋ.[1]

37. In the second class, i.e. the use of normal sounds in wrong places, or the insertion or omission of sounds, are the pronunciations haɪtθ (haɪt), ɒpəsaɪt (ɒpəzɪt), gʌvəmənt (gʌvənmənt), ɛərɪeɪtɪd (ɛəreɪtɪd), wɛstmɪnɪstə (wɛstmɪnstə), rɛkənaɪz (rɛkəgnaɪz), sɛkətrɪ (sɛkrətrɪ), klɜ·k (klɑ·k), kjuˑpɒn (kuˑpɒn), lenθ (leŋθ), etc.

38. The first kind of mistake is by far the more difficult to correct, and the teacher's work should be mainly concerned with this—the teaching of new sounds that the pupil does not possess. The Cockney child says tïü because he cannot say tuː, and generally cannot imitate the teacher's pronunciation; the Yorkshire child

---

[1] These dialectal pronunciations will be better understood after the chapters on vowels and consonants have been read.

says kʊm because the vowel ʌ does not exist in his speech; the Midlander says sɪŋgɪŋg because he cannot say the sound ŋ followed by a vowel or finally: he always adds a g sound. It is the business of the teacher, therefore, if he is going to attempt the task of teaching pronunciation, to find, when imitation fails, some other means of making his pupil pronounce the sounds which he thinks desirable.

39. In modern language teaching the old idea that one could " pick up " a good pronunciation is exploded, and the best modern language teachers now realise that pronunciation, like every other branch of language work, has to be taught, and taught scientifically. The problem of teaching a new pronunciation of the Mother Tongue is almost the same as that of teaching a foreign language; the pupil cannot make certain sounds which the teacher wishes him to make. It is, in fact, more difficult than teaching the pronunciation of a foreign language, since the pupil has acquired fluency in " incorrect" usages, and his " bad" habits must be broken. These pronunciation difficulties must be analysed and the most suitable method of treatment applied.

40. The phonetically trained teacher will be able to do this best, as he will realise not only what the right sound is which he is going to teach, but what the wrong sound is that his pupil is using, and the relation of the one to the other. Having this knowledge, he is able to invent exercises which will produce the required sound and help the pupil to get rid of the wrong one. In this book, suggestions for exercises of this type will be given in the detailed description of the vowels and consonants.

41. The correction of the second class of mistake, the misplacing of existing sounds, sounds the pupil already knows, is of little difficulty compared with the first kind. These mistakes are not made because the pupil is unable to say the normal sound—he can say klɑ·k as easily as klɜ·k—but because he has been accustomed to hear and use these pronunciations. Many of the mistakes are due to false analogy with other words; he says haɪtθ and deɪtθ and wɛstmɪnɪstə because he says lɛŋθ and brɛdθ and mɪnɪstə; and if he is told the correct pronunciation he can use it without difficulty.

42. It is generally found that the teacher who has had no scientific training in the analysis of English speech either does not realise or cannot tackle the first type of these mistakes; and unless the children can imitate with ease, he leaves them alone, concentrating entirely upon mistakes of the second type. Indeed, he often lays himself open to the charge of making wrong corrections on these lines, and of teaching an artificial pronunciation which is never heard outside a classroom. Thus he will insist on the word *sailor* being pronounced 'seɪlɔː; *captain* is taught as 'kæpteɪn, *oval* as 'ouvæl, *movement* as 'muːvmɛnt, and *conduct* (verb) as kɒn'dʌkt, *parliament* as pɑ·lɪəmənt, etc. This is because he has not the power of analysing exactly what people say, and, in spite of the inconsistencies of English spelling, he imagines the spoken word has a close resemblance to the written word. Such people consider speech as made up of a number of syllables, each pronounced in connected speech as it would be if said in isolation : *o-r* spells ɔː, therefore *s-a-i-l-o-r* spells seɪlɔː. They ignore entirely the changes which sounds undergo in connected speech under the influence of stress and rhythm, and try to teach not what is a good current pronunciation of certain words, but what they think the pronunciation ought to be. This point is dealt with in the chapters on "Spelling Pronunciations" (Chap. VII) and on "Sounds in Connected Speech" (Chap. XVI, §§ 324–8).

Note.—To illustrate this fact, an extract is given here from a speech-training scheme for primary school children which was submitted to the present writer.

"Distinction must be made between the final syllables of the following pairs of words:

leopard, shepherd	parrot, garret
fatal, battle	cousin, cozen
porridge, college	carrot. carat
bacon, taken	

-age must be pronounced, not *-ige* in *cabbage, village,* etc.
-ent   ,, ,,   ,,   ,, *-unt* ,, *excellent, benevolent*
-ence ,, ,,   ,,   ,, *-unce* ,, *patience, silence*
-et   ,, ,,   ,,   ,, *-ut* ,, *wicket, basket*
-ness ,, ,,   ,,   ,, *-niss* ,, *witness, kindness,*
                                                                etc."

Does anyone say feɪtæl, kærɒt, kæbeɪʤ, bɑskɛt, saɪlɛns? The scheme was in reality no speech-training scheme, but a list of hints for the teacher for the dictation lesson to ensure correct spelling,—of little value also in the teaching of spelling.

Chapter IV

QUALIFICATIONS OF THE TEACHER

43. A consideration of the different types of mistake in pronunciation and the problem of dealing with them, brings us to the question as to what qualifications are necessary for the teacher who is going to attempt this difficult task.

Ear-Training.

44. The basis of all speech-training is ear-training. A teacher who can hear only the most outstanding divergencies of pronunciation is at a loss when he wants to deal with subtler differences. He knows, but vaguely only, that something is not quite right, instead of being able immediately to put his finger on the spot and say *exactly what is wrong*. It is essential, then, for a teacher to have an ear trained to recognise fine distinctions in speech sounds if he is going to correct pronunciation.

45. To train his ear for speech sounds, the student must accustom himself to listening to sounds, not only in the ordinary speech of different people but in systematic exercises devised for the purpose. Such practice is given by the teacher of phonetics, who dictates meaningless words which the student writes down in phonetic script. The reason for the choice of meaningless words for ear-training is that by this method, the student has no other preoccupation than with the sounds themselves; he is not thinking of the associations which real words would call up, the ordinary spelling, his own or the teacher's pronunciation, or the meaning; he concentrates on the sounds alone, and in this way is able to train himself to observe even minute differences in pronunciation. The teacher can see by the written exercise if the student has heard correctly or not, and if he has made a mistake, the teacher can further help him by repeating alternately the sounds which the student thought he heard, i.e. the ones he has written down, and the ones which were actually said. In this way, he will gradually come to perceive the acoustic differences between the sounds which he has confused. Such a training, if carried out systematically and for a considerable period of time, should enable a student to recognise exactly the differences between his pupils' pronunciation and the one he is trying to teach.[1]

TRAINING FOR CONTROL OF THE ORGANS OF SPEECH.

46. The student of pronunciation who is going to attempt to correct wrong sounds, must not only be able to recognise the wrong sounds when he hears them, but he must also be able to *make* them. This is a matter of mouth gymnastics, which will enable him to use his speech organs in a way to which he has been hitherto unaccustomed. Such training involves considerable practice in making speech sounds of all kinds, not only those of normal English, but also many dialectal and individual variants, and the sounds of foreign languages. In this way the student will gain such control of the speech organs as will enable him to make at will any sound he wants, i.e. he will be able to imitate correctly the wrong sounds his pupil makes, and will consequently know *how* they are made. This training, obviously, cannot be obtained from books or lectures, although, as in the

---

[1] Ear-training exercises are added in Appendix II.

present book, exercises can be suggested; it is best obtained by careful study with a competent teacher, who will tell the student what to do with his organs of speech, and give him exercises to help him to carry out these instructions.[1]

KNOWLEDGE OF THEORY.

47. The third qualification of a teacher, who is going to use phonetics to teach pronunciation, is that he shall know how the sounds of English are made, i.e. what position the organs of speech take up in the formation of all the sounds of the language, and how they are used in connected speech. This knowledge of theory can be obtained from books and lectures, in which the sounds of English are described, and a study of the theory, together with a careful observation of his own speech habits will give a student a good working knowledge of how English speech sounds are made.

48. In the first two requirements, however, books play a secondary rôle; they may describe certain types of mistake, and suggest methods of dealing with them, but they can do no more. The teacher must analyse for himself the pronunciation of the pupil he is dealing with, and for this he must rely on his own trained ear.

49. When the student has these three qualifications, viz. the knowledge of the formation of the correct sound, the power to recognise the wrong sound and the ability to make it, he is in an excellent position to use phonetics in the teaching of pronunciation, i.e. to attempt to cure any mispronunciation he may come across. His theoretical knowledge and practical skill will enable

[1] Certain exercises are added in Chapters VIII and IX for the student to practise.

him to devise exercises to get rid of wrong and teach correct sounds in the quickest way possible.

50. A few words of warning should be given here. It is not advocated that phonetic theory should be taught in schools. The aim of the teacher is, presumably, to teach a good pronunciation, and in the quickest time possible. Phonetics is a science *for the teacher to know and apply in a practical fashion in the teaching of pronunciation*. In some cases, it may be interesting and profitable to introduce a certain amount of phonetic theory, where time allows; children like to know what they do in their mouths when they talk and they like to hear about other speech habits than their own, and to compare pronunciations, but this is not essential to the teacher's primary purpose. Also it cannot be too strongly stated that a knowledge of the formation of speech sounds on the part of a student does not necessarily mean that he can make the sounds correctly, nor does detailed information about the functions of the organs of speech imply that he has control over these organs. Moreover, the idea that to know a phonetic alphabet is either to know phonetics or to possess a "correct" pronunciation, or be able to teach it—an idea common enough, though perhaps not actually stated—should not be allowed currency. Knowledge of a phonetic alphabet is no guarantee whatever of the pronunciation of the user of it. Phonetic transcription is a useful adjunct to phonetics,[1] but it does not *teach* sounds. Phonetics is a science of great practical value in linguistics, and a theoretical knowledge only of the subject is of little use.

[1] See next Chapter.

Chapter V

PHONETIC TRANSCRIPTION

51. Phonetics is the science which analyses and records sounds and other elements of speech, and their use and distribution in connected sentences. For the purpose of *recording* speech sounds *in written or printed form*, without fear of ambiguity, it is necessary to use a phonetic alphabet, i.e. an alphabet based on the principle of "one letter per phoneme" (see Ch. X). Without such an alphabet, an accurate description and record of speech usages would be clumsy and awkward, and liable to misinterpretation. It should be remembered, however, that a phonetic alphabet is not phonetics, nor does it *teach* sounds; it is a most useful, in fact, almost indispensable accompaniment of phonetics, in that by means of it, a ready way is found of writing down the pronunciation of individual words, and of showing with fair accuracy and without ambiguity how sounds are used in connected speech. A phonetic dictionary can show the pronunciation of individual words, can even give alternative pronunciations, strong and weak forms,[1] etc. (see Ch. XVI), and can show how words are stressed, but it cannot indicate *when to use* the strong and weak forms in connected speech; nor can it show how the normal word stress is changed under the influence of sentence stress. This is possible only in a phonetic transcription.

52. The student is advised to learn to recognise and make the English sounds in isolation and in words,

[1] See D. Jones, *An English Pronouncing Dictionary* (ed. A. C. Gimson).

and the symbols which represent these sounds, and then
to practise writing down his own speech in sentences
by means of a phonetic alphabet. He will find in this
way that a phonetic transcription is a valuable aid to
the study of pronunciation. It will help him, in the
first place, to get rid of the natural idea that the conventional spelling represents pronunciation; we are
still very much the slave to the written word. Secondly,
it will enable him, as no other method could, to realise
his own speech habits; he will find that he uses far more
"weak forms" and that he drops more consonants
and makes more assimilations than he is aware of,
and does not pronounce every syllable in connected
speech as he would do if it were said in isolation.

53. In this connection, it should be remembered
that the *interpretation* of a phonetic transcription requires an understanding of phonetics. Critics of the
subject are apt to criticise the whole science adversely
on seeing and attempting to read a phonetic transcription without the necessary knowledge; they judge that
it represents a slipshod speech. This is generally due
to either or both of two reasons; the reader not trained
in speech analysis does not realise his own speech habits,
he still thinks the spelling more or less represents the
pronunciation; he does not realise, for example, that
he pronounces no vowel in the second syllable of *mutton*,
or that he does not pronounce the second syllables of
mountain and *attain* alike. Or, as he is unfamiliar
with a phonetic transcription, he deciphers it word
by word, or even syllable by syllable, when it was
written to represent natural quick connected speech.
When this occurs, he sees the word *was* written as **wəz**,

i.e. *unstressed*, and he gives it undue prominence, and turns it into wɜz, which, of course, does not occur in the English language in anyone's speech. In this way, because of his ignorance of the subject, he condemns phonetics, by misusing a phonetic transcription.

54. Just as a phonetic transcription can show a student with fair accuracy his own speech habits, so it can serve to represent the similarities and differences in the pronunciation of individuals and of dialects: e.g. the difference between N. and S. pronunciation of words like *plant*, *after* (N. plænt, æftə, or plant, aftə; S. plɑ·nt, ɑ·ftə), the Cockney diphthong in *lady* (laɪdɪ) as compared with the Received pronunciation leɪdɪ; the difference, not dialectal but individual, between the two pronunciations of the word *associate* (əsouʃɪeɪt and əsousɪeɪt), etc. The student of dialects will find an accurate knowledge of a phonetic alphabet invaluable for recording dialect speech of any kind.

55. In Chapter IV, on the training of the teacher of pronunciation, the importance of *ear-training* was stressed; in order to do adequate ear-training, a phonetic alphabet is necessary; without it only the simplest form of ear-training is possible.

56. In this book the phonetic transcription used is that known as the "narrow" transcription. The differences between "broad" and "narrow" are set out on p. xiii. Many phoneticians make use of the "broad" transcription of English,[1] in which length marks (ː) are used to show a difference in quality as well as in length. This can be justified as adequate for representing, with certain well-defined conventions, the

[1] Prof. D. Jones uses it in his *Outline of English Phonetics*.

normal pronunciation of English. Here, however, where we are comparing somewhat fine dialectal and personal differences, it has been thought better to use the "narrow" transcription, and to make length marks represent length only and not quality also.

Note.—A phonetic orthography based upon the principles of the International Phonetic Association has been established for the writing of many African languages. The name "Africa" script is given to this. (See Memorandum on Orthography published by the International Institute of African Languages and Cultures.)

Note to 4th Edition. An extra broad transcription has been used in Scott's *English Conversations* and by P. MacCarthy (see Bibliography), which simplifies the phonetic alphabet somewhat further.

Example of the Simplified Phonetic Transcription taken from N. C. Scott's "English Conversations."

'hʌ'lou! 'raːðə 'lʌk 'rʌniŋ intə 'juː. ai 'traid tə 'get juː on ðə 'foun, bət juː 'wəːnt 'ðeə.—'ʍwen wəz 'ðat?— 'ou, əbaut 'haːf ən auər ə'gou.—'ou, 'jes, ai d 'left bai 'ðen. 'did juː 'wont miː fə 'sʌmθiŋ 'speʃəl?—'aː juː 'duːiŋ eniθiŋ in pə'tikjulə ðis 'iːvniŋ?—ai dount 'θiŋk sou.

See p. xvii for the value of the letters used here.

CHAPTER VI

APPLICATION OF A KNOWLEDGE OF PHONETICS
TO THE TEACHING OF ENGLISH

57. In Chapter V of this book, phonetics is defined as the science which analyses and records speech. This analysis is the work of the phonetician, who is an observer with an ear trained to fine distinctions of sound. When such analyses and records have been made by the phonetician, there are several uses to which this knowledge may be put. In the present book we are concerned with its use in the teaching of English. It was assumed at the outset that teachers wish to teach a clear and distinct articulation and a pronunciation free from outstanding dialectal peculiarities, i.e. to "cure" an accent. This is, of course the most obvious use of phonetics to the English teacher, —and in this book it takes the chief place. The differences and similarities between articulation in speech and in song, between every-day speech and what is popularly known as "elocution," can be dealt with by phonetics, which should be used in teaching both elocution and singing.

58. Besides attempting to change an accent, the teacher can apply phonetics to the cure of specific speech defects, such as lisping of various kinds, inability to pronounce various consonants, such as *r*, *k*, etc. Children who have defects of this kind can generally be taught by phonetic methods to get rid of them: those children whose speech is slow in development can be helped, and those who have had cleft palate successfully

operated on can be taught to speak much better by a phonetically trained teacher.[1]

59. Teachers of the deaf have generally to undergo a phonetic training of some kind: this use of phonetics— the teaching of speech to the deaf—is one of the most useful applications of phonetic science.[2] A few experiments have been made in the teaching of reading in its initial stages by phonetics.[3] A description of such an experiment is published by the International Phonetic Association (University College London), under the title *Phonetics and Phonetic Tests in the Teaching of Reading*, by R. Jackson, M.A. [out of print].

60. A further use of phonetics lies in its application to the study of philology. Existing dialects can be analysed and recorded with great precision by a student with a trained ear and a knowledge of good phonetic notation, and the pronunciation of previous ages can be reconstructed and the development of modern pronunciation from Early English can be traced with considerable accuracy. In fact, without an exact and scientific knowledge of phonetics, philology becomes a mere history of the written word.[4]

[1] This side of the work is dealt with in the writer's *Defects of Speech : their Nature and Cure*. Dent & Co. [Out of print.]

[2] Miss Iza Thompson, Hugh Myddelton School for the Deaf, London, has written on work of this kind in various magazines on the teaching of the deaf. See *Volta Review*, July, 1927.

[3] [In recent years notably by means of the Initial Teaching Alphabet (see J. Pitman and J. St John, *Alphabets and Reading*).]

[4] Sweet, Preface to *Handbook of Phonetics :* "Without a knowledge of the laws of sound change, scientific philology— whether comparative or historical—is impossible, and without phonetics, their study degenerates into a mere mechanical enumeration of letter-changes."

CHAPTER VII

SPELLING PRONUNCIATIONS

61. A comparison of the pronunciation of certain words at the present day with that of other periods throws interesting light on tendencies and developments that have shown themselves in the history of English speech. Pronunciation changes are of two kinds: (*a*) Those gradual changes, which have taken centuries to develop, and which have changed Early English into the speech of to-day; and (*b*) those changes which are somewhat sudden, and which are, in the first place, a *deliberate* alteration of the established pronunciation for some purpose or other. In this book, it is not possible to deal with the first class, but the second class it will be advisable to examine, as this habit of deliberate alteration of an established pronunciation, which has shown itself for some generations, is still active to-day.

62. The main purpose of such alterations has been the desire to bring pronunciation more into line with the spelling, and for this reason the term " Spelling Pronunciations " is given to them.

63. Spelling pronunciations arise through some person who deliberately adopts a new pronunciation because he thinks it better; it is an affectation on his part. At first it is probably regarded as a false refinement by those who do not use it, but gradually by frequent repetition, the new pronunciation spreads, and a succeeding generation acquires it as its natural pronunciation. This tendency to change is marked at the present day, but it is by no means of recent development; it probably began with the grammarians and purists of the early eighteenth century. Until then people had written more or less as they spoke, and had certainly not let the written word affect their pronunciation. Since that time the tendency seems to have grown and an examination of modern speech shows it to be still going on.

64. Those who are interested in this aspect of pronunciation should consult Professor Wyld's *A History of Modern Colloquial English*, Chapter VIII, and *Studies in English Rhymes from Surrey to Pope*, and the sources he quotes. Most of the examples given here are collected from these books or from seventeenth and eighteenth century writers on English grammar and pronunciation.

EXAMPLES OF SPELLING PRONUNCIATIONS.

65. I. *Consonant sounds introduced.*

(a) The pronunciation of k in *perfect*, *verdict* (pɜˑfɪkt, vɜˑdɪkt) is a spelling pronunciation. The word *perfect* as introduced into English from Norman French was *parfet* or *parfit*; the *c* was re-introduced into the spelling in order to show the derivation of the word from Latin, and the pronunciation was altered to fit the spelling. Elphinston,[1] writing in 1790, says that *c* is not pronounced in *perfect*, *verdict*, *indict*. In the last-named it is still silent; we say ɪndaɪt; cf. also *victual* (vɪtl), in which it is also silent. In the same way the *d* was introduced into *adventure*, which was originally *aventure*; in *language*

---

[1] Elphinston, *Inglish Orthography Epittomized.*

(from *langage*) the *u* was introduced under the influence of the Latin *lingua*, and was afterwards
pronounced as the semi-vowel w (læŋgwɪdʒ); *equal*,
written as *egal*, acquired its w in a similar fashion.

(b) The habit of dropping *t's* and *d's* is not altogether
a modern one; indeed, examples go to show that
t's and *d's* dropped regularly in the seventeenth and
eighteenth centuries have been re-introduced into
the pronunciation in a number of words under the
influence of spelling. Jones,[1] writing in 1701,
gives a list of words in which he says *t* or *d* is not
pronounced: *often, Christmas, costly, ghostly, mostly,
roast beef, husband, pageant, Wednesday, wristband,
Wiltshire, friendly, handmaid, fondle, candle, handle,
children.* In some of these it has been restored,
and in others it is still not pronounced. (In the
Yorkshire dialect *fondle, candle, handle, kindle,* are
pronounced fɒnl, kanl, hanl, kɪnl.) In *Wednesday*
and *often* the process of " restoration " is seen at
work, some people pronouncing wɛnzdɪ, ɒfn, and
others wɛdnzdɪ, ɒftn (or even ɒftən); but we have not
yet attempted to restore *t* in *castle, listen,* etc.,
though the writer *has* heard *apostle* and *epistle*
pronounced əpɒstl and ɪpɪstl in the pulpit, and
pestle is often pronounced pɛstl.

(c) *p* is said to have been silent in *prompt, tempt,* etc.,
and *b* in *tumbling, Cambridge, chamber, humble* (cf.
Yorks. dialect tʊml for *tumble* and tʃɛːmə for
chamber). The *p* in *corpse* is intrusive: *corse* (kɔrs),
which was the normal spelling and pronunciation
in Tudor times, is still found in poetry.

[1] Jones, *The Expert Orthographer.*

(*d*) The present *th* of *theatre, anthem, author, Catherine*, has replaced a previous *t*; the spelling was first altered and later the pronunciation.

(*e*) The words *woman, Edward, forward, backward inward*, were formerly pronounced ʊmən (written *'ooman*), ɛdəd (*Ed'ard*), fɒrəd, bækəd, ɪnəd; the *w* is now pronounced in these words (cf. *towards*, tɔːdz and tʊwɔːdz). But *Greenwich* and *Norwich* remain grɪnɪʤ and nɒrɪʤ; cf. also *answer* ɑːnsə, *pennyworth* pɛnəθ, *hussy* hʌsɪ or hʌzi (from *housewife*), and the so-called vulgar pronunciation sʌmət for *somewhat*.

(*f*) The 1 sound in *fault, falter, vault, Walter, falcon, almanac, cauldron, falchion, Talbot, St. Albans*, is a spelling pronunciation. The word *fault* was *faute* when it came into English; the *l* was introduced in the spelling and then into the pronunciation. Jones (1701) says that the *l* in most of these words, and in *almost, Falmouth*, and *Chelmsford* is not pronounced; cf. *chalk, calf, almond, alms*, where it is still silent, and the name *Ralph*, which some people pronounce rælf, some as rɑːf, and others as reɪf. The *l* in the pronunciation of *soldier* is of comparatively recent introduction, the spelling *soger*, found frequently in the seventeenth century, indicating the pronunciation soʤə or sɒʤə, a pronunciation heard probably well on in the nineteenth century.

(*g*) The pronunciation of *h* in *habit, horror, homage*, and in *herb, hospital, humour*, is due to the influence of spelling, all these words having lost their *h* sound in French before they came into English. In the first three the *h* was re-introduced somewhat early, in the last three it is comparatively recent, and *humour* is still pronounced by some of the older generation as **juːmə**. *Hermit*, *horizon*, *hostler*, *heretic*, *hypocrite* are given by the seventeenth century writers as pronounced without *h*.

(*h*) Initial *h*, in words of other than French origin, seems also to have been frequently omitted, as the spellings *Amton Court*, *alff*, *at ome*, show. Its regular pronunciation nowadays in all but un-educated speech is probably due to the influence of spelling; the phrase *at home* may still be heard as **ət oʊm** from a number of educated speakers.

(*i*) Professor Wyld finds words like *white*, *when*, *wheat* spelt as *wite*, *wen*, *wete* as early as the fifteenth century, indicating the pronunciation **w** not **ʍ**. The pronunciation **ʍaɪt**, etc., is due to the influence of spelling in Southern and Midland English (but not in Scottish or Northern English, where *wh* has always been pronounced **ʍ**). Writers on pronunciation in the eighteenth century (as to-day) deplore the omission of *h* in such words, and say that it should be pronounced, a fact which seems to prove that both pronunciations were heard, and that the use of **w** for **ʍ** is not, as many are inclined to think, a recent degenerate tendency.

(*j*) The pronunciation of the termination *ing* is in-teresting. In words like *running*, *fishing*, *hunting*, etc., the pronunciation **ɪn** seems to have been common as early as the fourteenth century. The pronunciation ɪŋ is probably due to the spelling, and is now generally considered correct, the use of ɪn, like the dropping of the h being thought to be a vulgarism. There are, however, a number of educated people of the older generation who still use ɪn for the termination *ing*. Poet's rhymes go to prove that *ing* was pronounced ɪn: Pope rhymes *garden* and *farthing*; Swift *garden* and *Harding*; and Cooper, a grammarian, writing in 1685, says that the final syllables of *coming* and *cummin*, *coffin* and *coughing*, are pronounced alike.

66. II. *Words in which assimilations were made and later dissimilation, under the influence of spelling, has taken place.*

The spellings *emedgetly, teges, ojus, hijjus, perfyjus* (found by Wyld in diaries and letters), indicate the pronunciations ɪmiːdʒətlɪ, tiːdʒəs, oʊdʒəs, hɪdʒəs, pəfɪdʒəs. These pronunciations, probably good colloquial usage at the time when they were so written, are nowadays considered vulgar and slipshod; the influence of spelling reversed the process of assimilation which had led to these forms, and the result is the present pronunciations of ɪmiːdjətlɪ, tiːdjəs, oʊdɪəs, hɪdɪəs, pəfɪdɪəs. For modern tendencies in this direction see Chapter XVI, §§ 344-5 on Assimilation.

67. III. *Changes in vowel pronunciation due to the influence of spelling.*

(*a*) Words written with *er* are interesting, for some of these have retained their original pronunciation of ɑː, though still spelt with *er*, e.g. *clerk, Derby, Berkshire, sergeant, Hertford* (cf. *University* and

'*Varsity*). But *servant, person, learn, vermin,
deserve, earn, universal,* and others, which must at
some time have been pronounced with ɑː (and still
are in some dialects), are now pronounced with ɜː.
The present writer has come across the surname
Learner in Norfolk which is pronounced by most
people lɑːnə.

(b) Words written with *au* such as *taunt, launch,
staunch, laundry,* and the place names *Launceston,
Taunton,* were formerly pronounced with ɑː; some
people still consider lɑːndri and lɑːnʃ correct, and
Launceston and *Taunton* are pronounced lɑːnstən
and tɑːntən by natives of these places.

(c) In words like *grovel, hovel, Coventry, Bromley,
Honiton,* the vowel was probably ʌ, but the spelling
pronunciation ɒ seems gradually to be replacing
this. Both pronunciations are heard of *accomplish,
Coventry,* and *Bromley,* while *accompany* is always,
and *constable* generally, pronounced with ʌ.

(d) The word *bowls*—the game of bowls—from the
French *boule,* like all other *ou* words, should have
developed into aʊ. Its present pronunciation, oʊ,
is probably due to the fact that it was spelt like
bowl, a basin, and has developed the same pronunciation. In the Yorkshire dialect a bowling
green is still called a baʊlɪŋ griːn.

(e) The sounds ju in certain words must be due to the
influence of spelling, for the words *nephews, monu-
ment, reputation* are found written as *nevys, moni-
ment, repetation,* obviously indicating the pronunciation nɛvɪz, mɒnɪmənt, rɛpɪteɪʃn.[1]

[1] See Luick, *Historische Grammatik der englischen Sprache,*
§§ 466, 597, 608.

68. IV. *Spelling pronunciations due to words being* seen *written and not heard.*

Place and family names (like foreign words) which are seen and not heard are frequently pronounced as they are spelt. Thus anyone unfamiliar with London would pronounce *Holborn* as houlbɔːn or hɒlbɔːn, *Marylebone* as mɛərɪləboun, not knowing that these names have in the course of time developed into houbən, mærɪbən (or mɑːlɪbən), pronunciations that are well established.[1] Place names ending in *-ham* are frequently given a spelling pronunciation which violates the original form of the first part of the word. Thus *Merstham* may be heard as mɜːsθəm and *Streatham* as strɛθəm (not by Londoners, however). *North Walsham,* in Norfolk, is pronounced by non-inhabitants wɒlʃəm, but by inhabitants wɒlsəm, the former being a spelling pronunciation. Note also the pronunciation of *Southampton,* sauθhæm(p)tən, as if it were South-hampton. In [its early] years the B.B.C. Advisory Committee had to consider the question of spelling pronunciations with respect to certain place names. *Daventry,* which had developed into deɪntrɪ during centuries of use, has by the force of spelling returned to dævntrɪ, since to large numbers of people who do not know the local pronunciation and who read the name daily in the papers, the old pronunciation would be unrecognisable. A fierce newspaper correspondence followed the B.B.C. pronunciation of the word *conduit* (*Conduit St.*). Here the purists insisted on kʌndɪt; the ordinary man in the street pronounces it kɒndjuɪt. What is the wisest line

[1] Marylebone seems, however, to be very frequently pronounced mærɪləbən.

to take in such a case? Surely here is a place for tolerance of a spelling pronunciation and for the purist few not to object to a pronunciation they themselves do not use.

69. V. *Modern tendencies in Spelling Pronunciations.*

There are two main ways in which the tendency towards Spelling Pronunciations shows itself to-day; the first is in reversing the assimilations that have been made by previous generations, and the second is in giving the strong vowel pronunciation in syllables where the weak vowel has been established for long years. The pronunciation əpri·sıeıt instead of əpri·ʃıeıt is an example of the first, and kɒnsɛnt, weıstkoʊt, pɑːlıəmənt, instead of kənsɛnt, wɛskət, pɑːləmənt, are examples of the second. Individuals who themselves imitate such pronunciations, however, are seldom consistent, using the careful spelling pronunciation form in some words and not in others. For the most part, such speakers use these pronunciations with the idea that they are making their speech more distinct. Both these tendencies are dealt with in the Chapter on " Sounds in Connected Speech," where Assimilation, Dissimilation, and the influence of stress and rhythm on the pronunciation of sounds are considered.

70. What attitude is the teacher to take in the matter of spelling pronunciations? Spelling pronunciations which are well established in the language will, of course, be accepted, but what must he do about fresh innovations? The main thing for the teacher to avoid is a false idea of the value of spelling in spoken language, an idea which will lead him to teach artificial pronunciations under the impression that he is teaching

" careful " speech. If he is trained to observe what are the actual usages in the spoken language, he will be less likely to fall into this mistake. Whether the tendency towards re-establishing a pronunciation that has long passed away is to be encouraged or not is a question upon which every person is entitled to his own opinion. But it is the safer and wiser plan for the individual teacher to confine himself to teaching good modern usages, rather than to set himself up as a maker of a new standard of correctness.

Chapter VIII

ORGANS OF SPEECH

71. The student should have an elementary knowledge of the construction of the speech organs and how
they are used in the formation of speech sounds. The
diagrams in this chapter show all that it is *essential* to
know; the student who is interested in physiology and
anatomy will find further information in books on these
subjects.

72. In the following diagram, the main organs of
speech are shown and named. The student should
familiarise himself with these terms and should examine
as far as he can with the aid of a mirror the inside of his
mouth, and try to realise the movements he makes. To do
this last easily will take some time, but he will gradually
acquire the power of feeling what he is doing and of
being able to describe it.

L.L. Lips.

T.T. Teeth.

T.R. Teeth ridge (alveoli or gums); convex part of
   the roof of the mouth, immediately behind
   the teeth.

H.P. Hard palate: concave part of the roof of the
   mouth.

S.P. Soft palate (velum): membranous curtain.

U. Uvula: pendulous end of the soft palate.

N.P. Nasal pharynx: space between the soft palate
   and the back wall of the throat.

P. Pharynx: space between the back of the tongue
   and the back wall of the throat.

Bl.   Blade of tongue, including tip; that part which
        lies opposite the teeth ridge when the tongue
        is in a position of rest.

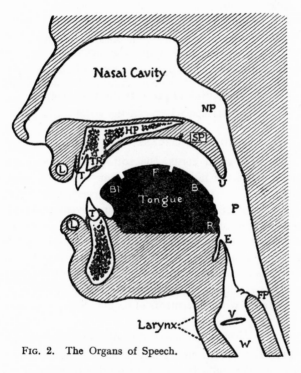

Fig. 2.   The Organs of Speech.

F.   Front of tongue: that part which lies opposite
      the hard palate when the tongue is in a
      position of rest.

B.   Back of tongue; that part which lies opposite
      the soft palate when the tongue is in a
      position of rest.

R. Root of tongue.

E. Epiglottis: this is drawn over the windpipe when swallowing.

W. Windpipe.

F.P. Gullet or food passage.

V. Vocal cords or lips[1]: membranes stretched from front to back across the larynx.

La. Larynx: the upper extremity of the windpipe (popularly called Adam's apple) which contains and protects the vocal cords.

Glottis: space between the vocal cords.

MOVABLE ORGANS OF SPEECH.

73. The vocal cords, the soft palate, the tongue and the lips are movable: the other organs of speech are fixed. The movable organs of speech can act independently of each other and their movements can be combined in different ways: consequently it is possible to make a very large number of different speech sounds. In any one language, however, the number of combinations is not very large. (See Section on voiced and voiceless sounds, where the action of the vocal cords is combined with movements of tongue, lips, palate, etc.)

HOW SPEECH SOUNDS ARE MADE.

74. The breath in passing from the lungs to the outer air is modified on its way by one or more of the

---

[1] "The vocal cords form a membranous reed-instrument, consisting of two elastic plates, stretched so as to leave a narrow fissure between them, so that when the current of air streams through the fissure, they are thrown into vibration."—C. H. von Meyer, *The Organs of Speech*.

movable organs of speech; and this gives rise to the various sounds of speech. In the following paragraphs the modification of the breath stream by each of the organs of speech will be examined in turn, and exercises suggested to enable the student to obtain full control over his speech mechanism.

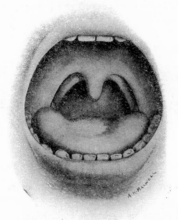

FIG. 3. Open Mouth.

THE VOCAL CORDS.

75. The vocal cords or vocal lips, as they may be called, for they resemble lips rather than cords, are stretched across the larynx from front to back. These cords can take up several positions, and in this way affect speech sounds.

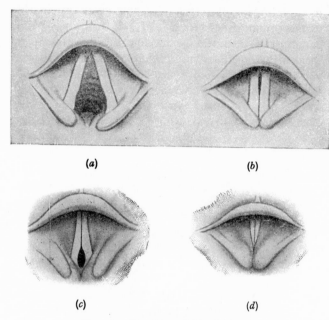

FIG. 4. Drawings of Vocal Cords.

(a) Vocal cords in position for breath.
(b)   ,,   ,,   during formation of a chest-note.
(c)   ,,   ,,   during whisper.
(d)   ,,   ,,   in position for a vigorous glottal stop.

(a) The vocal lips can be apart, leaving space for the
     breath to pass through without any obstruction of
     any kind. This gives rise to what is known as
     breath (heard purely in the English sound h).
     Fig. 4(a) above.   The vocal cords are in this
     position for the consonant sounds p, t, k, f, θ, s, ʃ.

(b)   The vocal lips can be brought together in such a
way that the air, forcing its way through them in
rhythmical puffs, opens and closes them regularly
and very rapidly. This, commonly called vibration
of the vocal cords, gives rise to a musical note,
which may vary in pitch and intensity according
to the number and extent of the rhythmical movements, and the note is called voice. Fig. 4(b) shows
the position of the vocal cords while a chest note
is being sung. All speech sounds which have this
musical accompaniment are said to be voiced. All
vowels are produced with this action of the vocal
cords; and the consonants b, d, g, m, n, ŋ, l, v,
ð, z, ʒ, r are voiced.

(c)   In Fig. 4(c) the position of the vocal cords is
shown which gives rise to whisper.

(d)   The vocal lips can be brought into complete
contact so that the air is entirely stopped for a
moment. This is the position taken up when one
holds one's breath, and is known as *closed glottis*
(Fig. 4(d)). On the sudden separation of the vocal
cords an explosion is heard, when the air, which
has been compressed behind the stop, escapes. This
sound is called the glottal stop [phonetic symbol
ʔ]. In an exaggerated form it is heard as a little
cough (ʔəhə, ʔəhə). The glottal stop is a common
speech sound in many varieties of English pronunciation (see Ch. XIV, § 250 d), but, as it has
no letter in English orthography to represent it,
its existence is not generally realised.

VOICED AND VOICELESS SOUNDS.

76. It has been observed that the actions of the movable organs of speech are independent of each other, and their movements can be combined in a large number of ways, and thus give rise to a large variety of speech sounds. The commonest combination is that of the action of the vocal cords with movements of the tongue, soft palate, and lips: i.e. when the lips, tongue and soft palate are in certain positions, articulating certain sounds, the vocal cords can be open or in vibration. Thus we speak of voiced and voiceless sounds; voiced sounds are those which are accompanied by the vibration of the vocal cords, while all the sounds in which the vocal cords are apart, as in Fig. 4(a), are said to be voiceless. All vowels are voiced sounds. Every consonant can be made with or without voice, e.g. f is voiceless, v is voiced; both are articulated in the same way, the difference between them being due to the action of the vocal cords. ʃ and ʒ, θ and ð are other pairs of consonants articulated in the same way; for the first of each pair, the vocal cords are open, allowing a free passage of the air, and for the second they are close together, and open and close rhythmically and very rapidly. The student is advised to practise distinguishing the presence or absence of voice; he can do so by saying the sounds alternately, at the same time covering the ears with his hands, or placing the hand on the top of the head, or feeling the outside of the larynx. For the voiced sounds a vibration can be felt. Not all English consonants are found in pairs, however; l, m, n, ŋ, r have voice, and their voiceless counterparts are not

considered normal English sounds. (They are sometimes heard in combination with other consonants; see Ch. XVI, § 334.) But it is possible to make a voiceless l, m, n, ŋ, and r, and the student is advised to practise making these sounds, as a good exercise for control of the vocal cords. The term "breathed" is sometimes given to those sounds in which the vocal cords are open; it is convenient to use this term for continuant sounds and "voiceless" for the plosive consonants—the latter because there cannot be a current of air passing between the vocal cords during the stop of a plosive, as would be implied by the term "breathed." Both, however, can be called "voiceless." Note that voiced and voiceless consonants differ not only in the presence or absence of voice, but in vigour of articulation and breath force; the voiced consonants are weaker in articulation and less breath force is used.

77. EXERCISES FOR CONTROL OF THE VOCAL CORDS.

(a) For pupils who have difficulty in voicing consonants. The pupil should pronounce the vowel ɜ (the vowel sound in *bird*), and while saying this, bring the bottom lip against the top teeth, making ɜːv. The voice should continue throughout; if the pupil thinks of the *vowel* all the time, the voice will go on through the consonant as well. If necessary he should sing it. The contact of lip and teeth may be light to begin with, but it should gradually become stronger.

(b) Similar exercises can be performed with z, ʒ, ð. When the pupil can carry on the voice into the consonant, he should try to pronounce the voiced consonant without the preceding vowel.

(c) The exercise of alternating breathed and voiced consonants is of great value—

| sz sz sz | θð θð θð |
| fv fv fv | ʃʒ ʃʒ ʃʒ. |

Each of these pairs of consonants should be repeated several times without a break.

(d) When the vocal cords are sufficiently under control to do these familiar pairs of sounds, the same exercise should be practised with other pairs of consonants, of which the voiced one only occurs in English, e.g. the pupil should say l, and then say it without voice; this gives l̥, the sound of Welsh *ll*. These two should then be alternated— l̥l l̥l l̥l. Similar exercises can be made with the nasal consonants m, n, ŋ; mm̥ mm̥; nn̥ nn̥; ŋŋ̥ ŋŋ̥. (The sign ₒ placed below any symbol—or above in the case of letters with tails—indicates that it is pronounced without voice.)

THE SOFT PALATE.

78.   The soft palate can take up two positions; it can be in the position marked (a) in Figure 5 (page 57), when the passage to the nose is open, or in the position marked (b) where it is raised to touch the back wall of the pharynx. When the palate is raised, all the air from the windpipe escapes through the mouth, giving rise to *oral* sounds; when the palate is lowered and the passage to the nose is open, the air can escape either entirely through the nose (if the mouth passage is closed), or through the nose and mouth. The lowering of the soft palate gives rise

to nasal, or nasalised sounds. Its function, as far as speech is concerned, therefore, is to close or open the passage to the nose, to close it for the production of those sounds which are not nasal, and to open it for the nasal sounds.

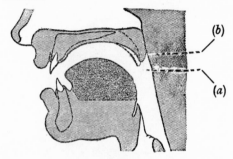

FIG. 5. Soft Palate raised and lowered.

79. The student of phonetics, especially if he is going to use his knowledge in the teaching of pronunciation, should be able consciously to control the movements of the soft palate. He should look into his mouth, say a very back variety of ɑ with considerable vigour, trying to lower the back of his tongue, and see how the palate rises. If he cannot do this at once, he should depress the back of the tongue with a tongue spatula (or a spoon handle) and watch the movement of his palate; then he should practise until he can do this at will, without the tongue being pressed down. Compare the two illustrations of the inside of the mouth (pp. 51 and 58). In the first the palate is lowered; in the second it is raised as high as possible. If the student cannot raise the palate easily, he should try the following exercise. Open the mouth wide, keeping the

tip of the tongue pressed against the bottom teeth; then yawn vigorously. The palate will be seen to rise.

FIG. 6. Open Mouth with Palate raised.

Relax the muscles thus stretched and the palate drops. A repetition of these two movements will help towards the control of the soft palate.   Another way of realising the movement of the palate will be found in pronouncing the word *mutton* (mʌtn) with considerable force.   The student must take care that he puts no vowel between the *t* and *n*; the explosion he can feel and hear is made as the soft palate leaves the back wall of the pharynx, and the air compressed below that place escapes through the nose.   A repetition of **tn tn tn** will help him to realise the movement of the palate and in time to control it.   (He should be quite sure that he is saying **tn** and not ʔn.) Similarly, he should practise **dn dn dn**, as in *sudden* (sʌdn), **kŋ kŋ kŋ**, **gŋ gŋ gŋ**, in each case without moving the tongue, and **pm pm pm** and **bm bm bm** without moving the lips. He should try to realise the position of the soft palate *before* the explosion is heard, i.e. when it is touching the back wall of the pharynx. A more difficult exercise is to alternate oral and nasal vowels, e.g. **aã aã aã**. This should be done without any appreciable movement of the tongue, and care must be taken not to add the nasal consonant **ŋ** to the vowel **a**.

THE TONGUE.

80. The tongue is, perhaps, the most important of the organs of speech, for it is capable of making many movements, and consequently of modifying the breath stream in numerous ways. It plays the chief part in the formation of vowel sounds, when its different positions alter the shape of the resonating chamber of the mouth and give rise to vowel sounds of various acoustic qualities. It is used in the articulation of many of the consonants, when it either blocks the air passage through the mouth at some point or other, or narrows it so that friction is heard. These movements will be dealt with in the chapters on vowels and consonants. Here it is necessary only to give a few exercises for the control of the tongue.

EXERCISES FOR CONTROL OF THE TONGUE.

81. The pupil should take a mirror, and where the mouth is sufficiently open to permit of it, he should watch the movements of his tongue while he does the following exercises.

(*a*) Touch with the tip of the tongue the top lip, the bottom lip, the left corner, the right corner of the mouth. Repeat this many times until it can be done very quickly and with great precision.[1]

(*b*) Open the mouth; alternately spread and point the tongue.

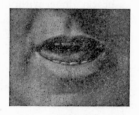
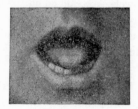

Fig. 7a   Fig. 7b

Photograph of Tongue spreading and contracting.

(*c*) For precision in consonant formation, repeat the following exercises many times, in whisper and in ordinary voice, concentrating on the movements of the tongue.

pɑ tɑ kɑ	kɑ tɑ pɑ	tɑ kɑ pɑ
bɑ dɑ gɑ	gɑ dɑ bɑ	dɑ gɑ bɑ
kɑ pɑ tɑ	pɑ kɑ tɑ	tɑ pɑ kɑ
gɑ bɑ dɑ	bɑ gɑ dɑ	dɑ bɑ gɑ
mɑ nɑ ŋɑ	ŋɑ nɑ mɑ	nɑ mɑ ŋɑ
nɑ ŋɑ mɑ	mɑ ŋɑ nɑ	ŋɑ mɑ nɑ

[1] This sounds a very childish exercise; but the writer has found many people unable to perform it.

sa ʃa sa ʃa	ʃa sa ʃa sa	sa ʃa sa	ʃa sa ʃa
za ʒa za ʒa	ʒa za ʒa za	za ʒa za	ʒa za ʒa
fa θa fa θa	θa fa θa fa	fa θa fa	θa fa θa
va ða va ða	ða va ða va	va ða va	ða va ða
fa sa fa sa	sa fa sa fa	fa sa fa	sa fa sa
va za va za	za va za va	va za va	za va za
θa sa θa sa	sa θa sa θa	θa ʃa θa	ʃa θa ʃa
ða za ða za	za ða za ða	ða ʒa ða	ʒa ða ʒa
la ra ma	ra la ma	ma la ra	
ra ma la	la ma ra	ma ra la	

82. These exercises should be pronounced with a vigorous articulation of the consonants; in this way they will prove useful to counteract a tendency to indistinct speech, as well as in giving quick control of the movements of the tongue. The teacher can vary them with different vowels, and can invent other combinations of consonants. It is well to do preliminary practice of this kind on meaningless syllables rather than on real words, so that the attention is not diverted from the main purpose, i.e. precise movements of the tongue.

83. For tongue control in the formation of vowel sounds, the following exercises should prove useful. The student should pronounce the vowel iː (the sound in *see*); while continuing the sound, he should round his lips without moving the tongue. This will give rise to a new vowel, not used in English (similar to French vowel in *rue*, phonetic symbol y). A useful exercise can now be made by alternating these two sounds, iy iy iy; the student will find it difficult at first to keep the tongue still, and he will want to pronounce his familiar **u** sound instead of **y**. If he finds difficulty in obtaining this new sound, he can reach it in another way, by first rounding the lips, and, while keeping them in this position, trying to say the vowel **i**. Similar exercises can be made from other vowels. Pronounce the vowel **e**; while continuing this sound, round the lips, and the new sound **ø** (similar to French vowel in *peu*), is produced; then **eø eø eø** can be practised. In the same way **ɛœ ɛœ ɛœ** gives a further exercise for control of the tongue.

Note.—In these and all similar exercises the student should practise on *one* note without any break: if he uses a different tone for each vowel, he may think he is making a change in the *quality* of the vowel, whereas the change may be one of *note* only. It would be advisable for the student to postpone the practice of these last exercises until the chapter on cardinal vowels has been studied.

THE LIPS.

84. The remaining organs of speech to be dealt with are the lips. The lips can articulate sounds themselves, and their movement can be combined with that of other organs of speech in the formation of both consonants and vowels. Like the vocal cords, the lips can take up four positions.

(*a*) They can be wide open, as in the sounds **ɑ** or **h**.

(*b*) They can be brought into contact so that the air is completely stopped for a moment and then released. This gives the sound **p** (with addition of voice, **b**).

(c) They can be brought close together, so that the air pushes itself through, making friction. This is the sound we make in blowing out a candle and is called *bi-labial f* (phonetic symbol ϕ); it exists as a speech sound in many languages, as does the voiced equivalent, bi-labial *v* (β). The student should practise these sounds, although they are not English, as such an exercise helps in the control of the lips. Care should be taken not to round the lips or raise the back of the tongue as for the English ʍ or w.

(d) They can be made to vibrate. This is the sound that babies are fond of making, and in some countries it is used to encourage a horse to go quickly. In Bavaria and Sweden it is used to command a horse to stop.

85. In addition to these positions, the lips come into play in the formation of vowel sounds. It has been shown in § 83 that rounding the lips alters the quality of vowels. Most English back vowels have a certain amount of lip-rounding, and most English front vowels are pronounced with neutrally open lips. (See photograph of lips in Ch. IX, p. 72.) When the front vowels are articulated with great vigour, the lips may be spread. Foreigners generally accuse English people of talking with closed mouth, and with very little lip movement, and although we dislike the exaggerated " mouthing " that is sometimes seen in recitation, it is well to encourage pupils to make a sufficient amount of lip movement to ensure that their speech is as clear and distinct as it can be.

86. EXERCISES FOR THE CONTROL OF THE LIPS.

(a) The student should practise with the aid of a small mirror the four positions described in § 84.

(b) For the sake of practice, he should make exaggerated movements in rounding and pushing out the lips and in spreading them. Alternate the following pairs of vowels with vigorous lip and jaw movement.

uːiː uːiː	ɑːuː ɑːuː	uːeː uːeː
ɛːoː ɛːoː	iːɑː iːɑː	ɑːiː ɑːiː
ɛːuː ɛːuː	ɔːiː ɔːiː	iːeː iːeː

(c) To keep the lips still, while the tongue moves, the student should say the sound uː (as in *soon*), and while keeping the lips in this rounded position, he should try to say the sound iː. The result will be the sound **y**, which has already been obtained in another way (see § 83). The two vowels can now be alternated **uy uy uy**. Similar exercises can be made from other vowels. If the student pronounces **o**, and with the lips in this position, he tries to say e, he will pronounce **ø** (see § 83). Now **oø oø oø** can be alternated, the student taking care that the lips do not move. Similarly if he pronounces ɔ, and with the lips in this position tries to say ɛ, he will pronounce œ. Now **ɔœ ɔœ ɔœ** can be alternated.

These exercises and those suggested in § 83 can be considered as exercises for both lips and tongue. In the one case the lips must be held still and the tongue must move, and in the other the tongue is still and the lips move.

CHAPTER IX

CLASSIFICATION OF SPEECH SOUNDS
VOWELS AND CONSONANTS
CARDINAL VOWELS

87. It is necessary for the purposes of phonetics to be able to describe all speech sounds of a language, and in order to do this accurately some method of classification must be adopted. Speech sounds are generally divided into *vowels* and *consonants*. The main difference between a vowel and a consonant is one of sonority; vowels are those sounds which have most carrying power; but certain consonants such as *l* and *m* also have considerable carrying power, so that a definition of a vowel must be such that it does not include these sonorous consonants.

88. In ordinary speech a *vowel* is a voiced sound in the pronunciation of which the air passes through the mouth in a continuous stream, there being no obstruction and no narrowing such as would produce audible friction. All other sounds are consonants.

89. A *consonant* is a sound accompanied or un-accompanied by voice, in which there is either a complete or partial obstruction which prevents the air from issuing freely from the mouth.

90. The old definition of a consonant as a sound which cannot be pronounced without a vowel is wrong. It is quite easy to pronounce a consonant, in fact, in many languages there are words consisting entirely of

consonants; tz, in Chinese, f, in Czech, krk, in Croatian,
are words; and in English we say ʃ when we want some-
one to be quiet, the word *from* often becomes frm in
quick speech (aɪ kʌm frm lʌndən), and we speak of
snt pɔːlz. For the classification of consonants see
Chapter XIV.

Classification of Vowels.

91. The difference in quality between one vowel and
another is caused by the movements of the tongue and
lips, which alter the shape of the resonance chamber of
the mouth. For the sake of describing and identifying
vowels, we classify them according to the position of
the tongue. The student is advised to look into his
mouth and watch his tongue as he pronounces ɑ - - iː;
then, i - - ɛ - - ɜ - - ɑ - - ɔ, keeping the mouth open as
wide as possible. He will see that for iː, the *front* part
of the tongue is raised to a considerable height, for ɛ it
is lower, for ɑ and ɔ it is the *back* which is mainly concerned, while for ɜ a part is raised that is *intermediate*
between front and back.[1] Consequently, vowels are
classified as *front*, *back*, and *central*, according to the
part of the tongue that is raised, and as *close*, *half-close*
half-open, and *open*, according to the *degree* of raising
which takes place. Thus i in *see* is a front close vowel,
æ as in *man* is a front half-open vowel, ɑ as in *half*
is a back open vowel, ɔ as in *all* is a back half-open

[1] See diagram on p. 49. The reader is reminded that the
front of the tongue lies opposite the hard palate and does not
include the blade and tip. The blade and tip play little part in
the production of vowel sounds except in the case of the retroflex
vowels of American speech and of certain English dialects. For
the formation of these, see p. 210.

vowel, ʊ as in *book* is a close back vowel, and ɜ as in *bird* is a central half-open vowel. It is not easy to know what one is doing with one' tongue in the formation of vowel sounds, and the student is advised to practise all the vowels he can say—his own natural ones, any others he can imitate, or any foreign ones he knows—and at the same time try to realize what part of the tongue is mainly concerned, how he is moving it, and what the vowel sounds like. In this way, he will learn to recognise from his own muscular sensations and from the acoustic effect, whether a vowel is back, front, or central, whether open or close.

92. English vowels, according to this scheme of classification, can easily be put into one of these categories, but the classification does not allow for the existence of several varieties of i, of ɛ, of ɔ, of ɑ, etc. It would, of course, be possible to say that one person's pronunciation of the vowel sound in *get*, for example, is more close or more open than another's, and if the two speakers are together, the difference between the two types of pronunciation can be heard. But if, in a book on phonetics, a writer refers to the vowel sound in the word *get*, the reader does not know which of the many varieties is meant.[1] Something else, therefore, is needed. If a vowel, in addition to being classified as a front, back or central vowel, close or open, can be compared to some known, unchangeable vowel, the student is in a much better position to realize exactly what the sound is. In most books on pronunciation,

[1] The close and experienced observer of pronunciation readily recognises that there are many varieties of most vowel sounds, even in educated speech. See Chapter XI.

whether of the Mother Tongue or of a foreign language,
a list of key words is given.   But as there are many
varieties of pronunciation in one language, these key
words, though possibly indicating roughly what a sound
is like, are valueless for exact study, as the reader is
likely to interpret them in a different way from that
in which the writer intended.   (Moreover, in the case
of a foreign language, it is impossible to describe the
pronunciation of one language in terms of another.)

93.   To avoid this difficulty, it is necessary therefore,
to have some *standard* vowels, which shall act as a kind
of scale or measure, with which to compare all other
vowel sounds, and which shall be constant.   It was
with this end in view that Professor Daniel Jones
devised a scheme of *cardinal vowels*.   These vowels
do not belong to any one language; they have been
chosen arbitrarily to represent certain well-defined
tongue-positions, and have a definite acoustic quality.
X-ray photographs have been taken of the tongue
positions of most of them, and gramophone records
have been made of them.[1]   They form an acoustic
sequence such that the intervals between any two con-
secutive ones shall be as nearly as possible equal.

94.   It is obvious that if these cardinal vowels are
going to be used at all, the student must know them;
he must be able to identify and say each one with
accuracy.   The best way to do this is to work with a
trained teacher who knows them.   If such a teacher is
not available, the next best thing is to try to imitate

[1] Records of the cardinal vowels have been made by the
Linguaphone Institute, ENG. 252–3 and 254–5, and are obtain-
able therefrom.

the gramophone. They should be pronounced with the tip of the tongue against the lower front teeth throughout, with tense muscles, with the extreme of the appropriate lip position (except for Nos. 4 and 5), and all on the same pitch. Once the cardinal vowels are learnt the work of the comparison of vowels can begin. The scheme is invaluable for the identifying and describing of the vowel sounds of a foreign language, for the comparison of the vowel sounds of two or more languages, and can be used with equal success in the comparison of variant pronunciations of the Mother Tongue, whether dialectal or individual differences. [1]

CARDINAL VOWEL FIGURE.

95. The cardinal vowel figure is made up from the accompanying diagrams of tongue-positions (Figs. 8 and 9).

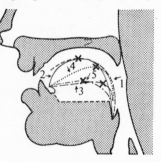

FIG. 8.

Tongue positions of Cardinal Vowels

i, a, ɑ, u.

1 – – – – – Vowel limit: the tongue moved beyond this limit, with normal breath force, would cause friction, and the resulting sound would be a consonant.

2 ———— Tongue position of the most forward and the closest vowel sound possible.

3 —— —— Tongue position of the lowest and most retracted vowel sound possible.

4 .... Tongue position of the furthest-back close vowel sound possible.

5 ·—·—·—·— Tongue position of the lowest and most forward vowel sound possible,

X Highest point of the tongue in each case.

[1] The cardinal vowel figure is now almost universally used in books on languages.

These four positions give the four " corners " of the cardinal vowel figure. Two intermediate tongue positions between i and a and between u and ɑ are chosen, giving e and ɛ as half-close and half-open *front* vowels respectively and o and ɔ as half-close and half-open *back* vowels respectively.

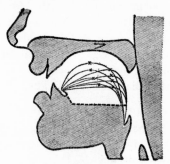

FIG. 9.
Tongue positions of the Eight
Primary Cardinal Vowels.

96.   The relation of these tongue positions can be more   easily   realised   in   diagrammatic   form   than

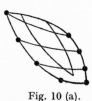

Fig. 10 (a).

in   a   drawing   like   the   one   given above. The true   shape   of   such a diagram should be Fig. 10 (a) which   is   made   by   a   line   joining   the   highest   point   of   the tongue of each vowel position, but for   practical   reasons   it   has   been found better to conventionalise it into the form represented in Fig. 10 (b)

97.   This gives a rough indication of the relative tongue positions of the *eight primary cardinal* vowels.

There are others, the learning of which it will be convenient to defer to a later time. When the cardinal vowels are known, any vowel can be placed on the figure and thus its relation to the nearest cardinal vowels can be shown. To do this accurately

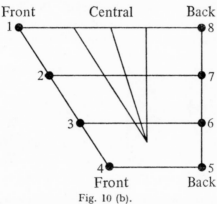

Fig. 10 (b).

requires a finely trained ear and much practice, but once such skill is gained, it is possible to show and interpret the relation of any vowel to any other with considerable precision.

98. In Chapter XI of this book the writer's English vowels are placed showing their relation to the cardinal vowels. The student should first master the cardinal vowels and then try to place his own vowels on the figure. English readers should note that the cardinal vowels are *pure* vowels, not diphthongs, i.e. the organs of speech remain in *one* position during the whole of the time that the sound is being made. They will need to watch particularly Nos. 2 and 7, in which a tendency to diphthongise is likely to show itself.

99.   It is convenient for reference to number the eight primary cardinal vowels.

1.	2.	3.	4.	5.	6.	7.	8.
i	e	ɛ	a	ɑ	ɔ	o	u

100.   In addition to the tongue, the lips are also concerned in the production of vowel sounds.   The lips can be either rounded or spread or in a neutral position.

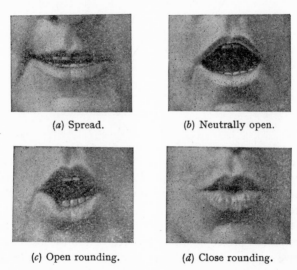

(a) Spread.   (b) Neutrally open.

(c) Open rounding.   (d) Close rounding.

FIG. 11.   Photographs of Four Lip Positions.

For i they are spread; for u they are close-rounded; for ɔ open-rounded; and for ɑ and ɜ they are neutrally open.

101.   In the cardinal vowels the four front vowels are pronounced with spread lips; cardinal ɑ has neutrally

open lips, and the back vowels ɔ, o and u have varying degrees of lip-rounding. The lip-position of the English vowels will be given in the detailed descriptions of each one. (See Chapter XI.)

102. Some phoneticians consider the tenseness or laxness of the muscles of the tongue as being of importance in the production of vowel sounds. For instance, i is often described as a tense vowel, and ɪ as the corresponding lax one; u is said to be tense, while ʊ is lax. But the tenseness or laxness of vowels has not yet been sufficiently well demonstrated for it to be of primary importance in the description of English vowels.

CHAPTER X

PHONEMES

103. The scientific study of pronunciation has revealed the fact that any one language contains far more speech sounds than is usually recognised. It is often stated that English possesses thirty-nine speech sounds, but an examination of facts shows that if the term speech sound is understood in its accurate sense, the English language has very many more than thirty-nine. For this purpose, the difference between a speech sound proper and what is termed a phoneme must be explained. " A speech sound proper is a sound of definite organic formation, and definite acoustic quality which is incapable of variation." [1] It is found that the sounds of a language group themselves into a number of families, that, for instance, a speaker does not use *one* ɪ sound and one only, one ɛ, one t, one l sound, but several varieties of ɪ, of ɛ, of t, and of l, etc. To these families of sounds the name *Phoneme* has been given. A phoneme is a family of sounds in a given language which are related in character and are such that no one of them ever occurs in the same phonetic context in a word as any other. By language in this connection is understood one person's pronunciation, and by phonetic context is meant surrounded by the same sounds and under the same conditions of length, stress and intonation.[2]

[1] *The Pronunciation of Russian*, D. Jones and M. Trofimov. 1924. (Cambridge University Press.)

[2] Definition given by Prof. D. Jones in *Outline of English Phonetics*, 3rd Edn. [In 9th edition, on p. 49.]

104. Examples will make this clearer. In the word *little* (lɪtl) the two *l*-sounds are of different formation (see Chapter XIV, §§ 262-3, on "clear" and "dark" *l*); the tongue position for **k** in *key* is different from that of **k** in *call*; in the pronunciation of many people the two vowel sounds in *city* (sɪtɪ) are different, the ɛ in *get* is different from ɛ in *well*; the u in *music* is different from the u in *cool*; the actual point of contact in making the **t** sound varies in the words *each* (iˑʧ), *eats* (iˑts), and *eighth* (eɪtθ) (see diagram, p. 137). That is to say, we must speak not of the English **k**, the English ɪ, the English **t** *sound*, since from these examples it is obvious that there is more than one **k**, one ɪ, one t, but of the English **k**, ɪ, **t** phoneme or family, meaning all the varieties of **k**, ɪ, **t**, etc., which are used in different combinations of sounds by one speaker.

105. Care must be taken not to confuse the various members of the phoneme with the different pronunciations heard from different people. The latter may be termed *variant pronunciations*; the different sounds constituting a phoneme occur in *one* person's pronunciation.

106. It is impossible to trace the history of all these groups of sounds, but many of the varieties are due to the influence of surrounding sounds and to position in the sound group. Thus the second ɪ in *city* is often more open than the first because it is final; the **k** in *key* is made in a more forward position than that in *cool*, because of the following *close, front* vowel iː; the **t** in *eighth* (eɪtθ) is made against the edge of the top teeth, and not against the teeth ridge (which is the commonest variety, and therefore the main member of the

phoneme) in order to be ready for the following θ sound; the u in *music* (mju·zɪk) is often more forward than the u in *cool* (kuːl) under the influence of the preceding j.

107. The native speaker of English, because he always uses one member of the phoneme in one position and another in another position is generally unaware of these differences in pronunciation, even when, as sometimes happens, they are in actual formation far removed from each other. There is a considerable difference in tongue position and in acoustic quality between the various *l* sounds which form one phoneme in English (see Chapter XIV, § 263–4), but because an Englishman uses a " clear" *l* before vowels and a " dark" *l* before consonants and finally, he finds it hard to realise that there *is* any difference.

108. For the purposes of language study, it is interesting and useful to note the existence of phonemes— a phenomenon that occurs in all languages. It is most important considered from the point of view of recording languages phonetically. The smallest number of symbols required for writing down a language unambiguously is the number of phonemes in that language. For the native speaker no more are needed, as he will generally use the subsidiary members in their right place naturally; and to have a separate symbol for even the important members of every phoneme would add unnecessarily to the alphabet and make it unwieldy. The student of English phonetics should know the habits of English people in the use of the subsidiary members of the phonemes, and be ready to observe them in his own pronunciation and in that of other people.

109. In the study of foreign languages a knowledge of the phoneme theory is extremely important. The sounds grouped into one phoneme in one language may belong to two or more phonemes in another language, and a speaker must be aware of this fact, or in keeping the phoneme usage of his own language, he may be be misunderstood; for the test of whether two or more sounds belong to one phoneme or to more, is that of significance. If the substitution of one sound for another makes a change in meaning, they belong to different phonemes. For example, to substitute "clear" *l* for "dark" *l*, or *vice versa*, in English, would not change the meaning, as they are members of one phoneme; such a pronunciation would only sound unusual. (Try it in the word *little*!) But in Russian, the substitution of "clear" *l* for "dark" *l* would change the meaning of some words, for in that language these two sounds belong to different phonemes.

110. But the present book is not concerned with the pronunciation of foreign languages. A knowledge of the ordinary usage in the matter of English phonemes is, however, important for the student of English pronunciation. In the first place, his ear should be sufficiently fine to distinguish the various members of the different phonemes, and to note their use by the people whose pronunciation he is studying. Secondly, if he is unaware of the existence of phonemes as opposed to speech sounds, he may try to teach a wrong member of the phoneme under a mistaken idea that he is teaching "the correct English sound." (The very frequent occurrence in elocution of "clear" *l* where "dark" *l* is usual may be due to this.) And thirdly, he will find it useful in the

correction of pronunciation, as he may have pupils whose phoneme usage is unusual and gives rise to certain peculiarities of pronunciation and even to misunderstanding. For instance, some speakers (particularly Cockney) use an ɪ vowel before dark *l* in words like *field* (fiːld), i.e. they substitute the ɪ for the i phoneme in this position. In this way they are likely to be misunderstood, as confusion arises between the words *field* (fiːld) and *filled* (fɪld), which are both pronounced fɪld. The present writer has been told that London primary school children often confuse these two words in pronunciation and in spelling.

111. It should be noted here that some people consider i and ɪ, u and ʊ, ɔ and ɒ, respectively, to belong to one phoneme. This can be justified by treating a certain degree of length as belonging to a particular member of the phoneme, i.e. going with a particular quality. They can only be so considered in the case of those whose speech shows a consistent relationship of length and quality, i.e. if i is always longer than ɪ under the same set of circumstances, ɔ longer than ɒ, u than ʊ. For those speakers who lengthen the so-called short vowels ɪ, ɒ, ʊ (who say, for instance : bɪːg, fɒːg, gʊːd,[1] etc.) i and ɪ, ɒ and ɔ, ʊ and u belong to different phonemes. In Scottish pronunciation i and ɪ are separate phonemes ; i occurs short and long, e.g. *agreed* is əgriːd and *greed* is grɪd.

112. In Chapters XI, XII, XIV of this book the usages in the matter of English vowel and consonant phonemes are described.

[1] See Ch. XVII, § 361 (vi), for this habit.

CHAPTER XI

ENGLISH VOWELS IN DETAIL

113. With the majority of English speakers, there are twelve pure vowel and nine diphthong phonemes. The symbols for these are numbered, as shown below, for convenience of reference.

1.	2.	3.	4.	5.	6.	7.	8.	9.	10.	11.	12.
i	ɪ	ɛ	æ	ɑ	ɒ	ɔ	ʊ	u	ʌ	ɜ	ə

13.	14.	15.	16.	17.	18.	19.	20.	21.
eɪ	oʊ	aɪ	aʊ	ɔɪ	ɪə	ɛə	ɔə	ʊə

114. METHOD TO BE OBSERVED IN CONSIDERING EACH SOUND.

(a) Each vowel sound and diphthong is described and placed on the vowel figure.

(b) The members of the phoneme are noted.

(c) The principal variants in the pronunciation heard in different parts of the country and from different speakers are discussed.

(d) Methods of teaching the sound are suggested.

115. In this chapter a paragraph is given under each vowel, suggesting methods of teaching the vowel and correcting dialectal peculiarities. It may be stated that these methods are based on a principle which can be illustrated at the outset. When a pupil pronounces one vowel and the teacher wishes him to say another, the latter uses his knowledge of the relative positions of (a) the pupil's wrong sound, (b) the sound he wishes to teach, and (c) any other sound which the pupil possesses

D

near to the desired sound. He can also use the method of exaggeration, i.e. the pupil says sound No. 1, the teacher wishes him to say sound No. 2, so he tries to make him say sound No. 3, which lies beyond 2, in the hope that he will say 2.

116. Both methods can be illustrated from the accompanying diagram. A pupil says the sound at A (ε); the teacher wishes him to say the sound at B (æ); he tells him to try to say the sound at C (a); the pupil probably produces a sound near to B, and with a little practice can

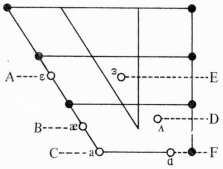

FIG. 12. Diagram illustrating Principles of Correction.

manage the correct one. The teacher wishes to teach the sound at D (ʌ) to a pupil who does not possess it; he possesses sounds at E and F, however (ɜ and ɑ); the teacher makes the pupil say ɜ and ɑ alternately and try to produce a sound between; or he tells him to make his ɜ sound more like ɑ. Thus the pupil arrives at a sound between the two. It may also be said that the methods suggested in this chapter are based on experience, but not every method fits every pupil—the teacher must try exercises on the lines suggested, and modify them to suit individual needs.

ENGLISH VOWELS PLACED IN THE CARDINAL FIGURE.

117. The writer's English vowels are shown in the following diagram in relation to the cardinal vowels.

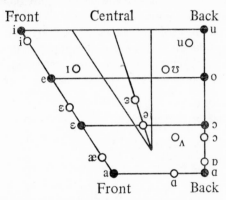

FIG. 13. Diagram illustrating English Vowels.

Note.—One pronunciation only can be shown here, other variants will be discussed under heading of each vowel. The student should practise placing his own and other people's vowels on the vowel figure.

118. *No.* 1. i, the sound in *sea, feel, read.*
Description.

(a) Front of tongue raised towards hard palate.

(b) Tongue raised almost to close position (near to Cardinal No. 1).

(c) Lips spread to neutral.

119. In the pronunciation of some people when the sound occurs finally, it is diphthongised, but not in a

closed syllable, i.e. *see* becomes sɪi (see next §), but *read* is riːd.

120.   Many people diphthongise this vowel to a greater or less extent in all positions; it is not a pure vowel, but the tongue starts from a somewhat lower position than the one marked on the figure, and moves up to a higher position. The commonest variety—a variety often used by educated speakers is ɪi (sɪi). In many dialects, however, the diphthong is more noticeable, the first element being retracted towards a central position, i.e. the diphthong becomes əi.

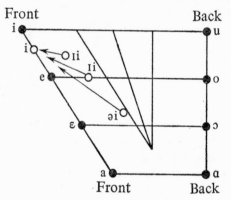

FIG. 14.   Varieties of the i Vowel.

This is a marked characteristic of Cockney speech, especially in a stressed position (e.g. gɪv ɪt tə ˈməi), and is heard, in a less pronounced form, in the Northern, Midland and Eastern counties.

121.   To correct this marked diphthongisation, the pupil should be told to say the sound i with considerable vigour.   A second method is to let him make a fricative

consonant corresponding to i, i.e. a fricative j; in this
way he raises his tongue high enough, and he can
easily get rid of the friction.

122. The student should notice that many words
which are pronounced with i when said alone, often
have an alternative pronunciation with the vowel ɪ or ə
when they occur in unstressed positions. Such words
are *he, she, we, be, the, been*.

E.g.   ˈwɒt dɪd (h)ɪ ˈseɪ?   wɪ ʃl ˈsuːn bɪ ˈðɛə.

      ˈdʌz ʃɪ (or dʌʒ ʃɪ).   ðə ˈbʊk.

      ˈʃæl wɪ ˈgoʊ?

      aɪ v bɪn ˈwɜˑkɪŋ ˈleɪt.

      wɛər əv jʊ ˈbɪn (bɪn for *been* is often used both
in stressed and unstressed syllables).

With some speakers the sound used in such positions
is a very short i.

123. In Cockney pronunciation the vowel i is
regularly replaced by ɪ before a " *dark l*," e.g.: stiːl is
pronounced stɪɫ. To cure this, it is necessary not only
to raise the ɪ to i, as shown in § 100, but to alter the
resonance of the *dark l*. (See Chapter XIV, § 268.)

124. *No. 2.* ɪ, the sound in *fit, did, little*.

Description.

(a) Front of tongue raised towards hard palate, the
highest point of raising being towards the central
position; i.e. it is considerably retracted from a
fully front vowel position.

(b) Tongue raised slightly higher than half-close
position (above Cardinal 2 line).

(c) Lips somewhat spread.

(d) Many people think that lax muscles are necessary for the production of ɪ.

125. Two or three varieties of ɪ sound can be distinguished in the pronunciation of most people, e.g. the ɪ in hɪl is more open than that in hɪt, and a final ɪ is generally of a low variety. This is particularly noticeable in words like *busy*, *smithy*, *pretty*, *chimney* (bɪzɪ, smɪðɪ, prɪtɪ, ʧɪmnɪ), where the two ɪ sounds occur in the same word.

126. In words of this type, however, i.e. when ɪ is final, there are several variant pronunciations.

(a) The commonest is the one noted above, where the final unstressed ɪ is lower than that in the stressed syllable.

(b) Some speakers, notably S. Africans, Scots, Northumbrians, use a No. 1 vowel finally, and say bɪzi (or bizi).

(c) Some speakers make no appreciable difference between the two vowels.

(d) Some speakers use such an open variety of vowel that it approaches to e or even ɛ, e.g. bɪze or bɪzɛ. In such cases it is frequently lengthened.

127. Note those words in which three ɪ sounds occur, e.g. *willingly*, *explicitly*, *probability*. With the speakers under (a) and (d), the final ɪ would be the lowest of all; with those under (b) the final vowel would be i. Note also an alternative pronunciation with ə, for some (but not all) of these words, e.g. ɪnfɪnɪtɪ or ɪnfɪnətɪ, sɪmplɪsɪtɪ or sɪmplɪsətɪ.

128. A low variety of ɪ is heard in such words as *ticket* ('tɪkɪt), *visit* ('vɪzɪt), *pocket* ('pɒkɪt), *market* ('mɑ·kɪt), *message* ('mɛsɪʤ), *frigid* ('frɪʤɪd), *modest* ('mɒdɪst)

fearless ('fɪəlɪs), *savage* ('sævɪʤ), *knowledge* ('nɒlɪʤ), *audible* ('ɔ·dɪbl).

129. For many of these words, however, there is an alternative pronunciation with ə, e.g. 'pɒkɪt or 'pɒkət, 'praɪvɪt or 'praɪvət, 'fɪəlɪs or 'fɪələs, 'ɔ·dɪbl or 'ɔ·dəbl. Some people use a vowel lying between ɪ and ə. Students should note also that, though many words written with *e* or *a* are pronounced with ɪ or ə, not all words of this type follow the same rules: e.g. *modest* may be pronounced mɒdɪst or mɒdəst (the vowel in the last syllable being a kind of neutral vowel in both cases; see § 184), but *contest, inquest, manifest* would generally have a strong vowel in this syllable, 'kɒntɛst, 'ɪnkwɛst, 'mænɪfɛst; *voyage* is vɔɪʤ, *savage* is 'sævɪʤ, but *outrage* is generally 'aʊtreɪʤ; *perfect* may be 'pɜ·fɪkt, but *prefect* is 'pri·fɛkt. This is not a question of the influence of stress, such as the difference between 'sʌbʤɪkt (noun) and səb'ʤɛkt (verb), nor of differentiation of function as in 'ɛstɪmeɪt (verb) and 'ɛstɪmət (noun), in 'dju·plɪkeɪt (verb) and 'dju·plɪkət (adj.), 'mɒdəreɪt (verb) and 'mɒdərət (adj.). It may be noted that those words in which the strong vowel is used are less common than those in which ɪ is used.[1] Note also that in the use of ɪ in words such as *fearless* and *subject* is not common in Northern speech (see Chapter XVI, § 327); they are generally pronounced 'fɪələs, 'sʌbʤɛkt.

130. The pronunciation of *pencil* as 'pɛnsɪl or 'pɛnsl, of *pupil* as 'pju·pɪl or 'pju·pl, *April* as 'eɪprɪl or ˌeɪprl, *passenger* as 'pæsɪnʤə or 'pæsɳʤə, seems to

---

[1] For explanation of this see Luick, *Historische Grammatik der englischen Sprache*, §§ 595, 605.

show that unstressed ɪ tends to drop out before an alveolar consonant, particularly when preceded by another alveolar continuant consonant.

131. In addition to the preceding differences in subsidiary members of the ɪ phoneme, there are several variant pronunciations.

(a) In London speech another phoneme is substituted for final ɪ in words like *busy*; this is pronounced bɪzəi, i.e. for final unstressed ɪ, the London pronunciation of No. 1 vowel is used: e.g. twɛntəi, prɪtəi, etc.

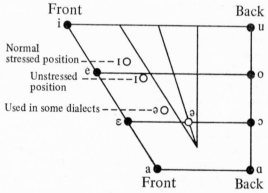

FIG. 15. Varieties of the ɪ Vowel.

(b) In some dialects ə is used regularly by educated speakers where S. England has unstressed ɪ, e.g. ɔˈdəbl, krɛdəbl, mɛsədʒ, mɒdərət, wɜˈθləs, bəfɔə, bəniˈθ.

(c) In many dialects, including Scottish, Irish, American, and West Country (I have heard it also in the West Riding of Yorks., and in Norfolk), a very retracted and lowered ɪ, approaching towards ə, is used in stressed as well as unstressed positions, e.g. *timid* is təmə́d, *bit* is bət. This form appears to be spreading in the speech of the younger generation in S. England. See § 361 (i).

(*d*) In some types of South African speech ɪ is a close variety, approaching i.

132. To cure the pronunciation indicated under (*a*) above should not be difficult, as the pupil already possesses an ɪ sound which he uses in words like *fit* (fɪt). The teacher should try to make him say this sound in isolation (which is not always an easy thing to accomplish, however), and use it at the end of a word. Sometimes it is only necessary to tell him to make the final sound very short. If it is desired to correct the pronunciation təmə́d, the pupil must be told to make a sound more nearly resembling his i sound, but it must be very short.

133. *No. 3.* ɛ, the sound in *bet, egg, bell*.

Description.

(*a*) Front of tongue raised.

(*b*) Tongue raised about half the distance between close and open (half-way between Cardinal e and ɛ).

(*c*) Lips neutral to spread.

134. If the three words given above are compared, it will generally be found that the vowel varies in each word; the ɛ in *bet* is somewhat closer than that in *egg*, and the ɛ in *bell* is more open than either of the other two. The phoneme varies, therefore, between a point just below Cardinal No. 2, and another one slightly higher than Cardinal No. 3. It should be noted again that the dark 1 of *bell* has the effect of lowering the vowel which precedes it.

135. Many variant pronunciations, ranging from e to ε, are heard. The Northerner uses an open variety, while the Cockney speaker uses a sound near to Cardinal e; in Hampshire a cardinal ε is often used, and in Devonshire and the West a diphthong eɪ is sometimes heard (eɪg, beɪd), while in many parts of the country a retracted and lowered variety of ε is heard. This

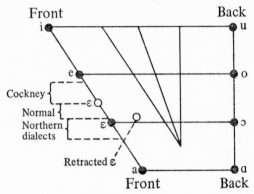

Fig. 16. Varieties of the ε Vowel.

is common in the West of England, in Yorks., and Lancs., and in the Eastern counties.[1] It is particularly noticeable before *r* in words like *very*, which often sounds like vɜrɪ. One type of American ε is also considerably retracted. Many Americans say gɛ°t for *get*, but do not use a diphthong in all words of this type. (See Ch. XVIII, § 368.) In Cockney speech ε followed

---

[1] Note the pronunciations of the word *breakfast*: brɛkfəst, breɪkfəst and briːkfəst. The last can be heard in Lancashire and Yorkshire, as can also stiːk for steɪk (*steak*). For explanation of this see Wyld, *History of Modern Colloquial English*, pp. 209 and 212.

by dark l is retracted to such a degree that it resembles ɔ
(and the l disappears), e.g. the London bus-conductor
says sɔˈfrɪdʒɪz or sɛɔfrɪdʒɪz for *Selfridges* (sɛlfrɪdʒɪz).

136. The correction of an ɛ will generally consist
in modifying an extreme variety—either close or open,
or of getting rid of a retracted variety. The first
correction is not difficult to make; it is generally only
necessary to make the pupil exaggerate in the other
direction. The correction of a retracted ɛ is more
difficult, and it is essential to attempt this, as retraction
of the tongue makes for vowels of an obscure and
indistinct quality. Many people find it difficult to
isolate an ɛ sound; in trying to pronounce it they say
something approaching ɜ.

137. In order to correct this tendency and to teach
a wholly front ɛ, it is well to begin with the diphthong
eɪ, in which the pupil probably pronounces a front e or ɛ
as the first element. The first element should be
lengthened e - - - ɪ, and the second part gradually
dropped. If the resulting e sound is too close, it is not
difficult then to teach a more open variety. A good
general exercise for obtaining a front vowel is to begin
with i, which most people can make well forward, and
then try to get the same quality of "frontness" into
e and ɛ.

138. *No. 4.* æ, the sound in *bad, catch*, etc.

Description.

(a) Front of tongue raised.

(b) Tongue raised approximately one-sixth of distance
from open to close: i.e. about half-way between
Cardinal 3 and 4.

(c) Lips neutral to spread.

(d) Some people consider this vowel lax, but sufficient investigation to prove this has not yet been made.

139.   In addition to the above details describing æ, there seems to be another factor in its articulation, namely, a certain amount of pharyngal contraction. It is a noteworthy fact that singers do not use this sound, as the quality of the voice is rarely so good in singing æ as in other vowels.[1]   æ is usually classed as a short vowel but the modern tendency is to lengthen it in many common words: eg. bæːd, stæːnd.

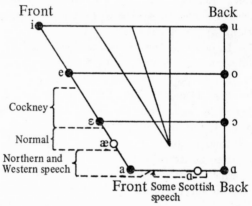

FIG. 17.   Varieties of the æ Vowel.

140.   The only subsidiary member of the æ-phoneme is a somewhat lower variety, nearer to ə when a "dark" l

[1] Another reason for the avoidance of æ by singers may be the fact that Italian singing masters were unable to pronounce this sound and substituted their own a vowel for it: and in this way, the tradition of using a or ɑ for æ has grown up.

follows; compare *shall* and *shally*; æ in the former followed by "dark" 1 is lower than in *shally*, which has a "clear" 1. The difference, however, is not very great.

141. Variant pronunciations between a very close æ verging on ɛ, and a or even ɑ are heard. The use of some kind of a, a sound round about Cardinal No. 4, is very widespread; it is an easily recognised characteristic of Northern, Midland, and, to a certain extent, of Western speech. In Scotland the sound ɑ is often heard, while in some types of Scottish town speech—sometimes called "Kelvinside" or "High English," an attempt has been made to imitate the S. English æ, with the result that the closeness of the vowel has been exaggerated and the pronunciation is practically ɛ, e.g. dʒɛks ə bɛd lɛd. In London dialect, the sound is much closer than the normal, reaching ɛ or even e in some cases, e.g. kɛb bɛŋk, kɛtʃ, bɛːd.

A tendency to diphthongise æ towards ə is observed to-day, particularly before alveolar consonants: thus *bad* is frequently pronounced bæˑd. This is an American variant and is also one of the newer developments of to-day. See Chs. XVII, XVIII.

142. For teaching, it is generally advisable to choose a middle variety of æ; in the North where a is heard from many educated speakers, it is wise to allow a variety that is not too open or too retracted towards ɑ. The pupil who uses ɛ or e should be made to keep his mouth wider open when he says the vowel, and should be told to modify his sound slightly in the direction of ɑ in *father*. The pupil who uses a retracted a or ɑ should be told to make the sound more like ɛ.

143. *No. 5.* ⓐ the sound in *father, calm, half.*
Description.

   (*a*) Back of the tongue concerned in the formation of this vowel.

   (*b*) Tongue quite low down in the mouth; an open vowel.

   (*c*) Lips neutrally open.

144. There are no subsidiary members of the phoneme differing to any marked extent from the main one.

145. In the educated and semi-educated speech of different parts of the country, there is little variety in the pronunciation of this vowel. In some Northern dialects, however, a forward variety of **a** is heard, faːðə or faðə (short), and in the extreme dialect fɛːðə is heard. In some forms of Scottish and in South African pronunciation a vowel near Cardinal ɑ is found. In London a very retracted ɑ used to be common, though at present a more forward **a** (faːðə) is frequently heard; ɑ is replaced by æ or **a** in some dialects, in words like *can't, half* (kænt, kæːnt, kant, or kaːnt). This is common in some types of Irish and some American speech. In those dialects (W. and S.W. English and American[1] chiefly) where **r** is pronounced (see Chapter XIV, § 271, iv) the quality of the vowel preceding *r* is affected and it becomes a front **a**, e.g. *harm* is pronounced haɹm.

---

[1] The analysis of one American's pronunciation showed that he had three sounds of the letter *a*, viz.: æ (a low variety), as in *bad*, **a** (about one-third of the way between cardinals **a** and ɑ,) for some words such as *can't, harm*, and ɑ (as in normal Southern English), for others like *calm, father*, etc. See, however, Chap. XVIII, § 371.

146. In order to correct a too retracted form of ɑ, tell the pupil to spread his lips and to modify his sound in the direction of æ. The opposite fault, a too forward a, can be corrected by telling the pupil to aim at ɒ, and to lengthen the sound.

147. There are a number of words in which many Northern speakers use a or æ, which in the South are pronounced with ɑ. Such words are *last, grass, after, dance, ask, plant.* Certain words, however, do not follow this rule: e.g. *lass* and *crass* are pronounced by Northerners and Southerners alike as læs, kræs (or in the N., las, kras); and a few words have two pronunciations with some speakers, indicating different meanings: e.g. *mass,* mæs, *heap*; mɑ·s, the religious service[1]; *ass,* æs, the animal; and ɑ·s, a term of friendly abuse. The pronunciation ɑ·frikə has been reported from South Devon; the present writer has heard it from a Scot (whose work was in Africa).

148. In Northern and Midland schools it would be unwise to try and insist on the pronunciation ɑ in such words as have been mentioned, for many educated people use æ or a, although it may be pointed out that this pronunciation is one of the obvious marks of a Northern or Midland pronunciation which anyone can recognise.

149. *No.* 6. ɒ, the sound in *not, long, box.*

Description.

(*a*) Back of tongue raised.

---

[1] See *Broadcast Word*, p. 104, for a note on the pronunciation of the words *mass* and *catholic*.

(b) Raising is very slight; a little higher than Cardinal ɑ; an open vowel.

(c) Slight open lip-rounding.

150. There are no subsidiary members of the phoneme worth noting.

151. In some parts of the country, particularly in Scotland, a vowel with a higher tongue position and more lip-rounding is used: i.e. the vowel resembles Cardinal No. 6,[1] and there are varieties between the two. Compare nɒt lɒŋ and nɔt lɔŋ. This is particularly noticeable in words written with *wa*, e.g. *watch*, *was*, *want*, which are pronounced wɔ·tʃ, wɔz, wɔnt. In the Midlands and some parts of S.W. England a vowel with the same tongue position, but with neutrally open lips, is used. The vowel then resembles Cardinal No. 5, hɑt, lɑŋ, ɑn ðə tɑp for hɒt, lɒŋ, ɒn ðə tɒp. This is one variety of American speech. In some dialects ɒ is replaced by ʌ: e.g. *not* is pronounced nʌt, *was* wʌz.[2]

152. If the unrounded variety ɑ is considered objectionable, it is easy to cure. To tell the pupil to round his lips while pronouncing the vowel is generally sufficient.

153. There are a good many words in which some people substitute for ɒ the vowel ɔ. Such usage is somewhat parallel to the use of æ and ɑ (see §147, p. 93), but in this case the division is not entirely a local one. The most important of these words are *cross*, *lost*, *off*,

[1] Grant (*Pronunciation of English in Scotland*) uses the symbol ɔ for this sound. Cambridge University Press. [Out of print.]

[2] The writer has been told that this is often taught in Edinburgh schools, probably as a correction of wɔ·z.

soft, often; probably ɒ is used by the majority, but a considerable number of people, including many educated speakers, use ɔ. The latter is not found in Northern pronunciation, and it is not at all general in the South. By those who do not use it, such a pronunciation is often considered vulgar.

154. There is no doubt that the use of the vowel ɔ in these words is dying out gradually[1]; the use of ɒ seems to have been a spelling pronunciation in Southern English in the first case, and it is extremely likely that eventually krɒs, etc., will be the only form. Educated speakers who use ɔ at the present day are mainly middle-aged, or conservative speakers. It is to be noticed that this alternation occurs in words where *s* or *ʃ* follow the vowel, and not in all these: *moss, boss,*[2] *scoff*, are rarely pronounced with ɔ, and tɔˑf for *toff* is considered Cockney; there are also people who would say krɔˑs but tɒs. At the present day it would be a waste of time to insist in schools on the pronunciation krɒs, since many educated speakers still use the form krɔˑs.

155. Occasionally a similar alternation is found when the letter *o* occurs before other consonants, e.g. *gone, dog, God*. The pronunciation dɔˑg used to be fairly frequent, but it is rarely heard now, and is considered decidedly vulgar; gɔˑd (*God*) is occasionally heard, sometimes as a particularly pious way of saying the word, but like dɔˑg, it is generally considered vulgar; gɔˑn is still heard from educated speakers. Of these

[1] "I was astonished to find recently, in a Council Central School in London (Marylebone), that the pronunciation krɔːs was laughed at by the children." *Broadcast English*, p. 161.

[2] bɔˑs is heard in American speech.

 see p. 45

three, it would certainly be advisable to correct dɔ˙g
and gɔ˙d.

156. A similar alternative pronunciation is found in
words which are spelt with *aus*, *ault*, *als*, *alt*. The
pronunciation ɔ in such words as *auspices*, *fault*, *false*,
alter, *Austria*, belongs to the South and ɒ to the North,
but here again the distinction is not entirely local.
Note the pronunciation of *because* (bɪkɒz and bɪkɔːz).
Some Irish speakers say bəkʌz.)

157. *No. 7.* ɔ, the sound in *saw, caught, all*.
Description.

   (*a*) Back of tongue raised.
   (*b*) Tongue raised to near the Cardinal 6 position:
      a half open vowel.
   (*c*) Lips considerably rounded. This vowel is some-
      times said to be *over-rounded*, i.e. the degree of
      rounding is greater than is usual in a vowel having
      such a tongue position.

158. In educated speech there are no notable subsidiary members of the phoneme.

159. The main variants in the pronunciation of
this vowel lie in the degree of lip-rounding used; the
tongue position does not seem to vary much. In
London pronunciation there is considerable lip-rounding
so that the vowel strikes the ear as being of an o-type:
e.g. *fall* becomes foːɫ, *caught* becomes koˑt, and *saw*
soˑə. This tendency of using close lip-rounding appears to
be spreading among educated speakers in the South. The
other extreme is heard in some parts of the country, i.e.
the sound is pronounced with very open lip-rounding. For
the Scottish pronunciation of words such as those given
above, see Grant, *Pronunciation of English in Scotland*.

160. It is not difficult to correct either of these tendencies; for the London pronunciation, if the pupil is told to open his mouth more, he will soon make the more normal sound; and the other extreme is corrected by rounding the lips more.

161. The words written with *or, ore, oar, oor, our* must be considered under the heading of this vowel, for many speakers in S.E. England use the vowel ɔ in all such words, e.g. *for, more, hoar, door, pour, fort, hoard, course,* etc. Speakers from other parts of the country, however, do not pronounce them all alike; the words fall into two distinct classes:

(*a*) Those words which have *or, ore, oar, oor, our* final and *oar, our*, followed by a consonant (e.g. *hoarse, court*), together with *some* words with *or* followed by a consonant (e.g. *fort*).

(*b*) Other words with *or* followed by a consonant (e.g. *corn*).

162. These classes have variant pronunciations. The main variants heard are:

When no *r* is pronounced—

(1) As stated above, both classes pronounced with ɔ in S.E. England.

(2) The first class pronounced ɔə and the second ɔ; this is heard from many English speakers from different parts of the country.

(3) The first class pronounced oə and the second ɔə or ɔ in many parts of the country.

When *r* is pronounced—

(1) The first class pronounced or and the second ɔr; this occurs in Scottish pronunciation.

(2) The first class pronounced oəɹ, the second ɔəɹ
or ɔːɹ. (For the retroflex *r*, see Chapter XIV
(§ 271 iv).) This is common in S.W. England.

163. The words written with *or* + a consonant
present an interesting problem, for there is nothing in the
modern form of the words themselves to indicate to
which class they belong,[1] but where any distinction at all
is made in these words, it is made, with very few
exceptions, in the same words by speakers from N.,
N.W., W., S.W. England, from Scotland, Ireland
and Wales. Thus *port*, with its derivatives, *report*,
etc., *sport, ford, sword, sworn, forge*, belong to Class 1,
and *cord, record, order, accord, short, adorn, morn, horn*,
belong to Class 2. A complete list of all the words
under consideration is to be found in Grant's *Pronunciation of English in Scotland*.[2]

164. In London dialect those words, particularly
where *or* is final, are pronounced with a marked oə
diphthong. Sometimes the two vowels o, ə form two
syllables with a kind of w between them, e.g. *door*
becomes doːwə, *four* becomes foːwə, and *more* becomes
moːwə. Other words in which there is no *r*, and which
are normally pronounced with ɔ, are by false analogy
pronounced in the same way. So that *saw* and *paw*
become soːwə and poːwə. Two things are necessary to
correct this; the pupil must be told to pronounce the
vowel with his mouth more widely open. This will
bring him near to ɔ; and to get rid of the diphthongisation,

[1] See, however, Jespersen's *Modern English Grammar*, Vol. I.
(Allen & Unwin), and Luick, *Historische Grammatik der englischen
Sprache*. §§ 567–8.

he must keep his mouth in one position and not move it during the pronunciation of the sound.

165. *No.* 8. ʊ, the sound in *put, book.*
Description.

(a) Back of tongue raised towards soft palate; the raising is slightly advanced from the full back position.

(b) Tongue raised to a little above half-close position.

(c) Lips generally close rounded.

(d) This vowel is considered by many to be lax.

166. There do not seem to be many important subsidiary members of the phoneme. With some speakers, however, ʊ followed by dark *l* has a lower and further back tongue position than when it precedes other consonants. Cf. *put, pull.*

167. This sound is sometimes replaced by an un-rounded vowel with a similar tongue position (phonetic symbol ɤ). It is especially noticeable in the word *good,* which is pronounced gɤd or gɤːd by a number of people ; this is an individual not a local pronunciation, and is often considered affected.[1] I have heard ɤ, however, as a regular sound from American speakers for all words which in normal English have ʊ. One variety of Yorkshire and Lancashire speech has a low type of ʊ sound, slightly unrounded in words like *put.* In Cockney the ʊ, followed by dark 1 in words like *pull, full,* resembles an o, i.e. it is markedly retracted and lowered from the normal.

168. In Scotland, words which in English are pronounced with ʊ have a short u sound, e.g. *put* is pronounced

[1] See Ch. II, § 22 (c) and Ch. XVII, § 361 (v).

put, *foot*, fut.   Such words as these do not differ in their vowel sounds from *food*, *rude*, except perhaps very slightly in length.   Compare the Scottish pronunciation of *full* and *fool*, *foot* and *food* (ful, ful, fut, fud). In the north of England ʊ in words like *cook*, *book*, *look*, is regularly replaced by u, often fairly long, giving **kuꞏk, buꞏk, luꞏk** (or **kʊuk, bʊuk, lʊuk**).   Note also the two pronunciations of the word *room*, ruːm and rʊm ; these are not purely local, though **rʊm** does not normally occur in Northern dialects.   In the S.W., *boots*, *soup*, *hoop*, *cooper* may be **bʊts, sʊp, hʊp, kʊpə.**

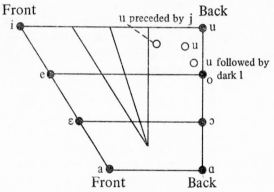

FIG. 18.   The u Phoneme.

169.   *No. 9.* u, the sound in *rude*, *fool*.
Description.

    (*a*) Back of tongue raised towards soft palate.

    (*b*) Tongue raised almost to close position.

    (*c*) Lips close rounded.

170.   In words where u is preceded by j, e.g. *music* (mjuꞏzɪk), u has a more forward position; where it is

followed by dark *l* as in *fool*, fuːl, a lower variety is heard. This is especially the case with Southern dialect speakers (see § 171). Many speakers would have one sound only in the words *music, rude, fool,* i.e. their phoneme consists of one member only. When the vowel occurs in a final position, it is often diphthongised: e.g. *do* is pronounced dʊu. (Compare sɪi, § 119.)

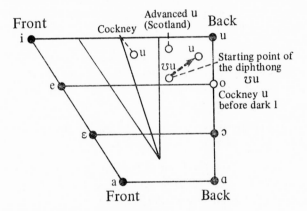

FIG. 19. Varieties of the u Vowel.

171. Many people diphthongise this vowel to a considerable extent, i.e. the tongue begins at a position near to ʊ and glides up to u (ʊu). Compare ɪi. In Scottish pronunciation the u is generally very much shorter and closer than in English; in some parts the u is of an " advanced " type, i.e. the tongue raising is further forward than a fully back position. In Southern English and to a marked extent in Cockney pronunciation the u is of a very " advanced " character, the raising being as far forward as half-way between i and u, i.e. it is a central vowel (represented here by ü). Generally words like *boots, shoes, moon, food,* are pronounced with the diphthong ïü, ï being a retracted i very nearly half-way between i and u, and ü a similar, though probably slightly further back tongue position, with slight lip-rounding. But when this sound occurs before dark l, the tongue position goes back almost to o. Compare in Cockney speech the words *food, fool* (fïüd, foːl).[1]

172. The Cockney ü is not easy to cure. Slight evidences of this sound often remain in speech that has lost almost all other signs of Cockney origin. Three methods may be tried.

(1) Let the pupil aim at o, i.e. tell him to say moːn, boːts; then let him modify this towards u.

(2) Hold down the front of the tongue with the finger or a tongue-guide (a small paper-knife, or a glass rod). This forces the back up into the correct position when he tries to say his u sound.

(3) Let the pupil whistle a low note. This gives the tongue position for u, and it should not be difficult after a time to pass from the whistled note to the spoken vowel. Sometimes a pupil can *sing* u when he cannot say it, and this can be used to get the spoken vowel.[2]

[1] Note, however, that *fooling* is pronounced fïülɪŋ.

[2] But an advanced u is frequently heard in the "crooning" songs of dance bands!

173. *No.* 10. ʌ, the sound in *but, mother.*
Description.

(*a*) Back of tongue raised, but not fully back; somewhat advanced towards a central position.

(*b*) Tongue raised not quite one-third of the total distance from open to close; near the Cardinal ɔ line.

(*c*) Lips neutral.

174. In educated speech there do not seem to be any outstanding subsidiary members of the ʌ phoneme. For dialect speech, however, see next paragraph.

175. Many variant pronunciations of this vowel are heard:

(*a*) In London pronunciation (and in Devonshire), it tends to become a kind of a vowel, somewhat approaching Cardinal No. 4, except before dark l, when the vowel is generally a kind of ɒ or ɔ, e.g. bʌlb, rɪzʌlt, mʌltɪplaɪ, become bɒlb, rɪzɔlt, mɔltɪplaɪ.

(*b*) In some parts of the country the tongue position is advanced towards the central vowel ɜ; I have heard the pronunciation lɜˑv, kɜˑm in Bristol and the S.W., and lɜv, kɜm from Northern speakers, where, however, it may be due to the avoidance of a typical Northern vowel. With some American speakers it is also somewhat more central. (See Ch. XVIII.)

(*c*) In the North of England, particularly in Yorks. and Lancs., and to a certain extent in the Midlands, the sound ʌ does not exist. The S. English more open ʌ strikes the Northern ear as a, and in attempting to reproduce it, the Northerner feels his pronunciation to be an exaggeration. In the broad dialect, it is replaced by ʊ, but in a more "refined"

dialect, the sound used is one lying between ʊ and
ʌ, a kind of ɤ partially rounded.   Most words in
which ʌ is now used were originally pronounced
with ʊ; in the South, the vowel ʊ has changed
gradually from ʊ to ʌ, going through many intermediate stages as far as tongue position is concerned, and also in losing lip-rounding.   In the
North this change has not gone so far as ʌ, and
the sound now heard is generally some type

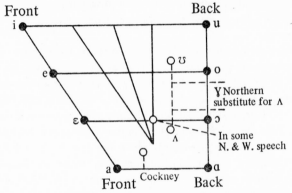

FIG. 20.   Varieties of the ʌ Vowel.

lying between ʊ and ʌ in tongue and in lip position.
But not in all words which were formerly
pronounced with ʊ has the vowel changed to ʌ,
cf. *put*, *but*, pʊt, bʌt.   Consequently speakers who
use ɤ where normal English has ʌ, confuse the
vowel in words such as *but*, *put*, *butcher*, *sugar*,
hunt.   Many Northerners and Midlanders have
difficulty in pronouncing ʌ before *r*, in words like
hurry (hʌrɪ) ; they use a kind of short ɜ vowel in
such positions (hɜrɪ), which sounds rather like hɜrɪ.

Note.—Speakers who have no difficulty in distinguishing between *but* and *put*, *bull* and *cull*, are apt to think that the Northerners invert the two vowels and say **bʊt** and **pʌt**. It is the writer's opinion, but this has not been verified sufficiently well yet for it to be a certainty, that practically one sound is used in all these words, viz. the one between **ʊ** and **ʌ**, marked **ɤ** on the diagram, and that when one expects to hear **ʌ**, and the speaker uses **ɤ**, the hearer thinks he hears **ʊ**, and when **ʊ** is expected and **ɤ** occurs, he thinks he hears **ʌ**; so that *Mr. Butler, the butcher* pronounced **mɪstə bɤtlə ðə bɤtʃə** sounds like **mɪstə bʊtlə ðə bʌtʃə**. There are some Northern speakers, however, who *do* invert the two vowels; it is often those people who have learnt that *two* vowels are used in these words and not *one*, and have not yet learnt in which words they occur.[1]

176. In order to get rid of the Cockney **a** sound, let the pupil make the sound more like **ɔ** without any lip-rounding. The pupil who makes the vowel like **ɜ** must be told to make it resemble **ɑ**. To teach the sound **ʌ** to Northern speakers who do not possess it, it is well to begin with **ɔ**, to make this without any lip-rounding and then to modify it—but not too far—towards **ɜ**. It is sometimes sufficient to make him say his own sound with exaggerated opening of the mouth. This is the first step towards getting rid of the confusion between **ʊ** and **ʌ**. When the pupil can make **ʌ**, then comes the second stage; he must learn in which words **ʊ** occurs, and which have the **ʌ** vowel. This latter stage is a question of memory.

[1] I have heard the word *woman* pronounced **wʌmən**.

177.   *No.* 11. (ɜ,) the sound in *bird, fur, learn.*

Description.

(*a*) Central part of the tongue raised.

(*b*) Tongue raised about half-way between open and close.

(*c*) Lips neutral.

178.   There do not seem to be any subsidiary members of the phoneme to be noted.

179.   The commonest variants in the pronunciation of this vowel occur with those people who make some attempt to pronounce the following *r*.   In some parts of Scotland where the *r* is rolled, ɜ is often replaced by ʌ, *bird* (bɜːd) is pronounced bʌrd.   In the N.W., W. and S.W. of England the r is pronounced with the tip of the tongue curled up (see § 271 iv), bɜɹd, and here the ɜ is of a closer variety than the one marked on the diagram.   It is also frequently found that, while the vowel is being pronounced, the tip of the tongue is curled up, not sufficiently to make a fricative consonant, but enough to modify the vowel sound.   Some types of American speech have a pronunciation similar to this.   In S. Lancashire and Cheshire and the Midlands generally, the ɜ has a more forward position, approaching towards ɛ, i.e. *fur* (fɜː) is pronounced rather like fɛː ; *Birmingham* is pronounced bɛːmɪŋgəm.

180.   If it is wished to teach ɜ without the inversion, it is only necessary to tell the pupil to press the tip of his tongue against the bottom teeth and keep it there. If he cannot do this without help, his tongue should be held down with a spatula or tongue-guide.   To correct

the Lancashire tendency towards a too front vowel, the pupil should be told to make his sound ɜ more like ʌ, and to lengthen it.

181. *No.* 12. (ə,) the first vowel in *alone* and the last in *butter*.

Description.

(*a*) Central part of the tongue raised.

(*b*) Tongue raised about one-third of the way from open to close.

(*c*) Lips neutral.

(*d*) The vowel is always very short.

182. The phoneme varies from a vowel of a half-close tongue position between two velar consonants, as in **bæk əgeɪn**, where the ə is distinctly close, to a position well below the Cardinal ɛ - - - ɔ line in final positions.

183. Like ɜ, this vowel is often pronounced in the W., N.W. and S.W. with the tip of the tongue inverted when *r* occurs in the spelling. Some speakers use a very much more open sound in final positions, a kind of ʌ, or even ɑ, e.g. **bʌtʌ**; and there are speakers who make a difference between words ending in *er* and those ending in *a* (where no *r* is pronounced), who say, for example, **ɔʊvə**, but **tʃaɪnʌ, soʊfɑ** or **soʊfʌ**.

184. The vowel ə is interesting because it replaces almost all other vowels and diphthongs in unstressed positions: i and ɪ, however, are exceptions to this: i is generally replaced by ɪ in unstressed positions, and ɪ remains the same: e.g. **ˈre-ˈname, ˈriːˈneɪm**, but *re*ˈ*main*, **rɪˈmeɪn**, *finish*, **fɪnɪʃ** (ɪ in stressed and unstressed syllables in this word). The strong form ði is replaced by

ðə before a consonant, ðə bʊk, and the termination *ible*
is sometimes pronounced əbl, though ɪbl is probably
more frequently used. Such pronunciations as bə'liˑv,
'sætən are occasionally heard.

185. *Examples of the Neutral Vowel ə Replacing
Strong Forms.*

ɛ in *pence* (pɛns),   but ə in *sixpence* (sikspəns)
æ ,, *valid* ('vælɪd)   ,, ə ,, *validity* (və'lɪdɪtɪ)
ɑ ,, *particle* (pɑˑtikl) ,, ə ,, *particular* (pə'tɪkjʊlə)
ɒ ,, *conduct*   ,, ə ,, *conduct* (kən'dʌkt)
        ('kɒndəkt)
ɔ ,, *ward* (wɔːd)   ,, ə ,, *backward* ('bækwəd)
u ,, *to* (as in *set to* (tuː)) ,, ə or ʊ in *today* (tə'deɪ or tʊ'deɪ)
ʌ ,, *some* (sʌm)   ,, ə ,, *handsome* ('hænsəm)
ɜ ,, *Bert* (bɜˑt)   ,, ə ,, *Herbert* ('hɜˑbət)
eɪ ,, *face* (feɪs)   ,, ə ,, *preface* ('prɛfəs)
oʊ ,, *most* (moʊst)   ,, ə ,, *topmost* ('tɒpməst)
aʊ ,, *mouth* (maʊθ)   ,, ə ,, *Plymouth* (plɪməθ)
ɛə ,, *there* (ðɛə)   ,, ə ,, *there isn't any* (ðər'ɪznt ɛnɪ)
aɪə ,, *shire* (ʃaɪə)   ,, ə ,, *Yorkshire* ('jɔˑkʃə)

186. These weak forms occur in conversational
speech[1]; in slow speech, however, it is customary not
to reduce the strong vowels completely to the neutral
vowel, but to use something more nearly approaching the
original vowel. If the speaker in his efforts to be very
clear and careful, uses the strong vowel in unstressed
positions, the result is very unpleasant. Such a habit
gives the effect of stressing unimportant words. For
example, a clergyman who says hu ɑˑt ðɪ ɔˑθər ɒv piˑs
ænd lʌvər ɒv kɒŋkɔˑd, sounds as if he were stressing

[1] See § 325 for the strong and weak forms of a number of
common words.

the unimportant words ði, ɒv, ænd. I have heard such
a preacher who also tried to say *sympathy* very carefully,
with the result that he said sɪmpɜˑθɪ. [1]

187. The best method of getting over the difficulty
is to say a vowel that lies in an intermediate position
between the strong vowels and the neutral ə.

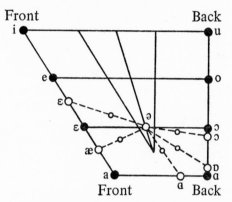

FIG. 21. Semi-weak Vowels.

188. The semi-weak forms of u and oʊ are generally
ʊ and o: thus *do* pronounced in its weakest form would
be də or d, as in wɒt d jʊ wɒnt: a more careful pronunciation would be dʊ. Similarly the words *obey*,
November, *protest*, *phonetics*, can be pronounced əˈe ɪ,
nəˈvɛmbə, prəˈtɛst, fəˈnɛtɪks (very weak), oˈbeɪ, noˈvɛmbə,
proˈtɛst, foˈnɛtɪks (semi-weak), and oʊˈbeɪ, noʊˈvɛmbə,
proʊˈtɛst, foʊˈnɛtɪks (very careful style). The middle
variety is probably the commonest.

189. It should be noted that those diphthongs
which can be reduced to ə in very quick speech, e.g.

[1] See Chapters XV, XVI.

ðɛə, baɪ, which can be ðə, bə or bɪ, should have their full value in more careful speech. In Professor Jones' Pronouncing Dictionary *my*, *myself* are given with two forms: maɪ, maɪsɛlf and mɪ, mɪsɛlf; *by* with the form baɪ, and as an *occasional* weak form bɪ. mɪ, bɪ were traditional stage pronunciations at one time, but their use has now died out; one example, however, remains in mɪlɔːd (*my lord*). mɪ, mɪsɛlf are still heard in colloquial speech, though perhaps less frequently than maɪ, maɪsɛlf.[1]

190. On pp. 152 ff. a summary is given of the main differences in vowel pronunciation between Northern speech and Southern English and between London pronunciation and Standard English.

[1] Note that in some dialects—as far apart as Yorkshire and Devon—*night* is pronounced naɪt, but *fortnight* as fɔ·tnɪt (fɔ(ɹ)tnɪt).

Chapter XII

ENGLISH DIPHTHONGS

191. It is customary to consider a diphthong as a combination of two vowel sounds, so pronounced as to form one syllable. In reality it is a gliding sound. The tongue starts in one vowel position and glides towards another vowel position by the most direct route. A diphthong is made by one impulse of the breath, i.e. there is no diminuendo—crescendo of breath force. This can be realised best by pronouncing slowly the English diphthong **aɪ**, a ---- ɪ ----, and then pronouncing the two vowels **a** - **ɪ**, with a fresh impulse of the breath on ɪ. (Take care not to insert a glottal stop.) The first will be felt as one syllable, the second as two; the first is a diphthong and the second is not.

192. English diphthongs, like those of most languages, are of the " falling " type, i.e. they have their greater prominence at the beginning; they are decrescendo diphthongs. English diphthongs are usually written phonetically with two letters, the first representing the starting point of the tongue, and the second the *direction* in which it moves. In the diphthong **aɪ**, for example, the tongue starts at the position of **a**, and moves towards, but does not actually reach, the ɪ position.

193. Diphthongs can be made by beginning at any one vowel and going in the direction of any other. so that the number of possible diphthongs is very large,

In English the majority of speakers possess nine diphthongs, which are represented by the symbols

13.	14.	15.	16.	17.	18.	19.	20.	21.
eɪ	oʊ	aɪ	aʊ	ɔɪ	ɪə	ɛə	ɔə	ʊə

194. They can be shown on the Cardinal vowel
figure as is indicated in the accompanying diagrams.

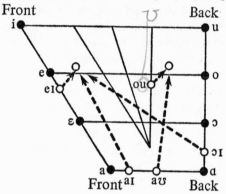

FIG. 22. English Diphthongs (a).

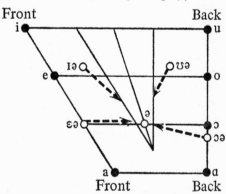

FIG. 23. English Diphthongs (b)

195. *No. 13.* (eɪ) the sound in *lady*, *make*.

Description.

The tongue starts in the position of a vowel somewhat below Cardinal No. 2, and moves towards the position of ɪ. As the movement is through a very small distance this diphthong is said to be narrow.

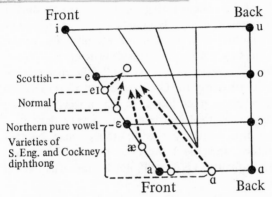

FIG. 24. Varieties of the eɪ diphthong.

196. In Scotland and many parts of the North of England, this diphthong is replaced by a pure vowel eː or ɛː. (The former is Scottish and Northumbrian, and the latter Yorks. and Lancs.). Thus the word *day* (deɪ) is pronounced deː or dɛː.[1] Another Northern pronunciation is an extremely narrow diphthong eɪ, where the starting point is a very close e vowel and the movement very slight. In the S. Midlands, S., S.W., and Eastern Counties, many varieties of wider diphthongs, ranging from ɛɪ to ɑɪ (through æɪ and aɪ), are heard. Thus the word *lady* is pronounced as leɪdɪ, lɛɪdɪ, læɪdɪ, laɪdɪ, lɑɪdɪ. The first two are generally

[1] See Ch. XVII for the modern pronunciation of words like *day*.

considered correct and the last three are looked on as markedly dialectal. A diphthong with the first element retracted towards ə, e.g. ləɪdɪ, pləɪs, is common in the Eastern counties, in the West of England, and with individual speakers.

197. The wider varieties of this diphthong can be corrected by exaggerating in the opposite direction, i.e. a pupil who says laɪdɪ must be told to make his sound more like leːdɪ, and the attempt will probably lead him to say a very good leɪdɪ or lɛɪdɪ.

198. The effect of a " dark *l* " following this diphthong, particularly the Cockney æɪ and aɪ, is to make the second element more like ə, so that a word such as *tale* is pronounced tæəl and taəl (with a very dark *l*). To correct this tendency the diphthong must be taught separately, and the 1 must be produced with a less " dark " quality, i.e. lᵘ or lᵊ, not lᵓ. (See Chapter XIV. § 268).

199. *No.* 14. ㅇㅜ, the sound in *go, home.*
Description
The first element of this diphthong is somewhat advanced from a fully back o, and there is not much movement of the tongue; hence it is, like eɪ, a narrow diphthong.

200. Many variant pronunciations of this diphthong occur in different parts of the country, the difference being due chiefly to the tongue position of the first element. In Scotland and in parts of the North of England a pure vowel is substituted for the diphthong, *I don't know* being pronounced aɪ doːnt noː. In the N. Riding of Yorkshire an open ɔ is used : aɪ dɔˑnt nɔː. (In the W. Riding broad dialect this would be a dʊənt nɔː.) A

very narrow oʊ diphthong is heard in educated Northern speech: in a less educated type of Northern speech, ɔʊ occurs in some words: e.g. nɔʊ (*know*). In Midland, Southern and Eastern pronunciation many varieties are found, ranging from ɔʊ and ʌʊ, in both of which the tongue starts in a much lower and further back position than in oʊ, to əʊ, æʊ, and aʊ, where the starting position is further forward, sometimes almost reaching that of a front vowel. Of these perhaps ɔʊ and ʌʊ are the commonest, while öü and ëü, which are made with a fronted position of each element, ëü, having the first vowel unrounded, are found in what is often called affected speech.[1] The difference between this pronunciation and one form of Cockney lies almost entirely in the quality of voice of the speaker; the diphthongs are practically of the same formation. In some dialects (e.g. Norfolk) the word *wholly* is pronounced hʌlɪ.

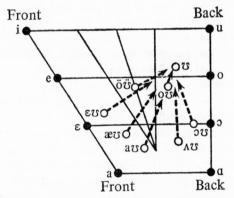

FIG. 25.   Varieties of the oʊ Dipththong.

[1] In some forms of "modern" pronunciation there is no lip-rounding whatever. See Ch. XVII, § 361 (v).

201. If the teacher wishes to get rid of ʌʊ or ɔʊ, the best way is to begin from ɜ. Let the pupil make this sound, then pronounce it with lip-rounding and pass to ʊ, gradually modifying the first element towards o. To get rid of a first element that is too far forward, make the pupil aim at a pure o, and then make a slight movement towards ʊ.

202. In certain words where oʊ occurs in an unstressed position, it is reduced to o; thus, *obey, November, going, phonetics, protest,* by some people are pronounced obeɪ, novɛmbə, goɪŋ, fonɛtɪks, proˈtɛst (alternative pronunciations əbeɪ, nəvɛmbə, fənɛtiks, prəˈtɛst; oʊbeɪ, noʊvɛmbə, goʊɪŋ, foʊnɛtiks, proʊˈtɛst).

203. *No. 15.* aɪ, the sound in *my, time.*

Description.

The tongue starts somewhere near the position of Cardinal a and moves towards ɪ; as the movement is considerable, aɪ is said to be a wide diphthong.

204. The main differences in the pronunciation of this diphthong lie in the starting point of the first element. This varies from æ, through various types of a, to ɑ and even ɒ, so that æɪ, aɪ, ɑɪ, ɑːɪ, ɒɪ are heard in addition to əɪ, where the first tongue position approaches that of a central vowel. æɪ is often considered affected, while ɑɪ, ɑːɪ, and ɒɪ are generally associated with Cockney pronunciation; and it is to be noted that this diphthong is often nasalised in London speech. In Yorkshire and Lancashire a diphthong beginning with a cardinal a rather lengthened is heard: aːɪ. In Southern speech the variant ɑɪ seems likely to become the commonest one, and it is heard very regularly on the stage.   It differs from one Cockney variety in length, and in the fact that it is not nasalised, but it is of practically the same tongue articulation. Another variety of London diphthong is æɪ, which is considered ultra " refaned " by many people, and it is possible that ɑɪ is a reaction against this pronunciation.

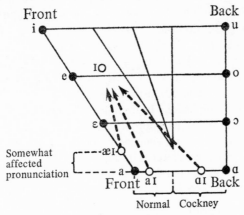

FIG. 26.   Varieties of the aɪ Diphthong.

205.   It is to be noted that aɪ followed by " dark *l*," as in words like *I'll*, *while*, *mile*, tends to become the pure vowel ɑː, ɑːl goʊ ɪn ə lɪtl wɑːl.   The London bus conductor calls out " tʃɑːlz ɪl " for *Child's Hill*.

206.   This pronunciation is found particularly in Southern speech, and is heard from speakers who have no other outstanding marks of Southern speech.

207.   It is generally considered desirable to modify the pronunciations of a too retracted aɪ, ɑːɪ and ɒɪ in the direction of aɪ, and this can easily be done by making the pupil exaggerate in the front direction; by attempting to say æɪ, he will probably say aɪ.

208. *No.* 16. aʊ, the sound in *now, round.*
Description.

This diphthong might well be written as ɑʊ, since the first element lies between a and ɑ, and is often near to the English ɑ as in *father.* The tongue starts at a point about half-way between Cardinal No. 4 and No. 5, and moves towards ʊ; it is a wide diphthong.

209. The diphthong varies in the starting position of the tongue, Northern speakers, especially Scottish, using a decided ɑ, Southern speakers tending towards Cardinal a and Cockney to æ, so that æʊ, aʊ, and ɑʊ are heard. In addition to these varieties, in the Eastern counties, a diphthong beginning with a centralised vowel is heard, something approaching əʊ, and in the West of England the second element becomes a front instead of a back rounded vowel, e.g. ay, wɪðayt, graynd.[1] In the broad Yorkshire dialect the diphthong becomes Cardinal a long, e.g. *now* is naː.

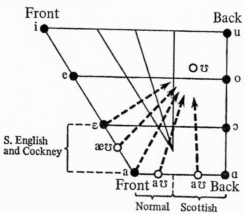

FIG. 27. Varieties of the aʊ Diphthong.

[1] I have heard this from a Kentish speaker.

210. In certain types of Cockney, a or ɑ are used where other Cockney speakers use æʊ, e.g. *about* (əbaʊt) becomes əbaːt, wɒt əbaːt ɪt or wɒr əbaː? ɪ?, *how* becomes aː, *out* becomes aːt, *cow* becomes kaː (kæʊ is a " refined " Cockney).

211. If these extreme pronunciations are to be corrected, the usual principle of making the pupil exaggerate in the opposite direction may be applied; if he says æʊ, make him try to say ɑʊ. If he says aː, after getting a further back a, make him add ʊ, a - - ʊ, making two syllables; gradually reduce the space between the two elements and let the tongue glide quickly to the ʊ position.

212. *No.* 17. ɔɪ, the sound in *boy, noise.*

Description.

The tongue position of the first element is a little higher than that of the English ɒ sound, and the movement is towards ɪ.

213. The different pronunciations of this vowel are due to the differences in the starting position of the tongue, and in some cases to the position of the lips. The varieties range from ɑɪ, where the first element is unrounded, a pronunciation which is heard in the Eastern counties, and, to a certain extent, in the West of England, to oːɪ, where the first position is closer and over-rounded. This pronunciation is found in London. bʌɪ (for *boy*) is said to exist in Devonshire and bwɔ or bɔ (spelt *bor*) in Suffolk.

214. If it is desired to teach ɔɪ instead of oːɪ, all that is necessary is to tell the pupil to open his mouth more at beginning the sound, while ɔɪ can be obtained

by telling the pupil who says ɑɪ or ʌɪ to round his lips.
This also produces the necessary tongue adjustment.

215. *No.* 18. ɪə, the sound in *here*, *beard*, *idea*
Description.

The tongue starts in the position of ɪ and moves
towards the neutral vowel ə.

216. Many varieties of this diphthong are founds
In Cockney the first element is very close, i, and it i.
often separated from the ə by the semi-vowel j,
" Darlin' Dora " in *Fanny's First Play* says ʌʊl diːjə.
and the London flower sellers say vɑ̃ːlɪʔs diːjə. iə is
heard in many parts of the country, and eə, ɪʌ, or ɪɑ,
in the last two of which the tongue moves beyond the ə
position, are met with in what is sometimes called affected
pronunciation. In those parts of the country where
final *r* is pronounced, the following variants occur:
iːr (in Scotland), ɪər (in many parts of N. England), ɪəɹ
and ɪə̣ (in N.W. and W.) with the tongue-tip curled up.
The two pronunciations of the word *year* should be
noted, jɪə and jɜː.[1]

217. To teach ɪə instead of iːjə, make the pupil
begin with a lower tongue position, i.e. let him aim at
e, and glide gently towards the ə.

218. *No.* 19. ɛə, the sound in *fair*, *scarce*.
Description.

The starting point of the tongue is near to Cardinal ɛ
position, the movement of the tongue in this case
being chiefly from front to back, towards the central
position.

[1] I have heard a lecturer pronounce *this era* as ðɪs jɜˑrə.

219. All varieties from iə to æə are heard. In the broad Yorks. dialect *there* is pronounced ðiə; Cockney pronunciation is ðeə, sometimes ðeːjə. In Southern English a more open first position is heard.[1] In addition to this, we find the varieties where some kind of *r* is pronounced, ðeːr, in Scotland, ðɛəɹ or ðɛə̣ (with the tongue-tip curled up) in the N. and N.W., and in S. Lancashire and in Cheshire, particularly in Liverpool and Birkenhead the pronunciation ɜ is heard, e.g. skɜˑslɪ, kɜˑfʊl.[2] The words *fur, hair*, in this part of the country are often pronounced fɛː, hɜː. It is probable, however, that a sound intermediate between the two is used for both, and that the hearer who is not accustomed to this pronunciation thinks the speaker is using ɜ in place of ɛ, and ɛ in place of ɜ.

220. To teach ɛə to pupils who say eːjə or ɜ, begin with an open ɛ sound, or with a sound resembling æ, and glide to the ə sound from that.

221. *No. 20.* ɔə, the sound in *more, board*.

Description.

The tongue starts a little below Cardinal ɔ position and moves towards the neutral ə.

222. A large number of South-eastern English speakers do not use this diphthong at all; for it, they use the pure vowel ɔ. The many different pronunciations of words in which this diphthong can occur were dealt with under the English vowel No. 7, ɔ §§ 161–163.

223. *No. 21.* ʊə, the sound in *pure, your*.

[1] This is the pronunciation indicated in *A Phonetic Reader*, by Mackenzie & Drew (Manchester University Press). [Out of print.]

[2] It is reported also from Devonshire.

Description.

The tongue starts from the ʊ position and moves to ə.

224.   Pronunciations vary from uːə, heard in the North, through ʊə, oə, ɔə, to ɔ, and there are also varieties where either an r is pronounced, e.g. puːr (Scotland), pʊər, pʊəɹ, or the vowel is made with inversion of the tip of the tongue. oə and ɔə and ɔ are heard in educated London speech, particularly in the word *poor*, while in *your*, perhaps jɔ is the commonest Southern pronunciation. A Cockney speaker pronounces these two words as pɔːwə and jɔːwə.

225.   To teach ʊə to a Cockney who says pɔːwə it is necessary to isolate the ʊ sound in the word pʊt, and make the pupil glide from that to ə; there should be no exaggerated lip movement, such as would give the semi-vowel w.

226.   It should be noted that in Cockney and other dialects in different parts of the country, there is a tendency to drawl the diphthongs. This is often a marked characteristic of dialectal speech, and should be corrected.   A Cockney says nʌ - - - ʊ or mɑː - - - ɪn, and a Yorkshire speaker says mɑː - - - ɪt, in which he differs from an educated speaker only in the "drawl," and probably voice quality.   To correct this tendency should not be difficult ; the speaker can be told to glide quickly from the first element, or it is often sufficient to tell him to say the sound vigorously.

TRIPHTHONGS.

227.   The groups of vowel sounds aɪə and aʊə, as in certain pronunciations of the words *fire* and *power* are often considered triphthongs.   They are not, however,

true triphthongs, for the first and last sounds in each group are more sonorous than the middle one, that is, they belong to different syllables, having a diminution of prominence between them. They often strike the ear, however, as one syllable, and are treated as such in poetry.

228. The diagram illustrates approximately the movements of the tongue in making these two groups

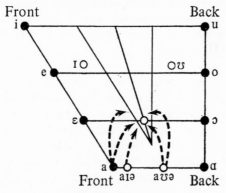

FIG. 28. Triphthongs.

of sounds. It will be noted that the starting position is known, that the tongue moves towards the ɪ and the ʊ positions, but does not nearly reach them, and then moves towards ə; aeə and aoə would be a closer representation of the sounds.

229. It is often found that these two triphthongs are reduced to diphthongs, that the words *fire* and *power* are pronounced faə and paə (the a in the latter being further back than the former: it could be represented as ɑə). Sometimes they are even reduced to a pure vowels aː and ɑː. Speakers who use this pronunciation for *fire*, distinguish between it and *far* (fɑː), the tongue position in the former being a little further forward than in *far*, and a suspicion of two syllables is added by a slight diminution and reinforcement of the breath force.   It is in the word *our* that this reduction is most noticeable: *our own*, often being pronounced aːr oʊn.   The pronunciation faː for *fire*, taː for *tire*, taː for *tower*, etc., is used by the younger generation in the south, and is criticised severely by people who do not use this type of pronunciation.   See Ch. II, § 22, and Ch. XVII, § 361 (iv).

NOTE.—The combinations of sounds written as eɪə, ɔɪə, and oʊə, as in *player*, *employer*, and *mower* can also be considered as triphthongs of a kind.   These groups, however, constitute two syllables in the pronunciation of many people.   The pronunciation vɔɪlɪn (vaɪəlɪn), vɔɪlɪt (vaɪələt) may be a mistaken spelling pronunciation due to a confusion of *oi* and *io*.

230.   On pp. 152 ff. a summary is given of the main differences in the pronunciation of diphthongs in Northern and Southern English, and in London and Standard pronunciation.

Chapter XIII

NASALISATION OF VOWELS

231. Nasalised vowels are not found in normal English speech, although there is no doubt that vowels which occur in the neighbourhood of nasal consonants are partially nasalised: e.g. in the word *man* (mæn), the soft palate is lowered for m and for n, and between these two sounds, it makes a movement towards closure for the vowel. But the time is so short that a complete closure is not possible; and in pronouncing the vowel, some of the breath escapes through the nose as well as through the mouth. If this nasalisation is too great, it becomes noticeable and is considered disagreeable.

232. Nasalisation (which is not due to physical defect) is often the result of bad habit, and is found in certain dialects and in some individuals. Cockney speakers add strong nasalisation to vowels in the neighbourhood of nasal consonants and sometimes where no nasal consonant occurs.

There aren't any becomes ðər ãĩʔ ɛnĩ.
I don't think so ,, ãɪ dãũ θĩʔ sʌʊ.

(Note the n of *aren't, don't* and the ŋ of *think* have disappeared; the nasalisation of the vowel takes their place.)

233. To cure nasality is not an easy task.[1] The teacher must try and work from sounds which are not

[1] See chapter on "Nasal Twang" in the writer's *Speech Defects: their Nature and Cure.* Dent & Co. [Out of print.]

nasalised. Sometimes the vowels are nasalised when not near nasal consonants. The open vowels lend themselves to nasalisation more readily than the close ones, and it is often found that i and u are free from nasalisation. If so, it is possible to work from these and gradually to get from i to ɪ and eɪ, from u to ʊ and oʊ, and so on to the more open vowels. ɑ is most subject to nasalisation, and should therefore be left till the last. Exercises for the control of the soft palate are useful, as they induce a more vigorous movement of the palate.

234. If all the vowels are nasalised, the teacher may begin with the consonant z, which loses its characteristic buzz if it is nasalised—which is a rare occurrence. Let the pupil practise zi, zi, zi; zu, zu, zu; then go on to ze, zɛ, zɔ, etc. When nasalisation begins to appear, it will be necessary to go back to a vowel which is not nasalised.

235. The vowels should be practised in isolation before there is any attempt made to use them in words. When they can be pronounced as purely oral vowels, they may be introduced into words. Words in which a nasal consonant occurs should be left to the last, and even then, the vowel should at first be separated from the nasal consonant by a complete break æ—nd, n—aɪs, the pause being gradually reduced until there is no break.

CHAPTER XIV
ENGLISH CONSONANTS IN DETAIL

236. Consonants are classified according to the *organs* articulating them and according to the *manner* of their articulation. This double classification lends itself to a useful diagrammatic form, the terms along the top of the diagram giving the *organs* by which they are articulated, and those down the side the *manner* in which they are articulated.

237. TABLE OF ENGLISH CONSONANTS.
See page 128.

Note.—Symbols which occur twice indicate sounds which have a double articulation, the secondary articulation being shown in brackets, thus ( ).

VOICED AND VOICELESS CONSONANTS.

238. In Chapter VIII, § 76, it was shown that it is possible to combine the movements of the vocal cords with the articulation of any consonant: i.e. consonants can be voiced (z, ʒ, b, g, l, m, etc.), or they can be voiceless (s, ʃ, p, k, etc.). In most languages there occur numbers of pairs of consonants, articulated by lips, tongue, teeth, etc., in exactly the same way, and differing in the presence or absence of voice (p b, f v, θ ð, s z, etc.). In the following table, where these pairs are shown, the first is voiceless, the second voiced. Many consonants (such as m, n, ŋ, r, l) have only their voiced form as usual speech sounds of English. These can be pronounced, however, without voice, and the student is advised to practise this as a good phonetic exercise. (See Chapter VIII, § 77 d.) It should also be noticed that voiceless consonants require more force

	Bi-labial	Labio-Dental	Pre-dental	Post-dental or Alveolar	Palato-Alveolar	Palatal	Velar	Glottal
Plosive	p b			t d			k g	ʔ
Affricative			tθ dθ	ts dz tʃ dɹ	tʃ dʒ			
Nasal	m			n			ŋ	
Lateral				l			(ɫ)	
Rolled				r				
Fricative		f v	θ ð	s z ɹ	ʃ ʒ			h
Semi-vowel	ʍ w					j	(w)	

of exhalation than voiced consonants and are articulated with greater vigour; there is a tighter closure for the plosives and a sharper release, and for the fricatives a smaller opening. To test the difference in breath force hold the hand before the mouth while θ and ð (or f and v, p and b) are pronounced alternately.

239. The voiced consonants in English in initial and final positions are not fully voiced: i.e. in initial position the vibrations of the vocal cords do not begin immediately the consonant is formed, but some way through the articulation; in final positions, the vibrations cease before the consonant is finished. Thus in *dog* (dɒg), the voice does not begin until perhaps half-way through the d, and it ceases before the articulation of the g comes to an end, i.e. it resembles t͡dɒg͡k in pronunciation. It is important for teachers to realise this, as some are apt to waste time in making children voice fully English consonants in final positions, under the impression that it is an essential of English speech. Thus they will insist on a voiced off-glide to a b, d, g, rɒbᵊ, sædᵊ, bɪgᵊ, which is not desirable even for very careful speech.

PLOSIVE CONSONANTS.

240. Plosive consonants are made by the stoppage of the air passage at some point. The air compressed behind the stop rushes out with a slight explosion when the stop is released. Thus a plosive consists of (*a*) a stop, (*b*) a release, and (*c*) some sound which follows the release. In forming p and b, the stop is made by the two lips; in t and d by the tip of the tongue against the teeth ridge; in k and g by the back of the tongue against the soft palate.

Voiceless Plosives.

241. The English voiceless plosives are said to be aspirated, i.e. on the release of the stop a slight **h** is heard before the following vowel, e.g. *park* is pʰɑ·k, *too* is tʰuː, *come* is kʰʌm. This aspiration is marked in *stressed*, but not in *unstressed* positions: thus, *ten* is

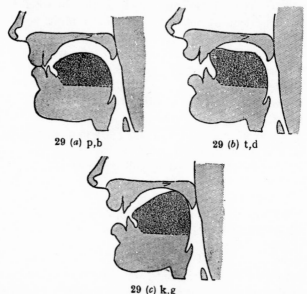

29 (*a*) p,b   29 (*b*) t,d

29 (*c*) k,g

FIG. 29.   English Plosive Consonants.

tʰɛn, but in *letter* (lɛtə), the aspiration is very slight. Compare the French and Italian voiceless plosives where the vowel sound begins immediately on the release of the stop; these are said to be *unaspirated*.

242. In Cockney speech, the consonants **p, t, k** are said to be over-aspirated; the puff of breath before the vowel sound is so great as to be noticeable, and such a pronunciation is thought undesirable. This is particularly the case with t, where strong aspiration, added to a lazy articulation of the stop and a slow release, results in ts, the s being heard as the tongue is removed slowly from the t position. Similarly the aspiration of k together with a slow release results in the affricative kx, the velar fricative x being heard as the back of the tongue is removed slowly from the k position. Thus a Cockney will say ə kxap əv tsəi for ə kʌp əv tiː. In Northern English, particularly in Lancashire and Yorkshire, aspiration of p, t, k even in stressed positions is either very slight or absent altogether.

243. In order to cure over-aspiration, it is necessary to tell the pupil to make the contact firm and the release vigorous. If after a vigorous pronunciation the aspiration is still too noticeable, he should be told to make his p more like b, his t more like d, and his k more like g.

244. Teachers of singing try to combat aspiration of p, t, k as it lets out a great quantity of breath, leaving little behind with which to sing the succeeding voiced sounds.

Incomplete Plosives.

245. In § 240 a plosive is shown to have three parts; but in English there are some cases in which all the three parts are not made, when the stop alone is formed, but no release. This occurs when two plosive consonants follow each other: in *act, stopped, doctor* (ækt, stɒpt, dɒktə), the first plosive in each pair is not exploded: we do not say ækʰt, stɒpʰt, dɒkʰtə. The same thing happens when the first plosive is at the end of one word and the second at the beginning of another, e.g. tɒp bɔɪ, lɒg kæbɪn, bæd gɜːl, hɒt pɒt, stɒp tɔ·kɪŋ, etc. When

the two consonants are the same, as in blæk kæt, gʊd dɒg, ðæt taɪm, stɒp pliːz, they form a long stop with one release. To explode the first plosive in such combinations does not add to distinctness even in slow speech ; in fact it detracts from clarity by the addition of an extra sound which does not belong to normal speech.

246.   When three plosives follow each other, in conversational speech, it is possible for the last one only to receive its full plosion: e.g. ə beɪkt tɑ·t, ækt tuː, ə lɒkt dɔə, ən æpt pju·pɪl, ə lɒpt triː, ə rɛkt trɔ·lə, tʊ ækt kaɪndlɪ.

FAUCAL OR NASAL PLOSION.

247.   In the pronunciation of such words as *button,*

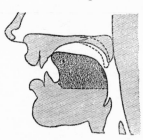

FIG. 30.
Illustrating Nasal Plosion.

hidden, shopman, oatmeal, the plosive consonant is immediately followed by a nasal consonant, bʌtn, hɪdn, ʃɒpmən, oʊtmiˑl, and the plosive is not exploded in the normal way. While the tongue or lips remain in the position for the plosive, the soft palate is lowered to allow the air to pass through the nose for the following nasal consonant. (See accompanying diagram, Fig. 30.)   The explosion that is heard and felt is made by the air rushing out through the nose, on the lowering of the soft palate. This is called faucal or nasal plosion.

248.   Examples of nasal plosion are found in the following words: sɪdnɪ, heɪpnɪ, beɪkŋ (alternative pronunciations beɪkn, beɪkən), ɔ·gŋ graɪndə (alternative pronunciation ɔgən graɪndə), oʊpm (alternative

pronunciations oʊpn, oʊpən), and in the phrases gʊd_naɪt, gʊd_mɔːnɪŋ, blæk_mædʒɪk, hiːz kʌm bæk_naʊ, pʊt ɪt_nɪə mi, hi sɛd_nʌθɪŋ, ə lɒt_mɔə, lɛt_mi goʊ. In such cases it is not necessary to explode the plosive normally, i.e. we do not say gʊd⁹ naɪt, ə lɒt⁹ mɔə, etc.

LATERAL PLOSION.

249. When a plosive is followed by an l sound, the explosion is made by the sides of the tongue leaving the upper teeth and the air rushing out along the sides of the tongue: e.g. lɪtl, mʌdl, rætl. This is called lateral plosion. The same kind of plosion occurs when one word ends in a plosive and the next begins with l: e.g. aɪ sɪt laɪtlɪ tʊ ɪt, ə bæd laɪt, ə big leɪk, etc.

250. NOTES ON THE PLOSIVE CONSONANTS.

(a) t and d before r are articulated on the teeth, not on the teeth ridge, in some types of Irish pronunciation and in North Yorkshire. Thus *true* has a dental t and a rolled r. This gives the impression of tθruː. (This word is often written *thrue* to indicate an Irish pronunciation.) (For dental t and d see Fig. 31a.)

(b) The substitution of d for t between two vowels is occasionally heard: e.g. sædədɪ for sætədɪ. Such a d tends to become a semi-rolled r; thus sædədɪ weakens into særədɪ, bɛtə becomes bɛdə and then bɛrə. This tendency is seen in the vulgar speech of many dialects in the phrase gɛr əweɪ for gɛt əweɪ. It is also a marked characteristic of American speech: e.g. lɛrə for *letter*, kɑ'rɪʤ for *cottage*. Compare *porridge* (pɒrɪʤ), which has come from *potage*. The London bus-conductor often calls *Swiss Cottage* swɪs kɒrɪʤ.

(c) A voiceless fricative *r* (ɹ̥) is used for final or inter-vocalic *t* by some Irish speakers : e.g. *better, sit* are pronounced bɛɹ̥ə, sɪɹ̥.

(d) *The Glottal Stop.*—The glottal stop (for description and diagram see § 75 d, p. 53) is a regular speech sound in English in the pronunciation of many people. It is used normally in the following cases:

i. For the sake of emphasis, when a stressed syllable begins with a vowel, a glottal stop is introduced before it, e.g.

> ɪt wəz ðɪ ''ʔoʊnlɪ 'θɪŋ tə 'duː.
>
> ɪt s əz ''ʔiːzɪ əz kən 'biː.
>
> [''Indicates extra emphasis.]

It is generally at the beginning of words that the glottal stop is used in this way, but particularly emphatic speakers use it in words like traɪʔʌmfənt, ɛkstrəʔɔ·dɪmərɪ, kriʔeɪʃn, ʔiːlɪ daɪʔɒsɪsn əsoʊsɪʔeɪʃn. This sound is not essential for English speech either for meaning or for emphasis, as it is possible to emphasize sufficiently by using extra force of breath without making a glottal stop.

ii. To avoid a hiatus between two vowels, e.g.

> pʊt ə kɒmə ʔɑ·ftər ɪt.
>
> liːnə ʔæʃwɛl (Lena Ashwell).

Some speakers use it instead of r in phrases like *better and better*, bɛtə ʔən bɛtə, *Westminster Abbey*, wɛstmɪnstə ʔæbɪ. It is possible, however, to make a smooth passage from one vowel to the next without either the glottal stop or r. (See §§ 273-4 for linking *r* and for intrusive *r*.)

(e) The glottal stop is used in all parts of the country
to replace other plosive consonants. This tendency,
probably of long standing, seems to be growing.
It is found to a marked extent in Scotland,
Yorkshire and Lancashire, in the Eastern counties,
in the Home Counties and in London. Most
people are familiar with the Scottish wɔːʔər or
wɒʔər for *water*, with the Cockney lɛʔə for *letter*,
and tɒʔnəm kɔːʔ rʌʊd; in *Stockport* the town is
often called stɒʔpɔːʔ, *Bradford* is called braʔfəd,
and all over the country *little* is found as lɪʔl,
lately leɪʔli, *exactly* ɛgzæʔlɪ, and *mutton* mʌʔn.
The Cockney newsboy calls out paɪʔə for *paper*;
in London I heard iːz biːn tɔːʔɪn əbaːʔ ɪʔ əbaːʔ
ɛɪʔiːn mʌ̃ʔs (He's been talking about it about
eighteen months); in Yorkshire I have heard
bɪʔwiˑn; and in the Eastern Counties aɪ tʊʊld ðə
pɔˑʔə tə pʊʔ ɪʔ ɪn ðə væn; ðeɪ ə kʌmɪŋ hɪə
ʔəmɒrʊʊ; mɛʔm; (*make him*); ðæʔ dəʊ̃ʔ mæʔə
s lɒŋ z jə gɒʔ ə tɪʔɪʔ, *That doesn't matter, so long as
you've got a ticket*; ðɪs hɒʔ wɛðə meɪʔs piˑʔl θĩʔ əbaʊʔ
teɪʔn hɒlɪdɪz (*This hot weather makes people think
about taking holidays*). In the last sentence the
glottal stop replaces p, t, k). It is easily recognised in the above examples, but before alveolar
and labial consonants, where it occurs very frequently, the glottal stop is not so noticeable, e.g.
ðæʔ sɔt əv θɪŋ, skɒʔlənd, aɪ dɔʊn? nɒʊ, dɔʊn? lɛʔ
mi kiˑp ju, nɒʔ bɪfɔə tuː, ðæʔ wʌn, pʌʔnɪ, mʌʔn.

(f) Many Southern and Eastern speakers insert a glottal
stop before a voiceless plosive in certain words:
e.g. njuʔtrəl (*neutral*), pɒʔpjʊlə (*popular*), mæʔtrɪs

(*mattress*), rɛ?klɪs (*reckless*), pɛ?trəl (*petrol*). This often gives the impression of a long stop on the p, t or k, i.e. njuˑttrəl, pɒppjʊlə, etc., but the glottal closure is almost always there in such pronunciations. This pronunciation is not confined to the uneducated.

251. If the glottal stop is to be got rid of—and it certainly makes for indistinctness—teachers will have to wage vigorous war against it. It ought not to be difficult to eliminate, for the pupil *can* pronounce the correct consonant, and always does so in stressed positions; he says bʌ?ə for *butter*, but never ?ɛn for *ten*. In actual practice, however, to get rid of the glottal stop is not easy. It is not a question of teaching a new sound, but of getting the pupil to remember to use a sound he already possesses, in unfamiliar positions, i.e. to lose an old habit and create a new one. Careful, slow reading in the first instance, paying particular attention to the articulation of the plosive consonants should make it possible for the pupil to cure himself.[1] The *over correction* of a glottal stop, however, i.e. the insistence of an off-glide to the t (e.g. sitʰ stɪl) is as unpleasant as the glottal stop itself. Where the glottal stop is inter-vocalic, it is useful, as a preliminary step, to break up the words in this way: pʊ - - - tɪ - - - tɒn ðə teɪbl.

AFFRICATIVE CONSONANTS.

252. A plosive consonant can be pronounced with either quick or slow separation of the articulating organs. If a slow separation is made, there is no noticeable explosion, but on the release of the stop a fricative

---

[1] See Ch. II, § 28 for the technique of "slowing up," which could be used here to get rid of the glottal stop.

consonant is heard. Such a method of articulating plosives gives rise to what are called *affricative* consonants.

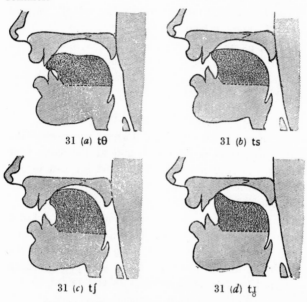

31 (*a*) tθ   31 (*b*) ts

31 (*c*) tʃ   31 (*d*) tɹ̥

Fig. 31.   Illustrating the starting position for
tθ, ts, tʃ and tɹ̥.

253. An affricate is a plosive consonant in which the articulating organs are separated less quickly than in the case of normal plosives, with the result that the corresponding fricative is heard momentarily as the organs separate.

254. To every plosive a corresponding affricate can be made, and the student is recommended to try to pronounce as many as he can.   In English, however,

those given on the table on p. 128 are the only ones that occur normally. E.g.

eighth, eɪtθ; *width*, wɪdθ; *eats*, iˑts; *beds*, bɛdz; *lunch*, lʌntʃ (alternative pronunciation lʌnʃ); *church.* tʃɜˑtʃ, *jump*, dʒʌmp; *German*, dʒɜˑmən; *bridge*, brɪdʒ.

tɹ and dɹ, as in the words *tree* and *draw*, may also be considered affricatives, the t and d made in this case with the tip of the tongue slightly curled up in readiness for the ɹ. [See Fig. 31 (d)].

NASAL CONSONANTS.

255. Nasal consonants are formed by closing the mouth passage at some point, and at the same time lowering the soft palate, so that the air can escape through the nose. In English there are normally three nasal consonants, m, n and ŋ.

256. The connection between nasal and plosive consonants can be seen by comparing the diagrams of Fig. 32 with those for p.b, t.d, k.g on p. 130, the difference being in the position of the soft palate, which is lowered for the nasal consonants and raised for the plosives. When for any reason—cold or adenoid growths—it is impossible for the breath to escape through the nose, something like the corresponding plosive is heard instead of the nasal consonant, e.g. *morning* (mɔːnɪŋ) is pronounced almost as bɔˑdɪg, a *strong man* (ə strɒŋ mæn) becomes almost ə strɒg bæd.

257. In the table on p. 128, the nasal consonants are given without their voiceless equivalents, m̥, n̥, ŋ̊. The student is recommended to practise these (see exercises in § 77 d). They occur occasionally in words like *ahem, humph* (ʔm̥m, m̥mm̥), and in mm̥m (*yes*).

258. The nasal consonants are often "syllabic," i.e. they form the most sonorous element of a syllable, e.g. mʌtn, hɛvn, iːvn, spoʊkn or spoʊkŋ, neɪʃn, prɪzm, oʊpm, klæpm, beɪkn or beɪkŋ. Some of these forms occur only in quick speech, oʊpən, beɪkən, klæpəm, etc., being a more careful form.

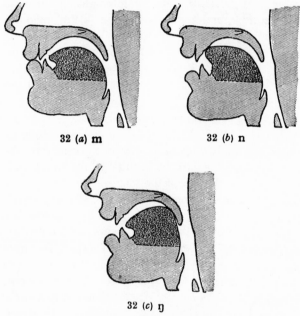

32 (a) m   32 (b) n

32 (c) ŋ

FIG. 32. Nasal Consonants.

259. The nasal consonants are extremely susceptible to the influence of other neighbouring sounds. For the changes which m, n, ŋ undergo, see the Chapter on Sounds in Connected Speech, §§ 335, 340—341.

260. The letters *ng*, pronounced as ŋ in words like *singer*, *singing* (sɪŋə, sɪŋɪŋ) are pronounced ŋg (sɪŋgə, sɪŋgɪŋg) in the Midlands. Words like *longer*, *finger*, *single*, normally pronounced lɒŋgə, fɪŋgə, sɪŋgl, become lɒŋə, fɪŋə, sɪŋl in some parts of Scotland, Yorkshire and the North Midlands. In Cockney speech *nothing* and *anything* have by false analogy become nafɪŋk, ɛnɪfɪŋk, and *kitchen* has become kɪtʃɪŋ; maʊntɪŋ and faʊntɪŋ pɛn can also be heard. What is known as *"dropping one's g's"* is replacing ŋ by n, e.g. goʊɪn, teɪkɪn. This practice is very widespread and is not confined to dialect speakers only. (See Chapter on Spelling Pronunciations, § 65 (j).)

LATERAL CONSONANTS.

261. The English *l* is termed a lateral consonant because the air passage is stopped in the centre by the tip of the tongue against the teeth-ridge, the air escaping along one or both sides of the tongue.

262. In English there are two well-defined types of *l* sounds; in both, the main articulation is that described above, i.e. the tip of the tongue against the teeth-ridge.

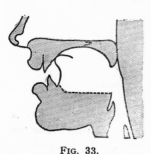

FIG. 33.
Primary Articulation of *l*.

263. They differ from each other in the position of the rest of the tongue. Where *l* occurs before vowels, the front of the tongue is raised towards the hard palate; when it occurs finally or before consonants, the front is slightly hollowed, and the back is raised towards the soft palate. The

former is called "*clear l*," and the latter, which has a somewhat obscure quality, is called the "*dark l.*" Some writers say that in "*dark l*" the contact of the tip of the tongue is further back than in "*clear l.*" This *may* be so with individual speakers, but it is not *necessarily* so; the difference in quality is chiefly due to the difference in the position of the main body of the tongue, not in that of the tip. The terms "clear" and "dark" are descriptive of the acoustic effect of the sounds and not a technical or scientific name; the correct phonetic terms are "palatalised" and "velarised,"

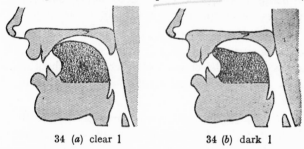

34 (*a*) clear l   34 (*b*) dark l

FIG. 34. Clear and Dark *l*.

i.e. palatalised means that the front of the tongue is raised towards the hard palate, velarised the back of the tongue raised towards the soft palate; in both cases this modification is a secondary articulation, the primary one being the tip of the tongue against the teeth ridge.

264. It is possible to make *l*, which is the most sonorous of all the consonants, with the resonance of any vowel. The English *clear l* has an ə resonance tending towards i, the *dark l* has an ʊ resonance. Many speakers use a kind of *mid l* instead of a *dark l*, i.e.

with an ɜ instead of an ʊ resonance. This is particularly noticeable in Northerners. Students should practise as a phonetic exercise, the making of *l* with the resonance of each Cardinal vowel in turn: lⁱ, lᵉ, lᵉ, lᵃ, lᵅ, lᵓ, lᵒ, lᵘ.

265. Like the nasal consonants m and n, l is often syllabic: e.g. lɪtl, ræbl, fɪkl, θɪmbl, etc. If it is required to mark l as syllabic, the symbol ļ is used, but it is unnecessary to use this symbol in a phonetic transcription, unless it is possible to make l either syllabic or non-syllabic: e.g. in bɒtl the l must be syllabic, while in bɒtlɪŋ it could be pronounced either bɒtlɪŋ (two syllables), or bɒt|ɪŋ (three syllables).

266. Voiceless *l* (ļ̥) does not occur as a speech sound of normal English. It is the sound of Welsh *ll*, and as a speech defect, is one of the common substitutions for **s**. In words like *please* the l is partially devoiced (pl̥iːz).

267. In Ireland and some parts of the North of England, a *clear l* is used in all positions, teɪblⁱ, piːplⁱ, bɛlⁱz. In Scotland and in some types of American and West Country speech, *dark l* is often found initially ɫeɪt, ɫɒŋ.¹ In London dialect, the *dark l*, instead of having an ʊ resonance, has that of o or ɔ, i.e. the vowel quality is that of a lower and more retracted vowel than ʊ. With this drawing back of the back of the tongue, there is a tendency for the tip to leave the teeth ridge; in such cases *l* is replaced by a vowel. E.g.

> *milk* is pronounced mɪlᵓk (with a very dark *l*) or mɪɔk
> *while*   ,,   waːlᵓ or waːɔ, (with no l),

¹ I have been told by a competent authority that *clear l* occurs in Galloway, even finally.

Bill is pronounced bɪɔ or bɪo,

sell ,,   sɛːɔ or sɛːo.

bowl ,,   boːl or bɔːl.

268. The " *dark* 1 " has a marked influence on vowel sounds which precede it. This is especially noticeable in London speech, and teachers should be aware of this fact, for often what is considered an incorrect vowel sound is due, not to inability to say a correct vowel, but to the influence of too dark an *l*, and if the 1 is put right, the vowel is generally easy to correct. This point is noted in Chapter XI under the head-

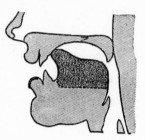

Fɪɢ. 35. Over-dark 1.

ings of the particular vowels. To correct the over dark 1, it is essential, in the first place, to insist on a firm contact with the tip of the tongue. Then tell the pupil to try and say 1 and ʊ at the same time; this should give the correct resonance for normal dark 1; it may, how-ever, be necessary to exaggerate a little towards a more clear 1, i.e. to say 1 with an ɜ resonance, or to aim at something approaching the pupil's sound of 1, which he uses before vowels.   When the " over-dark " 1 is corrected, then comes the teaching of the use of it after vowels, so that the vowel quality is not too much altered. It is well to separate vowel and con-sonant, e.g. bɛ.., 1, fi...1, as a first stage, insisting on the correct pronunciation of both. Then the pupil can gradually reduce the pause between the two.

ROLLED SOUNDS.

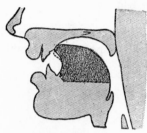

FIG. 36.   Rolled *r*.

269. The rolled r is made by a rapid succession of taps of the tongue-tip against the teeth ridge.

270. This sound is not common in Southern English, the letter *r* being more usually pronounced as a fricative consonant. In many parts of the country, *r* is not pronounced finally, e.g. hɜː, ðɛə, or before consonants, hɑːd, gɜːl.

271.   DIFFERENT KINDS OF *r* SOUNDS.

i. The rolled *r* described above is used in Scotland in all positions, even before consonants and finally, e.g. hɑrd, gɛrl or gʌrl, In North Yorks., where it is used after *t* and *d*, the *t* and *d* are dental, truː, draɪ. (To roll an *r* after an alveolar consonant is very difficult for English people.)

ii. A semi-rolled or one-tap *r* (special symbol ɾ), consisting of one tap of the tongue, is commonly used between voiced sounds. e.g. vɛɾɪ, kwɒɾl and frequently after the pre-dental fricatives, θ and ð, e.g. θɾuː, brɛðɾɪn.

iii. A fricative *r* (special symbol ɹ) is used in many parts of the country in positions where an *r* is sounded at all. It is the usual *initial r* in all parts of the country except Scotland.

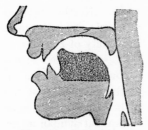

FIG. 37. Fricative *r*.

iv. An "inverted" *r*, i.e. a fricative made with the tongue-tip curled up considerably, is used finally and before consonants in many parts of the West Country (N. and S.), in the South as far east as Surrey, and in Ireland and America (hɑɹd, gɜɹl). It is heard in the pronunciation of many educated speakers in these districts. The inversion of the tip of the tongue may, and often does, take place while the preceding vowel is being pronounced, so that the vowel quality is affected. If the space between the tip of the tongue and the palate is not narrow enough to justify the sound being called a consonant, the effect of the inversion can still be heard in the vowel. Recent ex-

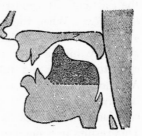

FIG. 38. Inverted *r*.

periments carried out in a Phonetics Laboratory prove that in some American speech, what sounds like an inverted *r* is in reality not a consonant at all—i.e. the space between the tongue and the roof of the mouth is too wide to allow any friction— but a vowel made with the tip of the tongue slightly curled up.[1] See p. 120, § 216.

[1] See Kenyon, *American Pronunciation*, p. 161, § 234.

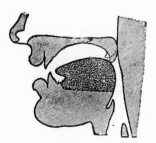

FIG. 39.   Uvular Rolled *r*.

v. In Northumberland and Durham a uvular variety of *r* is heard: this is formed either by the vibration of the uvula against the back of the tongue (special symbol **ʀ**), or by a narrowing between the back of the tongue and the uvula (special symbol **ʁ**): e.g. dɒʀəm or dɒʁəm (for dʌrəm, *Durham*).

272. Those students who cannot roll an **r** should practise the following exercise. Pronounce tədɑtədɒ, the **t** articulated against the *teeth* and the **d** against the *teeth ridge*. When these sounds are said very quickly, a one-tap **r** takes the place of **d**. This can be developed gradually into a fully rolled **r**; but a rolled **r** is not easy to acquire and takes long and patient practice. Another word that can be used to teach a one-tap **r** is *body*. Say bɒdɪ : then say it with rather lazy articulation, making the **d** very rapid and very light. This results in a one-tap **r**.

"LINKING r."

273. When *r* in spelling occurs at the end of a word or phrase, it is generally not pronounced in Southern English: e.g. gɪv mi səm mɔə, hɪə nɒt ðɛə. But when such a word is followed by another word in close connection with it, beginning with a vowel, the **r** is introduced by many speakers.

E.g. gɪv mi səm mɔər əv ɪt.
   hɪər ən ðɛə.

Westminster is pronounced wɛstmɪnstə, but wɛstmɪnstər æbɪ is often heard. (Some people insert a glottal stop instead of r in such combinations, wɛstmɪnstə ʔæbɪ.) The linking r is generally omitted when the syllable begins as well as ends with an r:

E.g. nɪərə ənd nɪərə, not nɪərər ənd nɪərə.[1]

"INTRUSIVE r."

274. An "*intrusive* r" where none exists in spelling is very frequently inserted between two words, the one ending and the next beginning with a vowel, in order to avoid what is felt to be an awkward hiatus. This is partly due to a false analogy with the linking r: compare aɪ v noʊ fɪər əv ɪt and aɪ v noʊ aɪdɪər əv ɪt. It is in this phrase, "*the idea of it*," and other similar ones, that the intrusive r shows itself most frequently; this pronunciation is heard among educated speakers who are quite unaware that they use it, and who would be horrified to learn it. I have heard from the pulpit or the stage:

> nɔər ənd hɪz fæmɪlɪ.
>
> ɪz sɪlvɪər ət hoʊm.
>
> pʊt ə kɒmər ɑ·ftər ɪt.

There is no doubt that the intrusive r is spreading; even in districts and among classes where it has not been known, the younger generation is using it. In Cockney speech the phrase "*I saw it*" is often pronounced aɪ sɔər ɪt or aɪ sɔːr ɪt. In this context, however, note that the preceding vowel is ɔː not ə, and in such a position intrusive r would not be used by the educated speaker.

---

[1] I heard recently on the radio, however, ðɪ ɛərɪər əv ɪt (*the area of it*), where intrusive r in this position was used.

Fricative Consonants.

275. Fricative consonants are formed by narrowing the mouth passage at some point, so that the air, forcing its way through, makes a rubbing sound. It is possible to make fricative consonants with the same articulating organs as the plosives; a glance at the table on p. 128 will show that there are more fricatives than plosives in English.

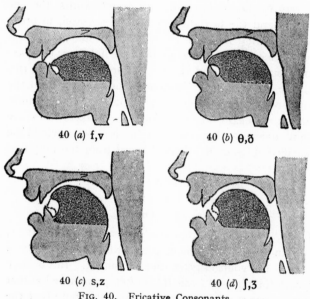

40 (a) f,v   40 (b) θ,ð

40 (c) s,z   40 (d) ʃ,ʒ

FIG. 40.   Fricative Consonants.

276. In the voiced consonants of this class it is sometimes difficult to recognise their fricative character. This is due to the fact that less breath force is used than

for the voiceless fricatives, and that the passage is not very narrow, hence there may be no audible friction.

277. The English fricative consonants are:

f, v; θ, ð; s, z; ʃ, ʒ; ɹ; h.

278. NOTES ON THE FRICATIVE CONSONANTS.

i. In Somerset, initial voiceless fricatives are replaced by voiced fricatives: e.g. vʊt, ðɪŋ, zʌm.

ii. The v of *of* (ɒv) often disappears in London and other dialects in familiar phrases such as ə glɑ·s ə bɪə, ə pɛər ə glʌvz.

iii. In Scotland and parts of N. England, *with* (wɪð) and *though* (ðoʊ) are pronounced wɪθ, θoʊ.

iv. In London dialect θ and ð are replaced by f and v, friː (θriː), mʌvə (mʌðə); θ is sometimes replaced by t in *months*—mʌnts (mʌnθs).

v. There is a tendency even among educated speakers to drop θ and ð in quick speech, when followed by s or z: e.g. klouz (klouðz), sɪkss (sɪksθs), mʌns (mʌnθs).

vi. h is a glottal fricative, i.e. the air passes through the glottis, and slight friction occurs between the open vocal cords.   A further element in its articulation is the sudden expulsion of the air from the lungs, and frequently some friction can be heard in the mouth after the sudden "jerk." h varies according to the vowel which follows it, i.e.

for the word hard (hɑːd), the tongue is in the position of ɑː while the h is being pronounced, for hʊd it is in the position of ʊ, for hiːd in the position of iː: i.e. the h in these words is similar to the unvoiced vowels (ḁ, u̥, i̥). h can be voiced (phonetic symbol ɦ). Many people use a voiced *h* between two vowels: e.g. əɦɑː (*aha!*), pəɦæps, ə ɦaʊs. This sometimes sounds as if the h were dropped. Voiced *h* is used more by men than by women.

vii. *"Dropping one's h's"* has been looked upon as a sign of lack of education, and the *h* is being re-introduced under the influence of spelling even in local dialects where it had quite disappeared or had never existed. In words like *he, his, her, have,* occurring in unstressed positions, however, the " *h* " is actually dropped in conversational speech by educated people. For instance, no one would pronounce all the *h's* in *he put his hat on his head,* hi pʊt hɪs hæt ɒn hɪz hɛd; *I should have thought so* becomes aɪ ʃʊd əv θɔ·t soʊ. In slow deliberate speech, however, the *h's* are generally pronounced even in unstressed unimportant words.

viii. "Intrusive *h.*" The pronunciation of *h* where there is no *h* in the spelling is perhaps not so frequent among the younger generation even of semi-educated or dialect speakers as it used to be and as it still is among older people in some parts of the country. Such use is due to lack of knowledge of the *distribution* of this sound and occurs mostly in those areas where the true dialect does not possess an *h.*

SEMI-VOWELS OR VOWEL GLIDES.

279. A semi-vowel may be defined as a gliding sound in which the tongue starts in the position of a close or half-close vowel and immediately leaves that position to take up one belonging to a more open vowel. There are two semi-vowels in English, w and j.

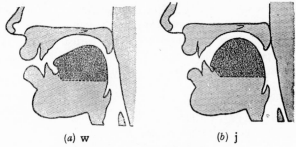

(a) w   (b) j

FIG. 41.   Semi-Vowels.

280. w has a double articulation; the primary formation is that the lips are rounded and pushed forward; at the same time the back of the tongue is raised towards the u position.

281. Voiceless *w* (phonetic symbol ʍ) is used by many people who distinguish *w* from *wh* in words like *witch* and *which*. Another method of pronouncing *wh* is to prefix *h*, i.e. **hw.** In Scotland and many parts of the North this distinction is regularly made, and by individual speakers in all parts of the country. Professor Wyld states that wɛn, wɒt, etc., have been established in S. English for hundreds of years, and says that the pronunciations ʍɛn, ʍɒt, are spelling pronunciations. (See Chapter VII, § 65 i.)

282. For the semi-vowel **j** the front of the tongue is raised towards the hard palate, and immediately leaves this position to take up that of the vowel which follows it. The voiceless glide corresponding to **j** is often heard in the pronunciation of words like *human*, *huge*, *Hugh*, which are pronounced çuˈmən, çuːʤ, çuː; instead of hjuˈmən, hjuˈʤ, hjuː. The acoustic difference between these two pronunciations is very slight: in the former the fricative element is heard more strongly. Note that in the word *ear* (ɪə) and other words with the group ɪə, some people use jɜː; thus *ear* may be jɜː, and *hear* and *here* are pronounced hjɜː by many people.

Summary of the main differences
between (a) Northern speech and Southern English
and (b) between London pronunciation
and Standard English

283. In this brief summary the main differences between these two types of speech and a more general standard are indicated. Most of the points will be found in the chapters immediately preceding, together with hints for the teaching of the recognised standard sounds. It is not the broadest dialect pronunciations that are noted here, but the slighter differences occurring in the speech of those who still show regional influences, which are not so easy to detect and which are even more difficult to correct. Many of the observations made on Northern speech apply to the Midlands and to the West, but the present writer is not competent to sum up the chief characteristics of these areas so well as those of the North and of London with which she is familiar.

284. (*a*) *Northern Pronunciation.*

  (i) *Vowels.*

    ɛ and æ : Very open ; æ is replaced by **a**.

    ɑ : Not used in certain words where Southerners use it ; **a** takes its place. Not very important to attempt to alter this unless the speaker definitely wants to adopt a Southern pronunciation.

    ʌ : Replaced by a vowel between ʊ and ʌ or by a central vowel near to ɜ (but short).

    ɜː and ɛə : Confused in South Lancashire and Cheshire ; a sound between the two is used for both.

    eɪ, oʊ : Pure vowels **e** and **o**[1] are used instead of these, often long eː, oː, or for oʊ a wider diphthong (ɔʊ : nɔʊ for *know*).

    The diphthongs ɪə, ɛə, ɔə, ʊə are wider than in Southern English ; there is considerably more tongue movement. Similarly in aɪə, aʊə all the elements are heard. This is not important ; indeed, it is good, if they are not slowed up too much and the first element not too long.

  (ii) *Consonants.*

    Use of the glottal stop before alveolar consonants and finally ; nɒʔ raɪʔ for *not right*.

    In the Midlands ŋg is used for ŋ in words like *singer*, sɪŋgə.

[1] The pure vowel replacing eɪ is not that which is noted as coming into use in Southern English pronunciation, but a closer type. (See Ch. XII, §§ 195–6.)

h is frequently dropped in Yorkshire (except in
the North Riding) and in Lancashire.

r : The Northumberland "burr" is the use of
uvular r.

(iii) *Other characteristics.*

The speech is often rather slow and gives the
impression of lack of precision.[1]   Unimportant
words and syllables frequently have "strong"
forms which sound as if they are stressed, and
with this characteristic, the rhythm changes.
Voice quality is often different ; some Northern
voices are hard and metallic or lacking in
resonance in some way ; this sounds to be the
result of pharyngal contraction and of forcing.
For the main differences in intonation see
§§ 319—20.

285. (*b*) *London Pronunciation.*

(i) *Vowels.*

ɛ and æ : Closer than standard.

ɔ : Very close, tending to o.

u : Centralised. Even in the less broad
Cockney this tendency is strongly marked.

eɪ : Low starting point of the diphthong, approaching ɛ.

ai : Not unlike modern educated Southern
English, but is frequently drawled and
nasalised.

ou : Open starting point, ɔ or ʌ.

---

[1] This in Lancashire in spite of a considerable amount of jaw
movement.

aʊ : Too forward a starting point, approaching æ.

In the type of speech considered here there is little nasalisation but sometimes undue lengthening of vowels and diphthongs.

(ii) *Consonants.*

Use of the glottal stop in many positions, including intervocalic.

"Intrusive" r is common, often after the vowel ɔ : aɪ sɔːr ɪt (*I saw it*).

Over-dark l is common and is especially noticeable after the diphthongs eɪ and aɪ. Note that it affects vowel quality to a considerable degree : eɪl is pronounced ɛəl and aɪl is pronounced ɑːl.

Affricated t's and d's in stressed positions.

(iii) *Other characteristics.*[1]

Voice is frequently produced with contraction of the pharynx and is often "husky," with little resonance ; it tends also to be adenoidal. Drawling somewhat affects rhythm and to a certain extent intonation patterns.

---

[1] See §§ 319–20, p. 177, for notes on the main differences between Northern and Southern speech in intonation.

Chapter XV

SOUND ATTRIBUTES: LENGTH, STRESS
INTONATION

286. When one hears English spoken or read aloud, one realises that a number of words or syllables stand out from the rest of the sentence. This standing out may be termed *prominence*. Recent investigations go to show that the effect of prominence is produced by the very intimate combination of length, stress, pitch, and inherent sonority of sounds, i.e. a sound or syllable has prominence when it stands out from its neighbours because (1) it is more sonorous, (2) it is longer, (3) it is louder, because of greater breath force, or (4) it has a different pitch. It is often extremely difficult to disentangle these elements and to say which is most important: the general effect of *accent* is often due to a combination of two or more of them.

287. An attempt is made here to show the recurrence of the prominent syllables in a number of sentences and to analyse what constitutes this prominence. The mark ' (the conventional stress mark) is used to denote prominence, while '' shows *special* prominence or extra emphasis. The notation to indicate intonation [1] is as follows:—Lines denote prominent,

[1] This is the notation used in *A Handbook of English Intonation*, by Armstrong and Ward.

and dots non-prominent syllables; a straight line ‾ shows
that the pitch of the syllable so marked is level, and
↘ and ⟋ that the pitch in these syllables falls or rises
respectively.[1]

288. The intonation[2] of the sentences should be very
carefully studied first. In the majority of the sentences,
one typical intonation has been given; there may, of
course, be others; there certainly would be other varieties
if emphasis were intended and *special* prominence given
to one part of the sentence.

(1) ˈgɪv ɪt tə ˈˈhɜː?

(2) ˈdɪd ju ˈgɪv ɪt tə hɜ.

(3) ˈðæt s wɒt aɪ ˈsɔː.

(4) aɪ sɔ ˈnʌθɪŋ əv ðəm.

(5) ˈwɛər əv ju ˈbiːn?

(6) aɪ v bɪn tə ˈtaʊn.

(7) ˈwɒt ə ju ˈgoɪŋ tə ˈduː əbaʊt ɪt?

(8) ˈwɒt dju ˈwɒnt?

ˈwɒt dəju ˈwɒnt?

ˈwɒt du ju ˈwɒnt?

(9) aɪ d noʊ aɪˈˈdɪə ju wər ɛnɪwɛə nɪə ˈˈhɪə.

[1] If a non-prominent syllable rises, as sometimes happens, it
must also be indicated by ⟋, as it would be impossible to show
a rise by a dot.

[2] See later §§ 301–18 for a summary of the intonation patterns
of English.

(10)　aɪ ˈdount maɪnd kənˈfɛsɪŋ ˈˈmaɪ ʃɛər ɪn ðə
　　　　mætə.　‾ · · — . ╲ . . . .

(11)　aɪ ˈwɪʃ hi ˈˈwʊd.　· ‾ · ╮ or · ╲ . ╮

(12)　ˈwɒt wʊd ju əv ˈsɛd tə ˈˈðæt?　‾ · · · — . ╲

289. Examine the sentences from these aspects—
the intonation of the prominent syllables, the breath
force used in saying them, and the length and quality
of the vowels used in them.

(1) It will be seen that the prominent syllables all
have a different pitch from that of the neighbouring
prominent syllables. Alter the pitch of these syllables
and note the effect. E.g.

(a) ˈwɛər əv ju ˈbiːn?　‾ · · ╲　*where* and *been* are
　　　　　　　　　　　　　　　　　　prominent.

(b) ˈwɛər əv ˈjuː bin?　‾ · ╲ .　*where* and *you* are
　　　　　　　　　　　　　　　　　　prominent.

(c) ˈwɛər əv ju bin?　╲ . . ╱　*where* only is
　　　　　　　　　　　　　　　　　　prominent.

(d) wɛə ˈhæv ju ˈbiːn?　· _ · ╲　*have* and *been* are
　　　　　　　　　　　　　　　　　　prominent.

(2) Try to say all these sentences with varying
intonations, with as *even* breath force as possible. It
will be noticed that the lack of strong breath force does
not affect the general result: the right effect is produced
by the intonation. This seems to prove that pitch is
an essential part of prominence. In fact if these
sentences are pronounced with extra breath force on

the *non-prominent* syllables, so long as the typical intonation is preserved, there is very little change in meaning. If, for instance, one pronounces *Heroes and Hero Worship* (ˈhɪərouz ənd ˈhɪərou wɜˈʃɪp) with the intonation ‾ ·· ⟍ ..., it matters little if one puts extra breath force on wɜˈʃɪp [‾ ·· ⟍. ⎯ .] so long as the same " tune " is kept.

(3) Although, as has just been stated, the right effect of prominence *can* be obtained without extra breath force if the intonation is right, this is not the normal usage and such effect is not dependent wholly upon intonation. All the syllables of a sentence are not pronounced with the same amount of breath, and those which are most important are pronounced generally with more breath force than the others. Thus stress or breath force seems to be a component part of prominence. It is customary in dictionaries to mark the stress of individual words of more than one syllable, and in phonetic texts to mark what is called sentence stress. The sentences given as examples should be said quite naturally and the breath force noted; the strongest force will generally be found to fall on the syllables marked as stressed.

(4) Now note the length of the vowels in the prominent syllables. In both the sentences ˈgɪv ɪt tə ˈˈhɜː and ˈdɪd ju ˈgɪv ɪt tə ˌhɜ? the word *her* occurs each time at the end of the sentence. The vowel in the first *her* is much longer than in the second. In the sentences ˈwɛər əv ju ˈbiːn and aɪ v bin tə ˈtaʊn note the difference in the length of the vowel in the two words *been*. In ˈwɒt ə ju ˈgoɪŋ tə ˈduː əbaʊt ɪt?

and ˈwɒt djʊ ˈwɒnt? note the words *do*: in the first, the vowel is long; in the second, the vowel has disappeared and the word consists of d. In aɪ ˈdoʊnt maɪnd kənˈfɛsɪŋ ˈˈmaɪ ʃɛər ɪn ðə mætə, compare the length of the diphthong aɪ in *mind* and the extra prominent word *my*. Compare the diphthong ɪə in *near* and *here*, in the sentence aɪ d ˈnoʊ aɪˈˈdɪə jʊ wər ˈɛnɪwɛə nɪə ˈˈhɪə. In the sentences aɪ ˈwɪʃ hi ˈˈwʊd and ˈwɒt wʊd jʊ əv ˈsɛd tə ˈˈðæt? compare the two words *would*. These examples show that vowel sounds in the prominent syllables are generally longer than those in non-prominent syllables.

(5) In English speech there is a well-established tendency for the vowel sounds in non-prominent syllables to be some kind of neutral vowel. Examine, in the sentences given, some of the words which are used in both prominent and non-prominent syllables. e.g. the vowel in *do* in sentence No. 7 has its full value u, whereas in No. 8 the word is reduced to dʊ, də or d. In sentence No. 5, pronounced with *have* prominent, wɛə ˈhæv jʊ ˈbiːn? the word has its strong vowel æ, whereas in ˈwɛər əv jʊ ˈbiːn? it is reduced to əv. Note in sentence No. 10 the word *confessing* (kənˈfɛsɪŋ). If the first syllable *con* is pronounced kɒn, the strong vowel ɒ gives the impression of prominence. The present writer has heard people, in criticising Northern speech, say that Northern speakers stress the first syllable in words like *confess*, *success* instead of the second. This is not true, i.e. they do not use noticeably more breath force on the first syllable than on the second, but the pronunciation kɒnˈfɛs, sʌkˈsɛs, instead of kənˈfɛs, səkˈsɛs, gives the *impression* of stress on the

first syllable, i.e. the use of the strong vowel adds
prominence. This seems to prove that vowel quality
plays some part in prominence.

290. These examples illustrate briefly that prominence is produced by a combination of certain elements
of speech, viz. pitch, stress, length and vowel quality.
Which is most important it is difficult to say. The
conventional method of marking breath force or stress
seems to answer well, especially for English people
studying their own language, as, with additional breath
force, they naturally alter the pitch, lengthen the vowel
and consonant sounds, and use " strong " vowels.

291. In considering English speech as a series of
"peaks" of prominence separated by "valleys," it is
perhaps useful to associate the positive elements of
outstanding stress and pitch as contributing to the
"peaks," and the negative weakening and shortening
of vowels as contributing to the "valleys." If the
syllables normally occurring in the "valleys" are made
stronger or longer, the valleys are raised somewhat and
the difference between them and the peaks is smaller,
i.e. the elements we may consider as subordinate are
given undue prominence; this in its turn detracts from
the importance of those words and syllables which
normally stand out, i.e. the "undulations" are less steep.
The teacher should be fully aware of this, lest he insist
on an undue strength being given to unimportant
elements. (See further, § 326-8, p. 183.)

292. Length, stress and intonation are generally
called *sound attributes*. The teacher of English should
be able to make his own observations on these elements

of speech. For convenience, the main rules governing
their use are summed up here.

293. _Length_.—(1) All vowels can be pronounced
long or short: the vowels i, ɑ, ɔ, u, ɜ, however, under
similar circumstances of stress and surrounding sounds
are longer than the remaining vowels, ɪ, ɛ, æ, ɒ, ʊ, ʌ, ə.
It is customary to mark length only in the case of the
long vowels i, ɑ, ɔ, u, ɜ in phonetic transcriptions,
because the varying degrees of length are difficult to
detect in the short vowels. The vowels æ and ɛ in the
pronunciation of some people may be considered long,
especially in a few odd words: e.g. æ in _bad_ is often
pronounced long, bæːd, and ɛ in _yes_ pronounced in a
hesitating fashion is long jɛːs.[1] Diphthongs are generally
considered long, though these also vary according to the
surrounding sounds and the stress. (See Sentences 9
and 10 in § 288.)

(2) Several degrees of length can be noted by the
trained observer; it is necessary, however, to show only
three degrees, viz. short, half-long and long. (Long
vowels are marked with ː, and half-long vowels with ·
following them.)

(3) As has been shown above in §289 (4), vowels
are generally longer when stressed than when unstressed.

(4) A vowel in a final position is longer than in a
non-final position: e.g. ˈwɒt dɪd ju ˈsiː?; aɪ ˈsi· jɔər
ˈpɔɪnt; ɪt ˈɪznt ˈfɑː; ɪt s ˈnɒt ˈfɑ·r əˈweɪ; ˈðæt s wɒt aɪ
ˈsɔː; aɪ ˈsɔ· hɪm ˈjɛstədɪ; ɪt s ˈkwaɪt ˈnjuː; aɪ ˈnju· hɪm
ət ˈwʌns.

[1] See Ch. XVII, p. 199 for modern tendencies in this respect.

(5) Vowels are longer when followed by a voiced consonant than when followed by a voiceless consonant.

In	liːv	the vowel		i	is longer than in			liˑf.
,,	haːv	,,	,,	ɑ	,,	,,	,, ,,	hɑˑf.
,,	nɔːd	,,	,,	ɔ	,,	,,	,, ,,	nɔˑt.
,,	ruːd	,,	,,	u	,,	,,	,, ,,	ruˑt.
,,	hɜːd	,,	,,	ɜ	,,	,,	,, ,,	hɜˑt.
,,	meɪd	,, diphthong		eɪ	,,	,,	,, ,,	meɪt.
,,	goʊd	,,	,,	oʊ	,,	,,	,, ,,	goʊt.
,,	laɪv	,,	,,	aɪ	,,	,,	,, ,,	laɪf.
,,	maʊð	,,	,,	aʊ	,,	,,	,, ,,	maʊθ.
,,	bɪd	,, vowel		ɪ	,,	,,	,, ,,	bɪt.
,,	bɛd	,,	,,	ɛ	,,	,,	,, ,,	bɛt.
,,	bæd	,,	,,	æ	,,	,,	,, ,,	bæt.
,,	bʌd	,,	,,	ʌ	,,	,,	,, ,,	bʌt.

Note also that ɜ is longer in bɜːnd than in bɜˑnt, and oʊ is longer in boʊld than in boʊlt.

(6) The oʊ in goʊ is longer than in goʊɪŋ (often pronounced, and therefore written, gɔɪŋ), the i in biːn is longer than in biːŋ, i.e. when a vowel or diphthong is immediately followed by another vowel, it is shortened somewhat. The ɜ in bɜːn is longer than in bɜˑnɪŋ, the ɔ in mɔːn is longer than in mɔˑnɪŋ, i.e. when the syllable in which a long vowel or diphthong occurs is followed by one or more unstressed syllables, the vowel becomes shorter. This is illustrated also in (4).

(7) Consonants may be pronounced short or long. They are longer when preceded by a short vowel than when preceded by a long vowel, e.g.

In bɪn the final consonant is longer than in biːn.
,, frl ,, ,,   ,,   ,,   ,,   ,, ,, fiːl.

Note also that:

In bɜːnd the n is longer than in bɜˑnt.

,, fɛld ,, 1 ,, ,, ,, ,, fɛlt.

(8) Consonants are often lengthened for the sake of emphasis, e.g.

<blockquote>

hiːz ə ''nnɔˑtɪ 'bɔɪ.

ɪt s ''ʔɔːfflɪ 'gʊd əv jʊ.

aɪ ʃl ''nnɛvə 'du ɪt.

ɪt s ə ''vvɛrɪ 'lɒŋ'wɛɪ.

ðə wəz ə trɪ''mmɛndəs 'bʌsl.

</blockquote>

Note.—There are individual speakers who habitually lengthen most of their consonants in initial positions in prominent words, e.g. ɪt wəz ttʌtʃ ən ggoʊ, haʊ ffʌnɪ, etc. This gives rather a deliberate effect to the speech. Some Northern and Midland speakers pronounce a long *t* in the numbers eɪtɪ, eɪtiːn (eɪttɪ, eɪttiːn or eɪʔtɪ, eɪʔtiːn).

294. The teacher should make himself aware of differences in length, for he may find among his pupils some who do not observe these usages, and who thus have a pronunciation which is not normal. An undue lengthening of the vowels and diphthongs gives rise to what is usually termed " drawling," and a drawling pronunciation lacks precision and vigour. It is often accompanied by a gliding or " portamento " intonation: e.g. nö - - - ʊ. Cockney pronunciation is known by its drawled vowels and diphthongs: e.g. nã - - - ɪs, sə - - - i, gɪv ɪt tə mə - - i ; and this habit is found in other parts of the country: e.g. Yorks. ha - - - ʊs, la - - - ɪk, 'dʊu jə 'la - - - ɪk ɪt? ɑ 'doˑnt 'nɔ - - - ʊ.

295. Such drawling speech can be improved by making the pupil move quickly to the second element of the diphthong; he may even, with advantage, exaggerate the second element, as a stage in working to the right length: e.g. rai - - - z, lau - - d, plei - - -.

296. *Stress.*—Every word of more than one syllable has its own *word stress*: e.g. ʹcountry, aʹbroad, emʹphatically, recoʹllect,[1] etc., but when words are combined into sentences, the word stress is often modified under the influence of sentence stress. This depends chiefly on the relative importance of the words in a sentence, and also on rhythm. It is impossible to do more than give a few examples of sentence stress here. English students, with practice, will be able to analyse their own speech from this point of view. Teachers will find it a useful exercise and of considerable help in the teaching of reading and recitation. Children like to find out the stress of new words; and the correct pronunciation of words which are commonly wrongly stressed becomes a matter of interest: e.g. ʹlamentable, ʹvehement, etc., ʹlæməntəbl, ʹvɪəmənt.

297. Certain English words differ in meaning according to stress: in some, the change in stress alters the vowels (see Chapter XVI, §§ 324–7), others differ in stress and to a slight extent in vowel length, e.g.

ʹincrease	ʹɪnkriˑs	inʹcrease	ɪnʹkriːs
ʹcompact	ʹkɒmpækt	comʹpact	kəmʹpækt
ʹconduct	ʹkɒndʌkt	conʹduct	kənʹdʌkt
ʹsubject	ʹsʌbdʒɪkt	subʹject	səbʹdʒɛkt

[1] In some long words another syllable bears considerable stress, and is said to have secondary stress, e.g. pɪˌkjulɪʹærɪtɪ, əˌbɒmɪʹneɪʃn.

298. The following observations on sentence stress, with examples, should be sufficient to put the student on the right lines to analyse his own stress. Word stress is marked in any good dictionary.

(*a*) In an ordinary statement, the most important words of the sentence are stressed, viz. nouns, principal verbs, adjectives, demonstrative and interrogative pronouns, and adverbs, e.g.

> He 'told his 'story 'quickly and with 'great en'joyment.
> They 'called to 'see him 'early in the 'day.
> 'Where are you 'going?
> 'This won't 'do.
> 'How do you 'like my 'new 'hat?

(*b*) Where it is desired to emphasize one idea above others in a sentence, the word expressing that idea receives an extra amount of stress, and the surrounding words lose a good deal of their stress.

> I 'don't know 'what he 'wants.   (Normal stress.)

> "I don't know what he wants.   (Implying someone else may know.)

> I 'don't know "what he wants.   (I've tried everything I can think of.)

> I 'don't know what he "wants.   (Impatience.)

I 'don't "know what he wants. (I've tried to
find out and cannot.)

Note the varying intonation in this sentence,
and compare the sentences in §§ 288 and 289.

(c) When compound words which normally bear a
double stress, e.g. 'home-'made, 'un'known, 'bad-
'tempered, occur in a sentence preceded or followed
by a stressed syllable, one of the two stresses
may disappear under the influence of the rhythm
of the sentence.

> ən 'ʌnnoʊn 'wɒrɪə; hiˑ z 'kwaɪt ʌn'noʊn;
> 'hoʊm meɪd 'dʒæm; ɪt s 'ɔːl hoʊm 'meɪd;
> ə 'bæd tɛmpəd 'dɒg; hi wəz 'ɔˑlweɪz bæd 'tɛmpəd.

(d) Contrast between two ideas expressed or unexpressed may be shown by varying the normal
stress, e.g.

> 'raɪs 'pʊdɪŋ but aɪ wɒnt 'raɪs pʊdɪŋ (not plum
> pudding).
> 'daʊn 'hɪl but hi wɛnt 'daʊn hɪl (not up).

This may be compared with (b), where the special
emphasis given to one word in the sentence often
implies contrast. Note also that the intonation
changes.

(e) English is a language of strongly marked rhythm,
and there is a tendency for stressed syllables to
occur at regular intervals of time.

> 'ðɛər aɪ 'fʌndə'mɛntəlɪ dɪsə'griː wɪð juˑ. | waɪlst
> əd'mɪtɪŋ ðət ɪndɪ'vɪdjʊəlz 'vɛərɪ ɪn kə'pæsɪtɪ, | aɪ
> bɪ'liːv ðət 'iˑtʃ 'wʌn | hæz ðə 'paʊər əv meɪkɪŋ

ʌn'lɪmɪtɪd 'prouɡrɛs, | ɪntɪ'lɛktjuəl ənd 'spɪrɪtjuəl. |
ðə 'tuː 'stʌmblɪŋ blɒks | ɪn ðə 'weɪ əv 'moust
piˑpl | ɑ ðɛər 'ɜˑlɪ 'mɪs-ɛdju'keɪʃn | ənd ðɪ 'ʌnɪn-
'spaɪərɪŋ ɛn'vaɪərənmənt | ɪn 'wɪtʃ ðeɪ hæv tə
'pɑːs 'moust əv ðɛə 'laɪvz.

In this sentence, the stressed syllables within
the breath groups occur at almost regular intervals
of time, and however many or few unstressed
syllables there may be between the stresses, they
seem to fit in to the time allowed. Many examples
can be found to illustrate this tendency, and the
skilled teacher will know how to apply this fact
to the rhythmic reading of prose, and also to obtain
variety of expression in the reading of both prose
and poetry.

299. The reader is advised to note carefully the
sentence stress marked in any phonetic reader, and to
compare this rendering with his own. For the manner
of stressing may vary to a certain extent from individual
to individual. There is, for example, considerable
divergence in the stressing of certain compound words,
e.g. *Christmas present* is stressed as 'krɪsməs 'prɛznt by
some, and as 'krɪsməs prɛznt by others.

Plum-cake is either 'plʌm'keɪk [‾‾ ╲] or 'plʌm
keɪk [╲.].

Shirt-sleeves is either 'ʃɜˑt 'sliːvz [‾ ╲] or 'ʃɜˑ
sliˑvz [╲.].

Hide and seek is either 'haɪd n 'siˑk [‾‾ · ╲] or 'haɪd n
siˑk [╲..].

[Note the intonation which goes with these different
stresses.]

300. As far as the present writer's experience goes, Northerners and Southerners have different habits in some compound words of this type (but not of all compound words, e.g. *blackbird* is always ˈblækbɜˑd [⌐ ˎ .], and *North Sea* is ˈnɔˑθˈsiː [‾ ˎ]), but a sufficient number of examples has not yet been collected to justify any authoritative statement being made about these varying usages.

301. *Intonation.*—Intonation is the term given to the rise and fall in the pitch of the voice in speech. Change in pitch is due to differing rates of vibration of the vocal chords.

302. Intonation varies somewhat from individual to individual, and considerably from district to district, each part of the country having its distinctive speech melody—a melody which often remains in the speech when all other signs of local dialect are absent. Students should practise analysing their own intonation and that of other people, and note how different kinds of feeling can be expressed by the " tune " of a sentence.

303. The different intonations used in various parts of the country have not been sufficiently well investigated to give examples here. The analysis of a typical Southern intonation has been attempted, however, in *A Handbook of English Intonation.* This book, although originally intended for foreign students of English, forms a basis on which to work for a further comparative study of English Intonation. Students are advised to read it, and see if the simple rules formulated and illustrated in it fit with their own habits in the matter of speech melody, and where there are

differences, to see in what these differences consist,
and if any reason can be given for them. A brief note
on some of the differences between Northern and
Southern intonation is given in §§ 319–20.

304. It will perhaps be useful to summarise very
briefly the main intonations used in English, which are
treated more fully in the *Handbook of English Intonation*.
What have come to be known as the two fundamental
"tunes" of English speech can be illustrated by the
following sentence:

The first clause has the tune of an unfinished group
(which we call Tune II), and the second that of a definite
statement (Tune I). It is convenient to consider first
sentences which are not unduly emphatic.

305. Normal Tune I consists of a series of stressed
syllables forming a descending scale, the last of these
having a fall in pitch. Unstressed syllables preceding
the first stressed syllable are usually low; those between
the stressed syllables are generally not far removed in
pitch from that of the preceding stressed syllable;[1]
final unstressed syllables are on a low level.

306. *Examples.*

[1] See D. Jones, *Outline of English Phonetics*, §§ 1025–6.

ɪt wəz ˈkwaɪt ɪmˈpɒsɪbl [. . ‾ · ＼ . .]
ˈhuː z ˈðɛə [‾ ＼]
ˈwɒts ðə ˈmætə [‾ · ＼ .]
wɛər ə jʊ gɔɪŋ [‾ ·· ＼ .]
ˈteɪk ɪt ˈɒf [‾ · ＼]
ˈʃʌt ðə ˈdɔː, pliːz [‾ · ＼ .]
ət ˈwʌns [. ＼]
ˈhaʊ [＼]

307. It will be seen that the tune can be spread over a considerable number of syllables or compressed into a small space; that the sentences given above are not very long; that definite statements, questions which begin with an interrogative word (and which cannot be answered by "yes" or "no"), and commands take this type of intonation.

When a group requiring Tune I is somewhat long, it is modified by raising the pitch of one of the stressed syllables before descending to the end of the sentence.[1]

ɪt ˈrɪəlɪ ˈstɑ·tɪd ˈfɔː ˈjɪəz əgoʊ [. ‾ ·—· ‾ ＼ . .]
aɪm ˈsɛndɪŋ jʊ ˈtuː ˈtɪkɪts fə ðə ˈθɪətə [. ‾ ·· ‾— ··· ＼ .]

308. Tune II, like Tune I, consists of a descending scale of stressed syllables with a rise from a low pitch at the end. The last stressed syllable is the lowest and if it is the last syllable of the group, it has a rise in itself; if not, any unstressed syllables which follow carry the rise. This tune is used, as illustrated above in § 304, in an unfinished sense group; it is also used in questions

[1] Note that the raising is generally on a more or less emphatic word, and frequently the sentences could be divided at this point into two groups, the first having Tune II.

of the type which can be answered by "yes" or "no,"
in requests, and in certain types of statement where
something is implied but left unexpressed in words.

309.   *Examples.*

(i) In unfinished groups.

ˈwɛn jʊ ə ˈrɛdɪ | ˈkʌm ən ˈkɔːl mi
                    [⎺·· __ · | ⎺· ⟍ .]
ə ˈfjuː ˈjaːdz ˈfɜˑðər ˈɒn | ðə ˈpɑːθ ˈwaɪdnd
                    [.⎺⎺— ·⟋ | .⎺ ⟍ .]
tə ˈtɛl ðə ˈtruːθ | ɪts ˈdʒʌst ˈtɛmpə
                    [.⎺·⟋ | .⎺ ⟍ .]
ɪn ˈðæt keɪs | aɪ ˈʃaːnt ˈkʌm [.⎺ ⟋ | .⎺ ⟍]
ðə ˈjɪə ðət ɪz ˈpɑˑsɪŋ | həz ˈbiːn tə ˈmiː | ˈmoʊst
ˈmɛmərəbl [.⎺··__· | .⎺·⟋ | ⎺ ⟍ ..]
(See p. 220.)

(ii) In questions requiring the answer "yes" or "no."

ˈaː jʊ ˈrɛdɪ [⎺·__·]
ˈwɪl jʊ ˈkʌm wɪð əs [⎺·__··]
ˈdjʊ ˈθɪŋk soʊ [⎺__·]
ˈhæv jʊ ˈbiːn hɪə ˈlɒŋ [⎺·—·⟋]
ˈdʌz ɪt ˈmiːn ɛnɪθɪŋ [⎺·__··]
ˈwɪl jʊ [__·]
ˈdʌznt hi [__·]

(iii) In requests.

ˈlɛt mi ˈnoʊ ˈsuːn [⎺·—⟋]
ˈdoʊnt ˈtrʌbl tʊ ˈɑˑnsər ɪt [⎺—··__··]
ɪksˈkjuːz mi ˈwʌn ˈmoʊmənt [·⎺·—__·]

Note that requests can also be said with Tune I.

ˈkʌm ən ˈsiː mi [⎺·⟍.]
ˈlɛt mi ˈnoʊ ˈsuːn [⎺·—⟍]

(iv) In statements in which something is implied.

ɪt ˈwoʊnt ˈteɪk ˈlɒŋ [. ‾ — ╱]
ˈðæts ˈɔːl, ʤɒn [‾ — ·]
aɪ səˈpoʊz ɪts ˈtruː [.. ‾ · ╱]

310. Note that in this type of sentence (iv), emphatic stress and its accompanying change of intonation is more usual than the unemphatic Tune II. If said with little emphasis and the intonation as indicated above, these sentences give the impression of casualness.

311. *Emphatic Intonation.*

Emphasis, an all-round increase of effort on the part of the speaker to express

(i) some added meaning or intensity ;

(ii) some extra prominence which he wishes to attach to a particular idea

is shown in part by intonation.[1]

312. *Emphasis for Intensity.*

Emphasis for intensity expresses in a higher degree the quality inherent in the word or phrase.[2] This is usually effected by widening the range of pitch.

ðə ˈmæn wəz ɪn ə ˈsteɪt əv ‖bɔɪlɪŋ ɪndɪgˈneɪʃn
[. ‾ ··· — · ‾ ··· ╲.]

[1] Note that means of emphasising other than by stress and intonation frequently accompany these two elements; different type of voice, use of pauses, use of glottal stop, lengthening of vowels and consonants, gesture and facial expression.

[2] Note that only words expressing measurable quality can have this type of emphasis. See D. Jones, *Outline of English Phonetics*, § 1046 and footnotes.

ˮsɜˑtnlɪ ˮnɒt [‾ ·· \ ]

ɪt wəz ə ˮmɑːvələs ˈdeɪ [‚ · ‾ ·· \ ]

An abnormal narrowing of the range of intonation can also be used to show intensity.

ˈpʊər ˈoʊld ˈθɪŋ [— — \ ]

ɪts ˈpɜˑfɪklɪ əbˈsɜːd [· ‾ ··· \ ]

313. *Emphasis for Prominence or Contrast.*

An examination of the following sentences will illustrate the changes in intonation which are used to show contrast.

ˈðæt ɪznt ˈwɒt aɪ ˈmɛnt [‾ ·ˑ—· \ ],
tune of the normal statement.

ˈðæt ɪznt wɒt aɪ ˮmɛnt [‾ ··· ⟍] *or* [‚···· ⟍],
"meant" with extra emphasis for contrast.

ˮðæt ɪznt wɒt aɪ ˮmɛnt [⟍ ··· ⟍],
"that" and "meant" with extra emphasis for contrast.

ˮðæt ɪznt wɒt ˮaɪ mɛnt [⟍ ·· ⟍ ·],
"that" and "I" with extra emphasis for contrast.

ðæt ˮɪznt wɒt aɪ mɛnt [· ⟍ ....],
the negative idea emphasised—a contradiction.

ˈðæt ɪznt wɒt aɪ ˈmɛnt [⟍ .... ⟋]
an implication here, but no extra emphasis.

ˈðæt ɪznt wɒt aɪ ˮmɛnt [⟍ .... ∿],
though I may have given the impression that it was.

314. It will be seen that the word to be strongly emphasised always has a fall in pitch from high to low; the greater the fall, the greater the emphasis as a rule. The emphasis is stronger if the stress of the remaining

stressed syllables is reduced somewhat, or if they are
treated, as far as the intonation pattern goes, as unstressed syllables.

Tune II with contrast emphasis on the final stressed
word has the fall belonging to that emphasis, followed
by the rise which is inherent in this tune. The fall-rise
may be spread over a number of syllables or compressed
into one, as will be seen from some of the examples
below.

315. *Further Examples.*

aɪm ‖sɒrɪ aɪ ˈkɑˑnt ɡoʊ ˈwɪð ju [. ⌍ . . __ . __ .]
ɪts ‖verɪ ‖sɪərɪəs [. ⌍ . ⌍]
ju ‖niːdnt meɪk soʊ mʌʧ ‖nɔɪz əbaʊt ɪt

[· ⌍ . . . . ⌍ . . ·]

ˈwɒts ðə ‖mætə [— · ⌍ .], cf. [‾ · ⌍ .]
‖evrɪbɒdɪ ˈwɒnts ɪt [⌍ . . __ .], cf. [‾ · · · ⌍ .]
aɪ ˈdoʊnt θɪŋk ɪts ‖raɪt [. __ · · ⌍], cf. [. ‾ · · ⌍]
aɪ ‖θɪŋk soʊ [· ⌍ ⌎]
aɪ ‖wɪʃ hi ‖wʊd [· ⌍ . ∿]
aɪ ‖hoʊp aɪ hævnt kept jʊ ‖weɪtɪŋ [· ⌍ . . . . ⌍ ⌎]
ɪts ‖soʊ naɪs tə ‖siː jʊ əɡeɪn [· ⌍ . . ⌍ . . ⌎]

316. Note that the use of Tune II in sentences with
an implication or reservation is very common in English
when emphasis is added. By this means we can express
many things which in other languages must be put into
words.

317. The intonation of King George V recorded in
the Christmas broadcast (see p. 220) is typical of normal
unemphatic speech with a purposely slow delivery.
The student is advised to study this and analyse his

own intonation of material of the same kind. President Roosevelt's speech (see p. 226) shows a considerable number of points of similarity in intonation, but some variations which have been pointed out. A short passage is added here which shows a mixture of emphatic and non-emphatic intonation.

318. æz ðeɪ ˈstɛəd ˈæŋgrɪlɪ ət wʌn ənʌðə, ðæt

mɪsˈtɪərɪəs ˈsɪmpəθɪ əv ðə ˈflɛʃ wɪtʃ wi kɔːl ˈfæmɪlɪ

ˈlaɪknɪs, ˈspræŋ ˈaʊt frəm ɪts ˈhaɪdɪŋ pleɪs, ˈstæmpɪŋ

ðɛə ˈtoʊtəlɪ dɪˈsɪmɪlə ˈfiˑtʃəz wɪð ən ˈɛlfɪʃ ɪˈfɛkt əv

ˈmjuˑtʃʊəl ˈkærɪkətjʊə. ɪt wəz əz ˈðoʊ ˈiˑtʃ ˈsɔː hɪmsɛlf

ɪn ə dɪsˈtɔˑtɪŋ ˈmɪrə, waɪl ðə ˈvɔɪsɪz maɪt əv biˑn

ˈwʌn vɔɪs wɪð ɪts ˈɛkoʊ.

"ˈlʊk "hɪər oʊld ˈtʃæp," sɛd ˈpiˑtə, rɪˈkʌvrɪŋ

himsɛlf, "aɪm "fraɪtflɪ "sɔrɪ. aɪ ˈdɪdnt "miːn

. ‾ . . \ . ⌣| . . ‾ \ . . ⌣|

tə 'lɛt maɪsɛlf 'goʊ laɪk "ðæt. ɪf jʊ "woʊnt "seɪ ɛnɪθɪŋ

. \ | \ . . | . ‾ ‾ . . \ . |

jʊ "woʊnt. 'ɛnɪhaʊ wɪər 'ɔːl 'wɜˑkɪŋ laɪk "bleɪzɪz,

. . \ . . . \ ⌣ . . . . ‾ \

ənd wɪə "ʃʊə tə faɪnd ðə "raɪt 'mæn | bɪfɔː vɛrɪ "lɒŋ."

319. A few notes on the main differences between Northern and Southern intonation are given below.

(1) The range of voice is generally greater in the north than in the south. Thus 'ðæts'raɪt [‾ ⌣] would have the pitch [‾ ⁄]; the rise and the interval are also probably greater in such a sentence.

(2) The Southern English descent of stressed syllables illustrated in the sentence (on p. 157) wɒt ə jʊ goɪŋ tə duː əbaʊt ɪt? [‾ · · ‾ · \ ...] is frequently replaced by a series of syllables on a high level tone with a big fall in the last [‾ · · ‾ · \ ...].

aɪ 'doʊnt θɪŋk aɪ 'kæn [· ‾ · · \ ]
                 instead of [. ‾ · · \ ]
'wɛər əv jʊ 'biːn [‾ · · \ ] instead of [‾ · · \ ]
ɪt wəz 'ɔːl əbaʊt 'sʌmθɪŋ ən 'nʌθɪŋ [. . ‾ · · ‾ · · \ .]
                instead of [. . ‾ · · ‾ · · \ .]
hi 'dɪdnt tɛl mi 'wɒt hi wəz 'duˑɪŋ [. ‾ · · · ‾ · · \ .]
'doʊnt teɪk ɛnɪ 'noʊtɪs ɒv ɪm [‾ · · · \ ...]

(3) Another alternative to this type of "tune" (used in a statement or in a question beginning with **an**

interrogative word) has frequent falls from the high level which often give the impression of emphasis.

ˈwɒts ðə ˈneɪm əv ðɪs ˈstriˑt [‾ ˑ ＼ . ‾ ＼]

ɪt wəz ˈmɪstɪ ən ˈfrɒstɪ ən əz ˈblæk əz ˈpɪtʃ

[ˑ ˑ ＼ ˑ ˑ ＼ ˑ ˑ ˑ ‾ ˑ ＼]

Again the same note is hit several times, and the range is wide.

(4) Similarly in the "tune" of an unfinished group and of a question requiring the answer "yes" or "no," a wide range is used and a high level pitch maintained until the last important word, when there is a sudden drop to the bottom limit of the voice before the rise which belongs to this tune.

ˈkæn jʊ ˈtɛl mɪ ˈɛnɪθɪŋ əˈbaʊt ɪt [‾ ˑ ‾ ˑ ‾ ˑ ˑ ＿ ˑ]

ˈwɪl jʊ lɛt mɪ ˈhæv ɪt ɪn ðə ˈmɔːnɪŋ [‾ ˑ ˑ ‾ ˑ ˑ ＿ ˑ]

dʊ jʊ ˈθɪŋk ɪt ˈmætəz [ˑ ˑ ‾ ˑ ＿ ˑ]

(5) The use of "Tune II" (the tune of an unfinished group) with a rise at the end, is frequently used in North and South for a statement with some reservation in the speaker's mind.

ðər ɪznt ˈtaɪm tə goʊ ˈbæk [ˑ ˑ ˑ ＼ ˑ ˑ ／],

the difference between the two being only in the range of pitch. But some northerners use this tune when one expects a more direct statement with the falling intonation of "Tune I," and this gives the impression of a reservation, particularly if it is some expression of opinion. I have frequently heard ˈjɛs, ɪts ˈvɛrɪ ˈnaɪs [＼ . ＿ ／], when on other evidence there was no reservation in the mind of the speaker, though to a listener who would not use this tune in this place, it

distinctly conveys an idea of a "but," or of a grudging
approval. It should be noted that this intonation in
some sentences is frequently an encouraging one : e.g.
kʌm əˈlɒŋ [‾ · ⟋] or [__ · ⟋].

320. The above observations refer mainly to Lancashire and Yorkshire speech. In North Yorkshire,
County Durham and Tyneside, an intonation pattern
which does not occur in the South is heard. This is a
variation of Tune II which ends on a falling pitch from
high to mid-level. Thus :

    hæz ˈɛnɪwʌn ˈsiːn ˈmɛərɪ ˈmɑˑtɪn [. __ .. __ __ . ⟋ ·]
    ˈwɒt djə ˈkɔːl ˈðɪs ˈθɪŋ [__ . __ ‾‾]
    ˈhaʊ djə ˈθɪŋk hiˑz ˈlʊkɪŋ [__ . __ . ‾ ·]

321. These brief notes are only intended to draw
the reader's attention to some differences in intonation
he may find in his investigations and to warn him that
what is called an "accent" is not merely a matter of
sound but is frequently due to variations from the
normal in intonation patterns. Moreover, an unexpected
intonation conveys to the hearer an impression which
the speaker does not intend (as under (5) above). Intonation is frequently the cause of real misunderstanding of attitude, since we interpret it as the expression of feelings we should have if we used that
pattern.[1]

[1] See *The Broadcast Word* (A. Lloyd James), pp. 8, 9, where the
question is treated from the point of view of foreign languages.

Chapter XVI

SOUNDS IN CONNECTED SPEECH

322. Our habit of reading written words is apt to make us think that the unit of speech is the word. From a grammatical and orthographic point of view, a sentence may consist of a number of separate words, but in the spoken language such is not the case; the word is not the unit of speech, nor are spoken words separated from each other by pauses, as the written words are by spaces. A short spoken sentence is continuous: " *It's a very fine day*," is as continuous as the single words *peculiarity* or *sympathetically*. A long sentence can easily be broken up into " sense-groups," and the number and complexity of these will vary according to the character of the sentence and the circumstances under which it is uttered. In somewhat careful and deliberate speech, such as one would use in reading aloud or in addressing a number of people, the sense-groups would probably be shorter and the pauses more frequent than in familiar conversation.[1]

323. The grouping of speech sounds in connected sentences brings them under the influence of new factors, and leads to modifications and changes which must be considered. In the chapter on Phonemes and in the description of the individual sounds of the language, the

[1] See the transcription of the speech of King George V, p. 220.

influence of the juxtaposition of one sound with another
has already been noted. Further changes may now be
considered.

THE INFLUENCE OF STRESS.

324. English is a language of widely differing degrees
of stress; strongly marked stresses occur at more or less
regular intervals of time separated by syllables bearing
little stress. It is in these unstressed syllables that we
must look for change. In the sentence, " *'What are you
'going to 'do to-'day,*" there are four stressed and five
unstressed syllables; the unstressed words pronounced
separately would be ɑː, juː, tuː, but the sentence is
pronounced 'wɒt ə jʊ 'gɔɪŋ tə 'duː tə'deɪ, i.e. *are* becomes
ə, *you* becomes jʊ, and *to* becomes tʊ or tə in the word *to*
and in the first syllable of *to-day*. The vowels in these
unimportant words are reduced to a kind of neutral
vowel under the influence of the stress and rhythm of
the connected sentence. In the following extract,
note the unstressed syllables where the original vowel
has been replaced by the neutral ə (or ɪ in the case
where the " strong " vowel was i, and ʊ where it was u).

'lɛt ðə 'mænɪʤmənts 'fɜːst əv 'ɔːl dɪ'praɪv 'leɪt-
'kʌməz əv wɒt ɪz 'naʊ ðɛə 'bɛst ɪks'kjuːs—'neɪmlɪ,
ðə 'kʌstəmərɪ 'leɪtnəs əv 'kɜːtn raɪz. ðeɪ 'kʌm 'leɪt
bɪ'kɒz, ðeɪ seɪ, ðə 'pleɪ 'ɔːlwəz bɪ'gɪnz leɪt. 'ɪf ðə
'θɪətəz wə junɪ'vɜːsəlɪ əz 'pʌŋktjʊəl əz ðə dɪ'pɑːtʃəz
əv ɪks'prɛs 'treɪnz, 'noʊ wʌn wʊd bɪ 'tɛmtɪd ɪntʊ
'oʊvər-'ɛstɪmeɪtɪŋ ə 'fjuː 'mɪnɪts 'greɪs. ə'nʌðə rɛmɪdɪ
ɪz tə prə'vaɪd 'leɪt-'kʌməz wɪð 'stuːlz əv rɪ'pɛntəns
ənd tʊ ɪn'sɪst əpɒn ðɛər 'ɒkjʊpaɪɪŋ ðəm.

STRONG AND WEAK FORMS.

325. The following words have strong and weak forms: the strong forms are used in stressed, and the weak forms in unstressed positions.

Word.	Strong Form.	Weak Form.
am	æm	əm, m
be	biː	bɪ
been	biːn, bɪn	bɪn
is	ɪz	z, s
are	ɑː	ə
was	wɒz	wəz
were	wɜː	wə
have (aux. vb.)	hæv	həv, əv, v
has ,,	hæz	həz, əz, z, s
had ,,	hæd	həd, əd, d
do	duː	dʊ, də, d
does	dʌz	dəz, dz
shall	ʃæl	ʃəl, ʃl
should	ʃʊd	ʃəd, ʃd
will	wɪl	l
would	wʊd	wəd, d
can (vb.)	kæn	kən, kn[1]
could	kʊd	kəd, kd
must	mʌst	məst, məs, mst, ms
you	ju	jʊ, jə
your	jɔː	jə, jɔ
he	hiː	hɪ, ɪ
she	ʃiː	ʃɪ
we	wiː	wɪ
me	miː	mɪ
him	hɪm	ɪm

[1] kŋ sometimes when followed by a word beginning with k, g or w.

Word.	Strong Form.	Weak Form.
her	hɜː	hə
his	hɪz	ɪz
us	ʌs	əs
them	ðɛm	ðəm, ðm
who	huː	hʊ
some	sʌm	səm, sm
and	ænd	ənd, ən, n
a	eɪ	ə
an	æn	ən
the	ði	ðɪ, ðə
not	nɒt	nt
or	ɔː	ə
at	æt	ət
for	fɔ	fə
from	frɒm	frəm, frm
of	ɒv	əv, v
to	tu	tʊ, tə
upon	əpɒn	əpən
but	bʌt	bət
as	æz	əz
than	ðæn	ðən, ðn
that	ðæt	ðət
there	ðɛə	ðə
my	maɪ	mɪ

326. The importance of considering the question of strong and weak forms lies in the fact that the speaker untrained in speech analysis does not realise that he makes any difference in these words. When he sees the

word *was* written, he thinks he always pronounces it wɒz, as he does when he says it in isolation.　Such a person is often shocked to find the number of neutral vowels in a phonetic transcription, and judges it as representing a slipshod and degenerate manner of speaking, the real fact of the matter being, that the transcription is an accurate representation of colloquial—and quite good— speech.　The student will find when he begins to analyse and write down his own pronunciation that the number of neutral vowels he uses is considerably greater than he at first realised.　This fact would be brought home to him if he heard a passage read, as it sometimes is, with all the unstressed vowels given their original "strong" forms.　Such a pronunciation creates the effect of emphasising unimportant words and syllables, and in its turn this weakens the important words.　I have heard pronunciation of this kind in schools in the reading lesson, where the teacher encourages his pupils to "speak each word and syllable distinctly, and not to slur them," thus giving rise to a wooden and unintelligent reading in which all the syllables have equal value.

327.　It is difficult to say how long this habit of weakening the unstressed vowel into ə or ɪ has been in existence—Professor Wyld thinks for many centuries; at present it is well established.　In the North of England, however, particularly in Yorks., and Lancs., the use of the strong form in unstressed syllables is very common, in the small, unimportant words, and in the unstressed syllables of longer words.　Thus one hears kɒn'sɪdə, sʌk'sɛs, 'ɒbdʒɛkt, 'pɜ'fɛkt, 'æksɛnt, 'spɛktɛklz, 'wɒt wɒz hi 'duɪŋ?, where in the South we should hear kən'sɪdə, sək'sɛs, 'ɒbdʒɪkt, 'pɜ·fɪkt, 'æks(ə)nt, 'spɛktəklz, 'wɒt wəz hi 'duɪŋ ?[1]

328. If this method of speaking is very marked, the effect, contrary to what one might expect, is not of a somewhat over-careful speech, but of a speech lacking in precision and finish. This the writer believes to be due to the fact that the important words and syllables are not given sufficient prominence and the characteristic rhythm of the sentence is lost.

ASSIMILATION AND SIMILITUDE.

329. The organs of speech moving in connected speech from one position to another are apt, because of the rapidity of these movements, to take "short cuts"— i.e. to drop out consonants or to modify their articulation. This phenomenon, which is common to all languages, is called *assimilation*. Assimilation is interesting to study because it is an important factor in the historical development of a language and is responsible for many changes in pronunciation.

330. Assimilation may be defined as the process of replacing a sound by another sound under the influence

---

[1] Many Southerners have said to me, "Northerners stress the first syllable in *success*, they say 'sʌksɛs [＼.]." As a matter of fact they do not stress the first syllable nor give the intonation which would accompany such stressing; they pronounce sʌk'sɛs [. ＼], but the use of the strong vowel plus the extra length this has in comparison with the neutral ə, gives the impression of prominence which the hearer associates with stress. (See Ch. XV, § 289 (5).)

of a third sound which is near to it in a word or sentence ; the coalescing of two sounds into a single sound may also come under the heading of assimilation.[1]

331.   There are two clearly defined kinds of assimilation, viz. historical and juxtapositional. Historical assimilation is that which has taken place in the course of the development of the language. We know, for instance, from various kinds of evidence, that the word *nature* was once pronounced næːˈtiur ; its present-day pronunciation ˈneɪtʃə is due, as far as the consonant tʃ is concerned, to this process of assimilation.

332.   Juxtapositional assimilation is an assimilation which occurs when words are juxtaposed in a sentence or in the formation of compounds, and by this juxtaposition, a word comes to have a pronunciation which is different from that used when the word is said in isolation. An example of juxtapositional assimilation is found in the pronunciation of the words *does she* as dʌʃʃi or dʌʒʃi, where the pronunciation of the word dʌz has been changed to dʌʒ or dʌʃ under the influence of the neighbouring ʃ.

333.   Many examples of this kind of assimilation occur in conversational English and the teacher will do well to observe these and note how far such changes may or may not impair intelligibility. He should beware of a too meticulous avoidance or correction of current assimilations of this kind, lest his pronunciation or that of his pupils should have that over-precision

[1] See D. Jones, *Outline of English Phonetics*, Third Edition, 1932, p. 202. [Ninth edition, on pp. 217–18.]

which draws undue attention to itself, and which is not in line with accepted usage.

334. It has been customary to consider other phenomena of similarity in the articulation of neighbouring sounds as examples of assimilation, but this term is better reserved for the two types of *change* of pronunciation illustrated above, i.e. to define assimilation proper as a process. The other similarity, to which the name *similitude* is given, describes an existing fact.[1] Thus in English when s, p, t, k are followed by m, n, l, r, j, w, e.g. in *small, snow, please, slow, try, pew, queen, curiosity,* the second of the pair is partially devoiced. These words are pronounced smɔ·l, snou, sou, pliːz, tʃaɪ, pçuː,[2] kwi·n, kçuərɪpsɪtɪ. (It is easiest to hear in tʃaɪ, pçuː, pliːz.) In these cases a subsidiary member of the m, n, l, r, j, w phoneme is used (the voiceless equivalent of each consonant) which has a greater resemblance to the preceding consonant (in its voicelessness) than the main member of these phonemes. There is no evidence to show that these sounds were ever pronounced in any other way than voiceless, hence it is not correct to say that they are due to assimilation, "When the sequence of two phonemes requires that a subsidiary member of one of them should be used, which has a greater resemblance to the neighbouring sound than

[1] Professor D. Jones is responsible for this division of what has previously been grouped under the one term assimilation. There is no doubt that the separation makes for exactitude and clarity. See *Outline of English Phonetics,* pp. 203–4. [Ninth edition, on pp. 217–19.]

[2] ç represents the sound of j pronounced without any voice. See Chap. XIV, p. 152, § 282.

the principal member has, there is said to be similitude between them.''[1]   Similitude has been illustrated fairly fully in the chapter on phonemes, where the use of the various members of the phoneme was shown to depend mainly on the proximity of some other sound : e.g. the use of a special kind of t (made on the teeth) before the θ-sound of *eighth*, and of another kind of t (made with the tongue-tip curled up) before the r of *tree*.

335.   A still further similarity in neighbouring sounds which is neither assimilation nor similitude occurs in words like *conquer, congregation, concrete, concord,* which are pronounced ˈkɒŋkə, ˈkɒŋgrɪˈgeɪʃn, ˈkɒŋkeɪv, ˈkɒŋkriːt, ˈkɒŋkɔːd, i.e. the neighbouring nasal and plosive consonants are both articulated at the same place.   Many writers have given the name of assimilation to this fact, but again there is no evidence to show that the *con*-prefix was ever pronounced as kɒn under the same set of circumstances of neighbouring consonants and stress. Nor can this fact be explained as similitude, according to the definition given above, since n and ŋ are not members of the same phoneme in English.[2]   Note that in all these words, either primary or secondary stress occurs on the first syllable.   In the words *conˈcur, conˈcussion, conˈcretion, conˈcordance,* when the stressed syllable follows the prefix, the latter is pronounced kən, kənˈkɜː, kənˈkʌʃn, kənˈkriːʃn, kənˈkɔːdns.[3]

---

[1] D. Jones, *op. cit.,* p. 202. [Ninth edition, on p. 217.]

[2] In Italian they are members of one phoneme and the pronunciation of *in casa* as ɪŋ kasa is an example of similitude in this language.

[3] Some people would use ŋ in these positions too.

336. A further example of similarity in neighbouring sounds occurs in Northern pronunciation in words like *climb, glow,* which are pronounced tlaɪm, dloʊ, i.e. t and d are articulated in the same place as l and replace the normal k and g. Such pronunciations as dlæd, tlɒk, intluːd are very common,[1] and the difference between them and the usual glæd, klɒk, inkluːd is not very easy to hear.

337. The points illustrated in the two previous paragraphs, though not examples of assimilation or similitude, are treated here because they have sometimes been considered as exemplifying assimilation, and because some of this type of similarity in neighbouring sounds may possibly be due to assimilations which can no longer be traced.

338. *Examples of Assimilation.*

Assimilation (and similitude) can be concerned with any of the organs of speech.

339. *Vocal Cords.*

(*a*) Voiced sounds have been replaced by voiceless sounds under the influence of a neighbouring voiceless sound; the v in faɪv is replaced by f in faɪfpəns because the voiceless p follows; the z of njuːz is replaced by s in njuˈspeɪpə; in quick speech the phrase aɪ juːzd tʊ becomes aɪ juˈst tʊ; with some speakers, particularly in the North, the d of *width* and *breadth* is pronounced t, wɪtθ, brɛtθ. *Bradford* is often pronounced brætfəd (or braʔfəd).

---

[1] I have heard strʌdl for *struggle.*

(b) A change from a voiceless to a voiced sound is seen in words like *raspberry* and *gooseberry* (rɑ·zbrɪ, gʊzbrɪ). The p has been lost in the b and the b has resulted in s being replaced by z. In some parts of the country, the North particularly, raspbɛrɪ, gu·sbɛrɪ, are still heard. In the plural of words like *bed, dog* (bɛdz, dɒgz),[1] the final sound is voiced owing to the influence of the previous voiced consonant.[2]

340. *Soft Palate.*—Nasal consonants often influence the plosives articulated in the same place, e.g. in *kindness*, kaɪndnəs, generally pronounced kaɪnnəs, the d, influenced by the preceding and following n, is replaced by n and then readily disappears ; grænmʌðə is another example of the same thing, and in hænsəm, the d has been dropped under the influence of the preceding n.

341. *Tongue.*—There are a large number of words in which the tongue position of a consonant is changed.

(a) The pronunciation in quick speech of beɪkŋ, broʊkŋ, tʃɪkŋ (*bacon, broken, chicken*) is an assimilation due to the dropping of the vowel and the bringing together of the two consonants ; these words would normally be beɪkən, broʊkən, tʃɪkɪn.

---

[1] The Early English plural *dogs* was probably *dogges*, dɒgəs; with the dropping of the vowel the two consonants have come together, and the s has been replaced by z; this is a case of historical assimilation.

[2] But note that although transcribed with z, like all final voiced consonants, the sound is only partially voiced. See § 239.

(b) A regular series of assimilations has been made in the language in words which were originally pronounced with s or z, or t or d, followed by i or j; these combinations have been changed into ʃ, ʒ and tʃ, ʤ respectively; e.g. *nation* pronounced as næːsjon in Shakespeare's day, has become neɪʃn; *occasion* is now əkeɪʒn from ɒkæˑzjon; *nature*, pronounced formerly as nætiʊr, has become neɪtʃə; *verdure*, from vɜˑdjur, has become vɜˑʤə.

342. How easy and natural this transition is will be seen from the accompanying diagram. In the word *nation* (næːsjon), the s followed by j has resulted in the sound ʃ, the tongue position of which lies between the two original sounds; while in *nature*, the t, under the influence of j, is pulled back to a point of articulation (see Fig. 31 *c*, p. 137), which makes the transition to ʃ extremely easy. It is to be noted that such assimilation has been made in unstressed syllables only; in stressed syllables it should be avoided: e.g. ˈneɪtʃə but məˈtjʊə.

343. In the two words *sure* and *sugar*, however, formerly (and still in some dialects) pronounced sɪʊr, sɪʊgər, the assimilation has been made in a stressed syllable. In Cockney speech it is made in words like *Duke*, *Tuesday*, *tube* (ʤuˑk, tʃuˑzdɪ, tʃuːb); these pronunciations are still considered examples of uneducated speech. (I have heard ʤʊerɪŋ

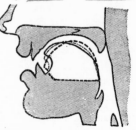

━ Tongue position for s
━ ━ ━ Tongue position for j
. . . . . Tongue position for ʃ

FIG. 42.

Illustrating Assimilation.

or ʤuˈrɪŋ for *during*, and ɪnˈʤʊər or ɪnˈʤuːr for *endure*
from educated Scottish speakers.) There are, however, large numbers of words in which the assimilation
is made by some educated speakers and not by others,
and in these words the process of assimilation is seen
working. For example, literature is pronounced by
some as lɪtrətjʊə, and by others as lɪtrətʃə,

education	as	ɛdjʊkeɪʃn	and	ɛʤʊkeɪʃn
associate	,,	əsoʊsɪeɪt	,,	əsoʊʃɪeɪt
immediately	,,	ɪmiˈdjətlɪ	,,	ɪmiˈʤətlɪ
issue	,,	ɪsjuː	,,	ɪʃuː
appreciate	,,	əpriˈsɪeɪt	,,	əpriˈʃɪeɪt
individual	,,	ɪndɪvɪdjʊəl	,,	ɪndɪvɪʤʊəl.

344. Many of the assimilated forms here given
would by many people be considered slipshod pronunciation, and by most would be avoided in careful
speech, but opinion would be by no means unanimous
on all the words, nor would one person necessarily be
consistent in using either all the careful forms or all
the assimilated forms. Fashion accounts for some of
these: for example, əsoʊʃɪeɪt is heard almost always
from older educated people, and əsoʊsɪeɪt from a younger
generation, while əpriˈsɪeɪt would be considered an
affectation by many who would say lɪtrətjʊə; and one
person will say tɪʃʊ peɪpə, and speak of the bodily
tɪsjuːz.

345. In the pronunciations əpriˈsɪeɪt and əsoʊsɪeɪt
a process the reverse of assimilation, viz. *dissimilation*, †
is showing itself. There is no doubt that əsoʊʃɪeɪt
and əpriˈʃɪeɪt have been well-established, good colloquial
forms of the language and the newer pronunciation is

† Not a standard use of this term
as it is used today (1977).

a somewhat pedantic effort to make a spelling pronunciation, conscious on the part of the first users of
it, but becoming unconscious and natural in others
who follow. Such *dissimilation* has already taken
place in certain words, the newer forms have
become well-established again, and the assimilated
forms are considered vulgar. (See Chapter VII on
Spelling Pronunciations.)

346. *The Lips.*—Assimilation affects the lips as well
as the other organs of speech, particularly in quick
speech. Words like *open, ribbon, tenpence* (oʊpən, rɪbən,
tɛnpəns) sometimes become oʊpm, rɪbm, tɛmpəns, i.e. the
alveolar consonant n is replaced by the labial m under the
influence of the preceding or following labial p or b.
(I have heard rɒbmsn for *Robinson* and sʌmʔm for
something.)

347. Vowels may also be subject to assimilation, the
influence being either that of a neighbouring consonant
or of a vowel in a neighbouring syllable. Thus the
pronunciation ʧʊldrən, prʊtɪ may be due to the influence
of the l and r which have an ʊ-quality together with
some lip-rounding. The plural of *man* and *mouse*, mɛn,
maɪs, is a case of historical assimilation; the old plurals
were manɪz, myːs[1] (from an earlier muːsɪz); thus the
influence of the ɪ of the second syllable resulted in the
replacing of a by ɛ, of u by y. This type of vowel
assimilation is often termed vowel harmony. There
are not a large number of examples of it in English.

[1] The change from myːs to maɪs succeeded that of muːsɪz
to myːs and followed the natural line of development of the
language, viz. myːs>miːs>meɪs>mɛɪs>maɪs. Note that
once it had become miːs it fell in with other words of this type
and followed the same course.

348. *Assimilation in Phrases.* (Juxtapositional Assimilation.)

Assimilations resembling those already described are often made in phrases, when a sound ending one word is changed under the influence of the first sound in the next word.

E.g. *Goodge Street* (guːʤ striːt) is pronounced by the bus conductor as guːʒ ʃtrit, or guːʃ ʃtrit;

I should think so (aɪ ʃʊd θɪŋk soʊ) is pronounced aɪ ʃt θɪŋk soʊ;

please shut the door (pliːz ʃʌt ðə dɔə) is pronounced pliːʒ ʃʌt ðə dɔə;

I can't go (aɪ kɑːnt goʊ) is pronounced aɪ kɑːŋ goʊ, or aɪ kɑŋk goʊ.

I can get it (aɪ kən gɛt ɪt) is pronounced aɪ kŋ gɛt ɪt.

In ten minutes (ɪn tɛn mɪnɪts) is pronounced ɪn tɛm mɪnɪts.

In bed is pronounced ɪm bɛd.

Cup and saucer (kʌp ən sɔːsə) is pronounced kʌp m sɔːsə.

Bag and baggage (bæg ən bægɪʤ) is pronounced bæg ŋ bægɪʤ.

Such assimilations as these, which may pass unnoticed in familiar conversation, are generally considered unsuitable for any other type of speech.

349. *Examples of Similitude.*

Similitudes show the same kind of varieties as assimilation.

350. *Voice and Breath.* (Vocal cords.)

The examples given under § 334 illustrate this type of similitude. A further example is provided in the pronunciation of voiced h (ɦ) in intervocalic positions, e.g. bɪfiaɪnd, ə ɦæt, etc. (See p. 150, § 279 h.)

351. *Soft Palate.* (Nasalisation.)

The chief example of this type of similitude occurs in the slight nasalisation of vowels in the neighbourhood of consonants. The soft palate lowered for the nasal consonant, remains lowered during the production of the following vowel for part or all the time; where the nasal consonant follows the vowel the palate is lowered before the end of the vowel sound to be ready for the nasal consonant, e.g. lõŋ, mãɪt.

352. *Tongue Position.*

The different members of the consonant phonemes described in the chapters on consonants and on phonemes illustrate similitudes affecting tongue position. The different t-sounds have been given as an example; the various kinds of h, k sounds provide other illustrations. (See Chs. X, XIV.)

353. *Lips.*

In the pronunciation of words like *queer*, *quite*, *quest*, *quick*, k is made with lip-rounding; similarly, g followed by w: e.g. *Gwendoline*, *language*. When f or v follows m or n the nasal consonant is often made with the bottom lip against the top teeth, to be ready for the f or v, giving rise to a labio-dental nasal consonant (phonetic symbol ɱ). This is seen in the pronunciation of some people in words like *conversation* (ˈkɒɱvəˈseɪʃn), *convenience* (kəɱˈviːnɪəns), *triumph* (ˈtraɪəɱf), *circumference* (sɜˈkʌɱfərəns), and occasionally when the *m* ends one word and the *f* begins another, as in *come forward* (kʌm fɔ'wəd). A similar change from bi-labial to labio-dental consonant is found in one pronunciation of *obvious*, where the b is replaced by a labio-dental stop.[1]

354. *Vowel Similitude.*

Vowel similitude is illustrated by the examples given of a front vowel followed by a "dark" 1; here the vowel and consonant approximate in vowel quality and that quality is not the same as the vowel has in other positions. Thus in *fill* (fɪl) the vowel is lower and more retracted than in *fit*, i.e. it approximates more to the ʊ-quality of the dark 1. Similarly the fronting of u preceded by j as in mjuːzɪk is another illustration.

DROPPING OF CONSONANTS.

355. Closely allied to the process of assimilation is the simplifying of groups of consonants in single words or phrases. The ease with which a consonant in a group is dropped is partly due to the fact that it generally bears some relation in articulation to one of the neighbouring consonants, either in the place or the manner in which it is made; for this reason, too, the loss of it is not so easily noticed by the ear.

356. The English language is full of examples of this process: here it will be possible to give only a few, but the student should add to this list from his own observations.

---

[1] Note that this pronunciation is regularly used by people who have prominent upper front teeth, and who consequently find it difficult to bring the lips together.

(a) In Words.

d has been dropped in *handkerchief* (hæŋkətʃɪf),
kindness (kaɪnnɪs),
grandfather (grænfɑ·ðə),
Wednesday (wɛnzdɪ),
t has been dropped in *castle* (kɑ·sl),
epistle (ɪpɪsl),
bustle (bʌsl), etc.,
        and by a large number of people in
often (ɒfn or ɔfn),
soften (sɒfn or sɔfn),
postman (poʊsmən),
Christmas (krɪsməs), etc.,
p is often not pronounced in
empty (ɛmtɪ), *tempt* (tɛmt),
k is often omitted from
anxious (æŋʃəs),
thanked (θæŋt),
and always from
blackguard (blægɑ·d),
p is omitted in *cupboard* (kʌbəd).

Note that in *recognise, Arctic, secretary, government*, the pronunciations rɛkənaɪz, ɑ·tɪk, sɛkətrɪ, gʌvəmənt are generally considered as uneducated pronunciations.[1] In these cases the dropped consonant is not articulated in the same place as the next one.

[1] I have heard sɛkətrɪ and gʌvəmənt from educated speakers. Note the dropping of occasional consonants in King George V's speech on p. 225; e.g. moʊs mɛmərəbl.

(b) In Phrases.

The same dropping of consonants occurs in phrases, under similar conditions, in colloquial speech, especially where the phrases are very familiar ones: e.g.

I don't believe it may be pronounced aɪ doŭ m bɪliːv ɪt,

I don't know is pronounced aɪ doʊn noʊ, or aɪ doʊ noʊ, or even aɪ də noʊ,

Bread and butter is pronounced brɛd n bʌtə,

Next Monday is pronounced nɛks mʌndɪ,

Breakfast time is pronounced brɛkfəs taɪm,

I must go is pronounced aɪ məs goʊ,

I've almost finished is pronounced aɪ v ɔˑlmoʊs fɪnɪʃt,

Last night is pronounced laˑs naɪt.

357. The student should note the assimilations and simplifications made in his own and other people's quick speech, and compare them with those he finds recorded in texts which represent colloquial speech. Note that in a slower and more careful type of speech, assimilation and the simplification of consonant groups is much rarer than in quick colloquial speech.

CHAPTER XVII

RECENT DEVELOPMENTS IN ENGLISH
PRONUNCIATION

" English, like all living languages, changes from generation to
generation: slight and imperceptible as the differences in the
pronunciation of father and son may appear to be, there is
always some change under ordinary normal conditions.[1] Hence
pronunciations which are vulgar in one century may become
fashionable in the next, sounds which are distinct in one
generation may be confounded in another, and new distinctions
may be made, new sounds may arise."

—Sweet: *The Sounds of English.*

358.   Readers of this book will have realised from
the chapters on Standard Pronunciation, on Spelling
Pronunciations and on Assimilation, that many changes
have taken place in the pronunciation of our language.
But it is not always easy to realise that changes are
going on in our own time and generation.   In 20 years
or so [up to 1944], a considerable number of changes
have been noted which it will be well to sum up here.

359.   The younger generation of educated Southerners
together with many of the products of the Universities
of Oxford, Cambridge and London show certain well-
marked tendencies in pronunciation.   Generally speaking, these are confined to persons—of both sexes—under
the age of 35, though I have heard them from occasional
people up to 45 or thereabouts.

360.   *Consonants.*

(i)   The treatment of the consonant **r** is interesting.
      While intrusive **r** is spreading in areas and among

---

[1] A Cockney girl, asked if her speech was like her father's,
answered at first, "Yes," but then said, "nʌu, wɛn mai
faːvə toːks əbaː? ə kwid, i sɛz paːnd : ai dʌʊ? sɛi paːnd,
ai sɛi pæund."

classes where formerly it was not used, there is also a tendency, in the type of speech we are dealing with, for the *"linking* r*"* not to be used.[1]　Thus

our own		is pronounced	aʊə oʊn and aə oʊn
moreover	,,	,,	mɔːoʊvə
wherever	,,	,,	wɛəɛvə
Sir Edgar Ede	,,	,,	sɜ ɛdgə iːd
Westminster Abbey	,,	,,	wɛsmɪnstə æbɪ
more and more	,,	,,	mɔː ən mɔː
anywhere else	,,	,,	ɛnɪwɛə ɛls

(ii) r is strongly labialised, i.e. pronounced with considerable lip-rounding.　This may be due to the fact that r has little or no friction ; it is a very weak consonant and the labialisation may be added unconsciously to strengthen it.

(iii) A kind of s which has a double articulation, viz. the lower lip against the upper teeth in addition to a tongue articulation is common.　This gives the effect of a slight whistling lisp.　The tongue articulation is not that illustrated in § 275 (p. 148), as can be proved by holding the lower lip free from the teeth, when the resulting sound resembles θ, not s, i.e. the slight friction heard is made between the tip of the tongue and the front teeth ; there is no narrow passage between the blade and the teeth ridge.

---

[1] Such pronunciation used to be considered a womanish affectation.

361. *Vowels and Diphthongs.*

(i) The front vowels, ɪ, ɛ, æ tend to be retracted in tongue position, in words like *bit, big, bed, bad*, etc. In *yes* this retraction has long been common, and it is heard in all types of speech. (See (iv) below for lengthening of vowels.)

(ii) The vowel ʌ is fronted and lowered in many cases, so that it is near to cardinal **a**.[1] †

(iii) There is a general tendency to replace the diphthong eɪ by a pure vowel ɛ: thus *pain* is pronounced pɛ·n, the ɛ being more open and retracted than ɛ in *pen*, from which it is clearly differentiated. This tendency is especially noticeable where the sound occurs in a final position: e.g. *play* is plɛ· (the vowel is sometimes even not long here).

(iv) The aɪ diphthong has a back type of **a** as its first element, i.e. it is the ɑɪ such as is described in § 203 (p. 116), (without the nasalisation belonging to the Cockney ɑɪ, however), and, like other diphthongs it tends to become narrower or flattened out as it were. Thus with little movement of the tongue ɑɪ sounds like ɑe. Similarly, aʊ sounds like aʌ (see below for lack of lip-rounding). The triphthongs aɪə, aʊə are regularly flattened as described in § 229 (p. 123). I have heard in a recent lecture *liability* pronounced lɑɑbɪlɪtɛ (with a slight re-inforcement of

[1] It has been suggested that this sound should be written phonetically with **a**.

† cf. Charles Dowsett's London bus.

breath between the two ɑ's, and a retracted ɛ in the final syllable), *environment* as ɪnvɑːrnmənt, *desire* as dɪzɑɑ (again with a little push of breath in the middle of the long ɑ). The same speaker used ɛ° in *sphere, experience, period*, which he pronounced sfɛ°, ɪkspɛ°rɪəns, pɛ°rɪəd, the vowel ɛ being very much retracted and lowered.

(v) The vowel ʊ and the diphthong oʊ have very little lip-rounding : *good* is pronounced guːd or gɤːd and *go* resembles gəɯ or gʌɯ.[1]

(vi) Perhaps one of the most noticeable features of change in English pronunciation in recent years is the lengthening of some of the vowels which have usually been considered short. This tendency has long been noted in the case of æ, which is regularly pronounced long in words like *bad, man*, etc., especially when extra emphasis is given to them. In *dog, fog, long, bed, said, men, this, bit*, the vowel is frequently lengthened and we have dɒːg (not dɔːg, which is now confined to uneducated speech), fɒːg, lɒːŋ, beːd, seːd, meːn (when stressed), ðiːs, biːt. The lengthening and unrounding of ʊ in *good* has been noted above. Some of these vowels (the front ones) are diphthongised somewhat, towards ə, as in certain types of American speech, but it would appear that the tendency to lengthening had begun before the influence of American speech of the moving pictures could have been felt : the diphthongisation *may* be due to America influence.

---

[1] ɯ represents unrounded u, ɤ unrounded o.

362. The lengthening of the traditionally short vowels and the monophthongisation of diphthongs, if these continue, are likely to introduce problems of phonetic transcription which we have not had to consider up to the present. The "broad" transcription (see Ch. V, § 56) in use in many books on English phonetics cannot represent all the variations of length and quality used by the younger generation of to-day, nor indeed, would the present "narrow" transcription used in this book be entirely adequate ; a still narrower one may be necessary.

363. It must not be thought in the summing up of modern tendencies in pronunciation attempted here that all Southern English speakers of the younger generation make use of all of them. The conditions under which lengthening takes place are rather obscure ; considerable investigations would have to be made to discover the rules, and the speech of a large number of typical people would have to be analysed. Nor should it be thought that these changes are all in the normal line of development of English pronunciation, and are certain to spread and be generally adopted. Some are doubtless due to an unexplainable fashion, and may change as unaccountably as they have developed.

364. *Intonation.*

It has not been possible up to the present to make accurate observations on any changes in intonation which may have taken place in the speech of the younger generation. The present writer has noted three intonation habits which are not familiar, however. One, observed mainly on the stage, is a tendency to use Tune II (see § 308, p. 171) in questions beginning with an interrogative word: e.g. '*What's your 'husband's 'name*? (heard in *Eden End*, by J. B. Priestley) had the pattern [‾ · — . ╱]. This occurs in a quarrel and gives the impression of a challenge, and as such would have the implication belonging to this pattern. The second, heard mainly in the broadcasting of news, is the habit of stressing the last word of a phrase, and with this stress is heard the accompanying high-fall in pitch. Thus: "*This was decided at a Cabinet meeting*" frequently has the intonation [‾ ·· — ··· __ ·· ╲ .] where the normal "tune" of the last two words would be [‾ ·· ╲ .]. It is most likely due to the desire to clinch some definite final statement, but there is no doubt that it plays tricks with the expected tune and often gives the impression of contrast stress and intonation, which actually is not meant or needed.

The following phrases were noted recently during the reading of a news bulletin, all of them final in a sentence.

The keystone of our policy [. ‾ ·· ╲ ··]

It would be dangerous to European peace
[··· ‾ ··· — ··· ╲]

For the next twenty-four hours [·· ‾ ··· ╲]

Copyright reserved [— ··· ╲]

He will describe it in to-night's 10 o'clock news
[··· ‾ ··· — ··· ╲]

Where they were given a warm welcome
[··· ‾ ·· — ╲ .]

The Madrid front [·· ╲╲]

Finally, a very monotonous intonation is used by commentators on news films (*not* in broadcasting) which consists mostly of Tune I, repeated many times with little variation in the range used, i.e. each group begins at the same height and descends in regular steps to a fall in the last syllable.

'Here is the 'bridge a'cross Ni'agara [‾· ‾· — · ╲ ..]
as it 'was before the 'recent 'storms
[.. ‾· — · · ╲]
and 'now you 'see what it 'looks like [.‾ · · · ╲ .]
when the 'rush of 'waters has 'done its 'worst
[.. ‾· — · · · ╲].

This habit is probably due to the effort to squeeze a great amount of comment into little time.

CHAPTER XVIII

BRITISH ENGLISH AND AMERICAN ENGLISH

365. An attempt is made in this chapter to summarise briefly some of the general differences between British English and American English. It must not be taken as an analysis of American pronunciation, since this obviously could not be undertaken within the limits of a short chapter nor without considerably more investigation on the part of the writer of the many types of American speech. American phoneticians who are best qualified for the purpose have made complete phonetic analyses of American pronunciation.[1] The points set out here are the result of personal observation of Americans in England and of the examination of gramophone records; they have been submitted to American phoneticians of note for confirmation. Records made in the Speech Department of Teachers' College, Columbia, by 17 students of Mrs. J Dorsey Zimmerman[2] are used to illustrate the general comparisons and contrasts which it is the aim of this chapter to outline. It is impossible to print all the phonetic transcriptions of these records here ; nor would it serve a useful purpose, since they illustrate many variant pronunciations of American speech which are outside the scope of this enquiry.

[1] See Bibliography, p. 246.

[2] These were put at my disposal by Mrs Zimmerman in August, 1937.

366. The sentences recorded have been taken from
A Handbook of English Intonation[1] (2nd edition, p. 36,
Nos. 1, 2, 4, 5, and pp. 49–59, Examples II*a*), and are
given below in the phonetic form found in that book
with the intonation marks.[2]

	—	•	•	\	•	|	•	•	—	•	—	•

(1) hi ˈfɛlt ɪn hɪz ˈpɒkɪt   ənd wəz glæd tə faɪnd hɪz

| — | • | • | ˋ | \ | • | \| | — | ⌣ | \| | • | — |

læˈtʃki ənd hɪz mʌnɪ   — fɔ wɪð ðiːz tuː   ə ˈmæn

| • | — | • | • | \ |

kəmˈɑːndz ðə ˈwɜːld.

| • | — | — | • | \| | • | — | • | — | • | • | ⌣ | \| |

(2) ðə ˈskɒtʃ ˈdaɪəlɛkt   ɪz ˈrɪtʃ ɪn ˈtɜːmz əv rɪˈprootʃ

| • | • | • | — | \ | \| | • | • | ⌣ | \| | • |

əgeɪnst ðə ˈwɪntə ˈwɪnd.   ðeɪ ər ˈɔːl ˈwɜːdz   ðət

| — | • | • | \ | • | • | • |

ˈkærɪ ə ˈʃɪvə wɪð ðəm.

| • | • | — | • | • | • | • | \| | • | — | ••• |

(4) hi ɪz ðə ˈdʒɒlɪəst əv ˈkəmpænjənz   ən ðə ˈstɛdɪəst əv

[1] *A Handbook of English Intonation*, Armstrong and Ward
(W. Heffer & Sons Ltd).

[2] These sentences form part of the gramophone records which
were made to illustrate the book and were spoken by Miss
Armstrong. The intonation marked is that of the record.

```
    \         .     . .    .        —   . .     —    . .
──────────────────────────────────────────────────────────
'frɛndz ənd pəhæps ðə moʊst 'dʒɛnjʊɪn 'bʊk-lʌvər
```

```
   .    \   .
──────────────────────────────────────────────────────────
in 'lʌndən.
```

```
   .    —.    —    .     — .  |   . .    .  \   .  |   — .
──────────────────────────────────────────────────────────
(5) hi 'nɛvə 'rɛd ðə 'peɪpəz   tɪl ðɪ 'iˑvnɪŋ   'pɑˑtlɪ
```

```
   . .       .   — .    ⌣   |   .        —   . . .    . .
──────────────────────────────────────────────────────────
bɪkɒz i 'hædnt 'taim   ənd 'pɑˑtlɪ bɪkɒz hi soʊ |
```

```
   — .      .      — . .    \     .
──────────────────────────────────────────────────────────
'sɛldəm faʊnd 'ɛnɪθɪŋ 'ɪn ðəm.
```

GENERAL OBSERVATIONS.

367. (1) The quality of vowels and consonants is influenced by a tendency to draw back the whole of the tongue somewhat and to raise the back towards the soft palate ; in many cases too, the back of the tongue appears to be hollowed, i.e. it has a furrow down the middle and the sides are raised a little.[1] As a result of this tendency, consonants articulated at or near the alveolar ridge have a secondary articulation ; they are velarised or "dark." Dark l is common in final positions and before consonants in most varieties of English. In American English it is also used in initial positions, as it is in Scottish. The exact quality of initial l varies with the following vowel and from individual to individual, but, generally speaking, "clear" l is not used in this position. The American velarisation of other alveolar consonants is not so easy to note, but it is

[1] "Sulcalised" is the phonetic term given to this tongue position.

recognisable in post-vocalic n, and the other consonants such as s, z, ∫, ӡ, r, t, d, are often made with some raising of the back of the tongue or a general backward pull, which contributes something to the effect of American as compared with British English. In the records, "dark" l is noticeable in words like *glad, latchkey, iolliest, London.*[1]

368. Vowel sounds are affected also by this action of the tongue, particularly the front vowels. Many of these are definitely more retracted in American speech than in English,[2] and some of them frequently are pronounced with an ə-glide before the following alveolar

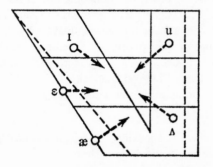

Fig. 43. Circles represent normal British English vowel positions; *arrows*, the direction towards the position in which the American vowels tend to be pronounced; the *dotted line*, roughly the front and back limit of American vowels.

[1] The whole word *London* sounds velarised and sulcalised.

[2] See, however, § 361 for a modern tendency towards this in England. See also the note on the President Roosevelt record. I heard recently in a broadcast of the speech by the President of Harvard the words *minimise* and *within* pronounced with a very much lowered and centralised vowel: these words sounded like mənəmaɪz, wəðən, the ə having somewhat of an ɛ quality.

consonant. Thus ɪ, ɛ, æ are frequently pronounced
ɪ°, ɛ°, æ°. The vowel i, however, does not appear to
be affected in this way, and is often very close. This is
illustrated in the majority of the records, where *wind,
friend, command* are pronounced wɪ°nd, frɛ°nd, komæ°nd
with a marked glide. The retraction of the front
vowels, together with an advancing of some of the back
vowels makes the vowel area smaller than in normal
British English.

369. (2) When the letter *r* follows a vowel in spelling,
the consonant is usually pronounced either with the
tongue-tip curled up or with a "bunching up" of the front
of the tongue.[1] This takes place during the pronunciation
of the vowel and affects the vowel quality by adding
to it something of the quality of a central vowel (ə).
Thus in the records the word *partly* is almost pɑɹtlɪ. It
is noticeable that with several speakers, post-vocalic r
is very lightly pronounced ; in some cases it is scarcely
perceptible.[2]

370. (3) Generally speaking, American English has a
weaker consonant articulation than that of British
English, a less vigorous contact and release. An inter-
vocalic consonant which is voiceless in British English,
in American speech has the weaker articulation which
normally belongs to a voiced consonant, and frequently

---

[1] See p. 145 for diagram and explanation of retroflex **r**. There
is often little or no friction, so that the pronunciation of vowel
+ **r** is vowel with retroflexion or bunching up of the tongue and
not consonant. See Kenyon, *American Punctuation*, p. 196.

[2] President Roosevelt does not use it except as a linking **r**
before a word beginning with another vowel. See p. 233, §383.

is voiced. Intervocalic **t** is so short as to be a very rapid "tap" or touch of the tongue-tip on the teeth ridge, and the voice goes on through this "vestigial" *t*. Thus *letter* is pronounced lɛtə in British English and lɛt̬r¹ in American. The difference between the two is not only in the voice introduced into the American type, but in the use of the weaker articulation which belongs to voiced consonants.

> *Example* : bɛt̬ɪ (*Betty*), θɜ-ɪt̬ɪ (*thirty*), lɪt̬l (*little*), wɪnt̬ɪ (*winter*),² ɔːt̬əm (*autumn*), ðət̬ ɪt̬ ɪz (*that it is*).

To English ears, intervocalic **t** pronounced in this way sounds like a one-tap **r**; *Betty* pronounced bɛt̬ɪ sounds like bɛri (*berry*), the **r** being a single tap and not the fricative variety. The consonants **p** and **k**, though pronounced with weak articulation in similar positions, are not so noticeably different from English **p** and **k**.

371. (4) While it is impossible to treat American vowel sounds systematically in this short chapter, there are one or two points to which attention is drawn. One of the outstanding difficulties of the British phonetician dealing with American speech is that of classifying the distribution of the vowels æ, a, ɑ, ɒ, ɔ. Many Americans use three sounds of the letter *a*, viz. æ, a, ɑ; the use of these, however, varies considerably from British custom. Thus *man* and *can't* are both pronounced with æ; *father* has frequently a more forward position than in English

---

¹ t̬ = **t** with some voice.

² The contact for **t** in this word in some of the records **is so** weak that it gives the impression that it isn't there: **wɪnɪ.**

(faːðɹ) while ɑ is used in words in which Englishmen use ɒ : nɑt (*not*). Again, ɔ occurs with many speakers where ɒ is used in England : *long* (lɒŋ) is frequently pronounced lɔːŋ. In the experience of the present writer, however, there are many variations in the use of these vowels among American speakers, and it is no part of this work to attempt a classification of their use, but merely to draw attention to this point.[1] In the records, *glad, latch* are pronounced by several speakers with a distinctly low and retracted variety of a (glad, latʃ), due probably to the influence of the initial dark "l," and the same speakers use æ in *man* (mæˀn) and *commands* (kɒmæˀndz) ; *pocket, Scotch, jolliest* are pronounced pɑkət, skɑtʃ, dʒɑlɹəst by many, and *wrong* is rɔːŋ. But it should be stressed once more that there is by no means uniformity in these pronunciations.

372.　(5) American usage in the matter of vowel length varies from that of British English. Certain vowels, which by the majority of English people[2] are considered short, are pronounced considerably longer in America, and some of the long vowels and diphthongs are also longer. The diphthongisation of the front vowels ɪ, ɛ, æ, which are considered short vowels in English, illustrates this point ; in American speech these are noticeably longer than in that of most English people. The question of length is also closely linked with that of rhythm and intonation. Examples of the differences in

---

[1] See Kenyon, *American Pronunciation*, pp. 60-63, para. 76. for a very full analysis of these vowels and their distribution.

[2] See, however, § 361 (vi).

this respect between the two types of English are given below.

373. (6) In all speech, vowels in the immediate neighbourhood of nasal consonants are nasalised to some degree; in some kinds of American speech, nasality in this position is more noticeable than in British English. This is one of the characteristics of American speech that the non-trained observer notes, but it should be pointed out that the degree of nasalisation varies widely, and that what is usually considered by Americans as the best type of speech is no more nasalised than the best British variety.   In the records examined, nasality is not marked in the majority of the speakers, nor is it noticeable in the Roosevelt record.

374. (7) It is perhaps in intonation, stress and rhythm that the greatest general differences are found between British and American English, and these are often subtle and difficult to analyse and to explain on paper without audible illustrations.

INTONATION.

375. (a) In American speech a falling intonation in a succession of stressed syllables appears to be common. This usually denotes emphasis in British English, so that a non-emphatic statement with these frequent falls gives the impression of an emphatic speech.   Thus:

ənd wəz glæd tə faɪnd hɪz lætʃki ənd hɪz mʌnɪ

ə mæn kəmændz ðə wɜrld

ɪn ə truːlɪ dɛməkræˈtɪk kʌntrɪ.

(President of Harvard's broadcast, Mar. 29, 1938.)

Curiously enough, however, emphatic speech sounds less vigorously stressed. American speakers on their side feel British English to be less stressed. The explanation of this difference lies, as far as the present writer has been able to ascertain, in the different methods of the two sets of people in applying stress. In British English, one way in which emphasis shows itself is by a more vigorous articulation of the consonants, i.e. a tighter and longer contact (or, in the case of fricatives, a narrower opening) and a sharper release ; this, of course, with increased breath force. The American who feels that he uses considerable effort, expends it rather on the vowel than on the consonant, i.e. it would appear that he has a stronger diaphragm movement and he lengthens his vowels, but the incidence of this extra force expended affects his consonants little. Thus the judgment on each side is subjective ; since he does not find the type of emphasis he uses himself, with its acoustic effect, each thinks that it is absent in the other. It should be possible to analyse by experimental methods these two types of producing emphasis, and confirm—or otherwise—what is put down here as a tentative suggestion, the result of careful observations and discussion with an American phonetician.

(b) It will be seen from the first sentences set out on p. 170 that a succession of stressed syllables in a descending scale, with a fall on the last one, is typical of an unemphatic statement in British English; it is rare to find these syllables on the same note. In American English, however, the same pitch is struck frequently, as is shown by the intonation given under (a) above, with, of course, the fall within the syllable. To English ears this gives the impression of monotony; the fall evidently gives the necessary variety to Americans. In the records examined, the men speakers particularly show this tendency; the limits of the voice within which they speak also are narrow, and the bottom limit in some cases is reached only at the end of a sentence.

(c) As far as intonation alone is concerned, the records illustrate the foregoing points. They also show that in the emphatic sentences the intonations of the two types of speech are not unlike. There are naturally variants where the speaker has made one idea more prominent than was done in the original recording. Thus: *How do you know it's wrong* has the intonation [· ·⌒\ . —], making *know* prominent and not *wrong* (which implies that the fact of its being wrong has already been stated). This is a normal reading of the sentence, and would be used by both Americans and English alike. Similarly, one speaker gives the sentence *It's not my business* the intonation [. . __ · ·] with extra stress on *my*, and using Tune II with its implication, which is quite as usual as [. ‾ — \ .].[1] The use of Tune II in

[1] I have been told that this sentence is not American English. An American would express the same idea by " That's none of my business."

statements is perhaps not quite so frequent in American speech as in English, and as far as the present writer has observed the pattern

> *I know what you mean* [· __ .. ⌣] is used rather than [˙‾ · · ⌣].

There is no material in the records, however, which can illustrate this habit. The following variations in the tune of an unfinished group which are not common in British English were heard in a broadcast from America :

 eɪ ˈmɔːr əˈtræktɪv ˈprogræˈm [.‾ · — .‾ ·]

hu du ˈnɒt gɔʊ tʊ ˈkɒlɪʤ [.. ⟍ ·· — ·]

ə weɪst əv ˈpreʃəs ˈfʌndz [.‾ · — . ⌒]

ei ˈmænjʊəl ˈwɜˑkər [.‾ · — ·] (the two last in a series).

One further point should be mentioned. The use of the two speech tunes varies. What is perfectly polite to American ears may sound somewhat casual to British ears, while a normal British tune may give the impression of a dogmatic or even rude utterance to the American.[1] In this connection it would be interesting to make a careful study of the intonation of the small change of greetings, farewells, familiar questions and sentences in the two types of speech.[2]

---

[1] See *The Broadcast Word*, by Professor A. Lloyd James, pp. 7–9, for the misunderstandings that may arise from differences in this particular bit of speech behaviour.

[2] The intonation [__ ⌒] for the word "Goodbye" at the end of a business interview gave to the present writer an impression of a casualness which was decidedly out of place. She has been told by Americans that it was in point of fact probably intended to be extra friendly and polite.

STRESS AND RHYTHM.

376. One of the main contributory factors to the difference between English and American rhythm is the fact that the American makes use of fewer "weak forms" and neutral vowels than the Englishman. This changes the rhythmic patterns entirely. The pronunciation of the words *vacation, necessarily, romance* illustrates this point as far as words are concerned. In British English they are pronounced vəˈkeɪʃn, ˈnɛsɪsərɪlɪ (or ˈnɛsəsərɪlɪ), roˈmæns (rəˈmæns), while in most types of American English they are veɪˈkeɪʃn, ˈnɛsɪˈsɛərəlɪ (or nɛsəˈsɛrɪlɪ), rouˈmæns (or ˈroumæns). There may or may not be secondary stress on the syllable which is unstressed in English, but in any case the use of the diphthongs eɪ, ɛə, ou in place of the short neutral vowel gives greater prominence to the syllables in which they occur, since they are longer and of a stronger quality. Thus the rhythm of the word and the relative length of the syllables is altered. When this habit is carried over into the sentence, and words which in British English have weak forms with the minimum of stress are pronounced with a stronger form and at greater length, it is easily seen how different the rhythmic patterns become. At the same time, the American usage of relatively long vowels where British English has short ones, and the greater length of long vowels and diphthongs also contributes to the variations in rhythm between the two types of speech. It should be noted that to the American the reduction of so many vowels to the neutral, and the occurrence of a succession

of unstressed syllables with a neutral vowel gives the impression of "clipped" speech, of the swallowing of syllables and of distortion of the word,[1] while the more deliberate American pronunciation sounds to the Englishman as if undue importance were given to unimportant words and syllables.

377. A considerable number of examples occur in the few sentences of the records under examination.[2] In unstressed syllables of single words, the only differences of this kind are *reproach*, pronounced rɪprouʧ, instead of rɪprouʧ, *genuine* as ʤɛnjuain,[3] and *partly* as paɹtli (with final i) by two or three speakers. Of the unimportant words, *of* is never anything but əv, except in one case where *the jolliest of friends* is pronounced ði ʤɑlɪəst ɒv frɛˀndz, where *the* is also pronounced ði. The women speakers mostly use h in unstressed his, but not the men: *you* is often ju and not jʊ as in the question *How many times have you been there?*, where *have* also has its strong form (but *been* is usually bɪn, where English usage would probably give fifty per cent. saying biːn): *with them* is almost always pronounced wɪððɛm and not wɪððəm; *and* is frequently ænd, and the article *a* is sometimes pronounced eɪ: eɪ mæˀn komæˀndz ðə wɜɹld. The words *winter wind* illustrate a different rhythmic pattern from British English; in the latter the two words take up the same time and have even stress; most of the records give the impression of a stronger stress on *wind* because (*a*) the vowel in it is longer, and the vowel in

---

[1] Several types of English dialect speech share, to some extent, this characteristic of American. See §§ 284 (iii) and 327.

[2] They are not all alike, however, in this respect.

[3] This is said to be an emphatic form and somewhat "rustic."

winter is shorter, and (*b*) there is a different relation of the pitch of the two syllables ; as far as time is concerned, the one can be represented as ♩.♪♩ and the other as ♪♪♩· .

378. In this brief chapter general differences between British and American English have been illustrated. Further illustrations of these points are given in the notes on the pronunciation of President Roosevelt's record, of which a phonetic transcription is given on p. 226–31. The writer would like to point out once more, however, that these are not to be considered as exhaustive nor of universal application. Moreover, it must be stated that in the great body of English pronunciation there are many more points of similarity than of variation between the two types of speech. A close comparison of the two would reveal subtleties difficult in the first place to analyse and in the second to record, and requiring a major work in which to do justice to the problem. It is to be hoped that such a work may sometime be forthcoming.

CHAPTER XIX

PHONETIC TRANSCRIPTIONS

The intonation given for the first two texts has been noted down from the gramophone record and is shown above each line.

379. KING GEORGE V'S MESSAGE TO THE EMPIRE, CHRISTMAS, 1935.

aɪ ˈwɪʃ ju ˈɔːl, maɪ ˈdɪə ˈfrɛndz, ə ˈhæpɪ ˈkrɪsməs.

aɪ v biˑn ˈdiˑplɪ ˈtʌʧt bə ðə ˈgriˑtɪŋz wɪʧ ɪn ðə ˈlɑˑst

ˈfjuˑ ˈmənɪts hæv ˈriˑʧt mi frəm ˈɔːl ˈpɑˑts əv ðɪ

ˈɛmpaɪə. lɛt ˈmiː ɪn rəsˈpɒnts sɛnd tə ˈʔiˑʧ əv ˈjuː

ə ˈgriˑtɪŋ frəm maɪˈsɛlf. maɪ ˈwɜːdz wɪl bɪ ˈvɛrɪ ˈsɪmpl,

bʌt ˈspoʊkən frm ðə ˈhɑˑt, ɒn ðɪs ˈfæmɪlɪ ˈfɛstəvl ɒv

ˈkrɪsməs. ðə ˈjɪə ðət ɪz ˈpɑˑsɪŋ, ðə ˈtwɛntɪ-ˈfɪθ ˈsɪns

maɪ æk'sɛʃn, həz 'biːn tə 'miː 'moʊs 'mɛmrəbl ɪt

'kɔːld 'fɔːθ ə ˌspɒn'teɪnɪəs 'ɒfrɪŋ ɒv 'lɔɪəltɪ ən aɪ

'meɪ 'seɪ, əv 'lʌv, wɪtʃ ðə 'kwiːn ən 'aɪ kən 'nɛvə

fə'ɡɛt. 'haʊ kʊd aɪ 'feɪl tə 'noʊt ɪn 'ɔːl ðə rə'dʒɔɪsɪŋz,

'nɒt 'mɪəlɪ rəs'pɛkt fə ðə 'θroʊn, bət ə 'wɔːm ænd

'dʒɛnərəs rɪ'mɛmbrəns əv ðə 'mæn hɪm'sɛlf, 'huː,

meɪ 'ɡɒd 'hɛlp ɪm, hæz biːn 'pleɪst əpɒn ɪt. ɪt 'ɪz 'ðɪs

'pɜːsnəl 'lɪŋk bətwiːn 'miː æn maɪ 'piːpl wɪtʃ aɪ

'vælju 'mɔː ðən aɪ kən 'seɪ. ɪt 'baɪndz əs tə'ɡɛðə

ɪn 'ɔːl aʊə 'kɒmən 'dʒɔɪz 'ænd 'sɒroʊz, æz 'wɛn 'ðɪs

'jɪə ju 'ʃoʊd jɔː 'hæpɪnəs ɪn ðə 'mærɪdʒ əv maɪ 'sʌn,

æn jɔː ˈsɪmpəθɪ ɪn ðə ˈdɛθ əv maɪ bəˈlʌvəd ˈsɪstə.

aɪ ˈfiːl ðɪs ˈlɪŋk ˈnaʊ, əz aɪ ˈspiˑk tə ju fər aɪ m

ˈθɪŋkɪŋ ˈnɒt so ˈmʌtʃ əv ðɪ ˈɛmpaɪə ɪtˈsɛlf, əz ɒv ðɪ

ˈɪndəˈvɪdɪʊəl ˈmɛn, ˈwɪmɪn ˈænd ˈtʃɪldrən hu ˈlɪv

wɪˈðɪn ɪt, ˈweðə ðeɪ ə ˈdwɛlɪŋ ˈhɪə ət ˈhoʊm ɔː ɪn

sʌm ˈdɪstənt ˈaʊtpoʊst ɒv ðɪ ˈɛmpaɪə. ɪn ˈjʊərəp ən

ˈmɛnɪ ˈpɑˑts əv ðə ˈwɜːld æŋˈzaɪətɪz səˈraʊnd əs. ɪt

ɪz ˈɡʊd tə ˈθɪŋk ðət aʊə ˈʔoʊn ˈfæmɪlɪ əv ˈpiˑplz ɪz

æt ˈpiˑs ɪn ɪtˈsɛlf æn juˈnaɪtɪd ɪn ˈwʌn dəˈzaɪə tə

bi ət ˈpiˑs wɪð ˈʌðə ˈneɪʃnz, ðə ˈfrɛnd əv ˈɔːl, ðɪ ˈʔɛnɪmɪ

ɒv ˈnʌn. ˈmeɪ ðə ˈspɪrɪt əv ˈɡʊdˈwɪl æn ˈmjuˑtʃʊəl

'helpfʊlnɪs 'groʊ, 'ænd 'sprɛd. 'ðɛn ɪt wɪl 'brɪŋ 'nɒt

'oʊnlɪ ðə 'blɛsɪŋ əv 'piˑs bət ə sə'luːʃn əv ðɪ ˌiˑkɪ'nɒmɪk

'trʌblz wɪtʃ 'stɪl bɪ'sɛt əs. tə 'ðoʊz hu ə 'sʌfrɪŋ ɔˑ

ɪn dɪ'strɛs 'wɛðə ɪn 'ðɪs 'kʌntrɪ ɔˑ ɪn 'ɛnɪ 'pɑˑt əv ðɪ

'ɛmpaɪə, aɪ 'ɒfə maɪ 'diˑpəs 'sɪmpəθɪ. 'bʌt aɪ wʊd

'ɔˑlsoʊ gɪv ə 'krɪsməs 'mɛsɪʤ əv 'hoʊp ænd 'tʃɪə.

ju'naɪtɪd baɪ ðə 'bɒnd əv 'wɪlɪŋ 'sɜˑvɪs, 'lɛt əs 'pruːv

aʊəsɛlvz boʊθ 'strɒŋ tʊ ɪn'djʊə ən 'rɛzəluˑt tʊ

oʊvə'kʌm. 'wʌns ə'geɪn əz aɪ 'kloʊz, aɪ 'sɛnd ju

'ɔːl æn 'nɒt 'liːst tə ðə 'tʃɪldrən hu 'meɪ bɪ 'lɪsnɪŋ

tə 'miˑ, maɪ 'truˑəst 'krɪsməs 'wɪʃɪz, ənd 'ðoʊz əv

```
  .  —  ╱  |  .  .  —  ·  |  .      _   · · |  · ·
```

maɪ ˈdɪə ˈwaɪf, maɪ ˈtʃɪldrən ænd ˈgræntʃɪldrən hu ɑ

```
  —  · ·  ╲  |  ·  ╲  |  .  —  ·      ╲  |  ·  ·  —
```

ˈwɪð mi təˈdeɪ. aɪ ˈæd ə ˈhɑ·tfɛlt ˈprɛə ðət wɛəˈɛvə

```
  · _  |  —  ·      —      .  —  ·  ╲  .
```

ju ˈɑː gɒd meɪ ˈblɛs ænd ˈki·p ju ˈɔ·lweɪz.

NOTES.

380. (1) The speech is deliberately slow; the sense groups are smaller and the pauses longer than in ordinary speech, but the normal rhythm is very little disturbed by this, nor is there much exaggeration of sound or any undue stressing. The slowing-up is in proportion. (See Ch. II, p. 19.)

(2) Certain of the unimportant words which in quicker speech would have a weak form have the full vowel here. These occur frequently after a pause and occasionally within the group when the slow speed would mean too great a length for the neutral vowel:

> bʌt ˈspoʊkən frm ðə ˈhɑ·t.
> hæz biːń ˈpleɪst əˈpɒn ɪt.
> ə ˈwɔːm ænd ˈdʒenərəs rɪˈmembrəns.

(3) The range of voice and intonation patterns are also without exaggeration and this in its turn strengthens the impression of sincerity. The intonations used illustrate the normal patterns of English unemphatic speech. Note, however, two examples of a character-

istic of public speaking, viz. a rather high-pitch ending
to a Tune II group:

  wɛðə ðeɪ ə dwɛlɪŋ hɪə,

and a low level ending of a similar group:

  bouθ strɒŋ tu ɪndjuə.

(4) The following details of pronunciation may be
noted.

 (i) The frequent use of ə where many people use ɪ :
  rədʒɔɪsɪŋz, rəspɛkt, bəlʌvəd.

 (ii) The ou is near to ɔu in many words : spɔukən
  but nout.

 (iii) A voiced h is used in *help* in gɒd hɛlp ɪm.

 (iv) "Linking r" is generally not used (but it occurs
  in fər aɪ m θɪŋkɪŋ) : ɔ ɪn dɪstrɛs, wɛə ɛvə juˑ ɑ,
  ɔ ɪn ɛnɪ pɑˑt əv ðɪ ɛmpaɪə. This is the only
  characteristic of those noted in Ch. XVII as
  belonging to the modern type of Southern
  English. In one place a glottal stop is used :
  auə ʔoun fæmɪlɪ əv piˑplz.

 (v) The occasional dropping of the d of *and*, and of t :
  mous mɛmərəbl, diˑpəs sɪmpəθɪ, and of h in unstressed positions. It should be noted that the
  record had to be played over a considerable
  number of times to decide whether these consonants were pronounced or not ; the omissions
  are not noticeable without very careful attention.
  This is another illustration of the naturalness
  of the speech.

PRESIDENT ROOSEVELT'S SPEECH: "FIRESIDE CHAT"

381. *Survey at the time of the special convocation of Congress, Oct. 13, 1937. First side of record.*

maɪ ˈfrɛnz, ðɪs ˈæˑftəˈnuːn aɪ əv ˈɪsjuːd ə ˈprɒkləˈmeɪʃn

ˈkɔːlɪŋ eɪ ˈspɛʃl ˈsɛʃn əv ðə ˈkɒˑŋgrəs tʊ kənˈviːn ɒn

ˈmʌndɪ, noʊˈvɛmbə ˈfɪfˈtiːnθ, ˈnaɪntiˑn ˈθɜˑtɪ ˈsɛvn.

a ˈduˑ ˈðɪs ɪn ˈɔˑdə tʊ ˈgɪv ˈtu ðə ˈkɒˑŋgrəs ən ɒpəˈtjuˑnətɪ

tʊ kənˈsɪdə ɪmˈpɔˑtnt lɛdʒɪsˈleɪʃn bəˈfɔˑ ðə ˈrɛgjʊlə ˈsɛʃn

ɪn ˈdʒænjʊərɪ, ˈænd tʊ əˈneɪbl ðə ˈkɒˑŋgrəs tʊ əˈvɔɪd

eɪ ˈlɛŋθɪ ˈsɛʃən ˈnɛkst ˑjɪə ɛksˈtɛndɪŋ ˈθru ðə ˈsʌmə.

aɪ ˈnoʊ ðət ˈmɛnɪ ˈɛnəmɪz əv dəˈmɒˑkrəsɪ wɪl ˈseɪ

ðət ɪt ɪz ˈbæˑd fə ˈbɪznəs, ˈbæˑd fə ðə træŋˈkwɪlətɪ əv

ðə ˈkʌntrɪ tə hæv ə speʃl seʃn   ˈiːvn ˈwʌn bɪˈɡɪnɪŋ

oʊnlɪ ˈsɪks ˈwiːks bəfɔː ðə ˈreɡjʊlə seʃn,   bət ˈaɪ həv

ˈnevə ˈhæd ˈsɪmpəθɪ wɪð ðə ˈpɔɪnt̮ əv ˈvjuː ðət ə ˈseʃn

əv ðə ˈkɒŋɡrəs   ɪz ən ˈʌnˈfɔːtʃənət ɪnˈtruːʒn   əv ˈhwɒt

ðeɪ kɔːl ˈpɒˈlətɪks   ɪntʊ aʊə ˈnæʃnəl (ə)ˈfeəz.   ˈðoʊz hu

ˈdu nɒt ˈlaɪk dəˈmɒkrəsɪ   ˈwɔːnt tə ˈkiːp ˈleʤɪsleɪtɔːz

ət̮ ˈfiːm.   bət ðə ˈkɒŋɡrəs   ɪz ən əˈsenʃl ˈʔɪnstrəmənt

əv ˈdeməkrætɪk ˈɡʌvənmənt,   ˈænd ˈdeməkrætɪk ˈɡʌvən-

mənt kən ˈnevə bi kənˈsɪdəd   ən ɪnˈtruːdə ɪntʊ ðɪ əˈfeəz

əv ə ˈdeməkrætɪk ˈneɪʃn.   aɪ ʃl ˈæˈsk ðɪs ˈspeʃl ˈseʃən

tʊ kənˈsɪdər əˈmiːdɪətlɪ ˈsɜːtn ɪmˈpɔːtnt leʤɪsˈleɪʃn wɪtʃ

ˈɒn maɪ ˈriˑsnt ˈtrɪp θru ðə ˈneɪʃn kənˈvɪnsɪz ˈmi ði

əˈmɛrɪkən ˈpiˑpl əˈmiːdɪətlɪ ˈniːd. ˈðɪs ˈdʌz ˈnɒt ˈmiːn

ðət ˈʌðə lɛʤɪsleɪʃn tʊ ˈwɪtʃ aɪ əm ˈnɒt rɪˈfɜɹɪŋ təˈnaɪt

ɪz ˈnɒt̯ ən ɪmˈpɔˑtnt paˑt əv auə ˈnæʃnl wɛl-ˈbiˑɪŋ, bət̯

ˈʔʌðə lɛʤɪsleɪʃn kæn bi mɔ ˈrɛdəlɪ dɪsˈkʌst æt ðə ˈrɛgjʊlə

ˈsɛʃn. ˈɛniwʌn ˈtʃaːʤd wɪð prəˈpoʊzɪŋ ɔ ˈʤʌʤɪŋ

ˈnæʃnəl ˈpɒˑləsɪz ˈʃʊd hæˑv ˈfɜˑst-hænd ˈnɒlɪʤ əv ðə

ˈneɪʃn əz ə ˈhoʊl. ˈðæt ɪz ˈhwaɪ əˈgeɪn ˈðɪs ˈjiər aɪ əv

ˈteɪkən ˈtrɪps tʊ ˈɔːl ˈpaˑts əv ðə ˈkʌntrɪ. ˈlæˑst ˈsprɪŋ

aɪ ˈvɪzɪtɪd ðə ˈsaʊθ-ˈwɛˀst: ˈðɪs ˈsʌmər aɪ meɪd ˈsɛvrəl

ˈtrɪps ɪn ðə ˈʔiːst: ˈnaʊ aɪ əm ˈʤʌst ˈbæk frəm ə ˈtrɪp

‾ · — · — · ＼ · · ｜ · ＼ · — · ｜ ·

'ɔːl ðə 'weɪ ə'krɒs ðə 'kɒːntnənt ənd 'leɪtə ðɪs 'ɔ·təm aɪ

‾ · — · ‾ · ＿ · ｜ · · ＼ · ｜ · ·

'houp tə 'peɪ maɪ 'ʔænjuəl 'vɪzɪt tə ðə 'sauθ-iːst. tʊ ə

＼ · · ＼ · ｜ · · ＼ ‿ · ＼ · — ·

'prezədənt əs'peʃəlɪ, ɪt̬ ɪz eɪ 'djuːtɪ tʊ 'θɪŋk ɪn 'næʃnəl

＼ ｜ · — · ＼ · · ＼ ‿ ｜ · ·

'tɜːmz. hiː məst 'θɪŋk 'nɒt̬ ounlɪ əv 'ðɪs jiə, bət əv

＼ · · ｜ · — · ＼ · · ＿ · ｜ ·

'fjuːtʃə jiəz wɛn 'sʌmwʌn 'ɛlts wɪl bi 'prezədnt. hi

· — · — · · — · · · · ·

məst 'luk bɪjɒnd ðɪ 'ævrɪʤ əv ðə prɒs'pərətɪ ənd 'wɛl-

＿ · · · — · ｜ · · ＼ · ‿ ｜ ‾ · · — · ＼

'biːɪŋ əv ðə 'kʌntrɪ bɪkɔz 'ævərɪʤɪz 'iːzəlɪ 'kʌvər 'ʌp

＼ · · ｜ · ＼ · ‿ · — · ＼ · · ｜ · ‾

'deɪnʤə spɒːts əv 'pɒvətɪ ənd 'ɪnstə'bɪlətɪ. hi 'mʌst

‾ — · ‾ · ＼ ｜ · · — · ＼ ·

'nɒt 'lɛt ðə 'kʌntrɪ bi də'siːvd baɪ ə 'mɪəlɪ 'tɛmpərərɪ

· ＿ · ｜ · · · · · · — · · ·

prɒs'pərətɪ wɪtʃ də'pɛndz ɒn 'weɪstful ɛksplɔɪ'teɪʃn əv

· ＿ · · ＼ ｜ · ‾ ‿ ｜ — · ‾

riː'sɔɪsɪz wɪtʃ kænɒt 'læɪst. hi 'mʌst 'θɪŋk 'nɒt̬ ounlɪ

əv ˈkiˑpɪŋ ʌs aʊt̯ əv ˈwɔː tuˈdeɪ,   bət̯ ˈɔˑlsoʊ   əv ˈkiˑpɪŋ

əs aʊt̯ əv ˈwɔːˀ ɪn ˈdʒenəreɪʃnz tə ˈkʌm.   ðɪ ˈkaɪnd əv

prɒsˈpərət̯ɪ wi ˈwɔːnt   ɪz ðə ˈsaʊnd ənd ˈpɜːmənənt kaɪnd

wɪtʃ ɪz ˈnɒt ˈbɪlt ˈʌp tempəˈræərəlɪ   ət ðɪ ɛkˈspɛns əv ɛnɪ

ˈsɛkʃn ɔ ˈgruːp,   ænd ðə ˈkaɪnd əv ˈpiˑs wi wɒːˀnt   ɪz ðə

ˈsaʊnd ənd ˈpɜːmənənt kaɪnd   wɪtʃ ɪz ˈbɪlt ʔɒn ðə ˈkoʊ-

ɒpəreɪtɪd ˈsɜˑtʃ fə ˈpiˑs   baɪ ˈɔːl ðə ˈneɪʃnz hwɪtʃ ˈwɒːnt

piˑs.   ðɪ ˈʌðə ˈdeɪ aɪ wəz ˈɑˑst tu ˈsteɪt maɪ ˈaʊt̯ˈstændɪŋ

ɪmˈprɛʃn ˈgeɪnd ɒn ðɪs ˈriˑsnt ˈtrɪp tə ðə pəˈsɪfɪk ˈkoʊst

ən bæk, ən ˈaɪ ˈsɛd ðət ɪt ˈsiːmd tə ˈmiː tə ˈbi ðə ˈdʒenərəl

ʌndəˈstændɪŋ ɒn ðə ˈpɑˑt əv ðɪ ˈʔævərɪdʒ ˈsɪt̯əzn ʌndə-

stændɪŋ əv ðə ˈbrɔːd əbˈdʒektɪvz ənd ˈpɒˑləsɪz wɪtʃ aɪ əv

ˈdʒʌst ˈautlaınd. ˈfaıv ˈjiəz əv ˈfıəs dısˈkʌʃn ənd dəˈbeıt :

ˈfaıv ˈjiəz əv ınfəˈmeıʃn θru ðə ˈreıdıou ənd ðə ˈmuˑvıŋ

ˈpıktʃə hæv ˈteıkən ðə ˈhoul ˈneıʃn tu ˈskuːl ın ðə

ˈneıʃnz ˈbıznəs.

NOTES ON THE PRONUNCIATION: INTERPRETATION OF THE PHONETIC TRANSCRIPTION.

382. *Vowels and Diphthongs.*

ı   A low variety is used ; it is difficult to say whether unstressed ı or the neutral vowel ə is used in words like *because, citizen,* which sound near to bəkɔːz, sətəzən. Final ı is closer than is usual in British English ; it is between ı and i.

ɛ   A fairly open variety is used ; in the word *west* it is lengthened and diphthongised, wɛɪ°st. When followed by r, e.g. in the word *American* it is very much centralised, nearing ɜ, and liable to English ears to be confused with ɜ + r. Comparison of the two words *American* and *referring,* however, shows them to be different, the former having a distinct ɛ quality and the latter being a rather close central vowel.

æ   A little lower than Southern English æ. It is often long and is diphthongised in the word *last* (læ°st). Note its use in *temporarily* (tɛmpərærəlı).

ɒ　This symbol has been used throughout the text, but must be taken to represent a sound somewhat like cardinal ɑ (cf. § 371, p. 211). It gives the impression of some slight lip-rounding, however. In stressed positions it is considerably longer than the corresponding sound in British English.

ɔ　A fairly close variety, with more lip-rounding than cardinal No. 6; it is very similar to British English ɔ. In the word *war* (the second time it is used when it has emphatic stress and a fall-rise intonation) it sounds diphthongised.[1]

ʌ　More central than the normal Southern English variety, nearing ɜ.

ɜ　A close variety, near the e–o-line.

ə　The neutral vowel is used very frequently where many English people use ɪ.

oʊ　The first element is verging on ɔ;[2] in the word *home*, a pure vowel is used, between o and ɔ.

ɑʊ　The first element is further back than in normal Southern English: in the word *outstanding* it is almost ɔʊ.

ɪə　In strongly stressed positions, where lengthening of the diphthong is a sign of emphasis, iə is frequently used: e.g. *five years*.

There is no noticeable nasalisation.

[1] There may also be retroflexion of the tongue, giving slight impression of ɻ.

[2] This wide diphthong ɔu was also noted in the speech of the President of Harvard, which was broadcast on 29th March, 1938, when the words *ago*, *both*, *only* were pronounced əgɔu, bɔuθ, ɔunlɪ.

383. *Consonants.*

(a) The letter r is not pronounced before consonants or finally except as a linking r.

(b) r is the retroflex fricative; the inversion of the tongue is noticeable between vowels, but not in the groups tr, pr, kr, gr, etc.

(c) t is generally voiced (t̬) between vowels unless there is a pause. In one or two places, however, it sounds voiceless.

(d) l is dark in all positions.

(e) ʃ is dark; it is noticeable in the word *impression*.

384. *Stress and Rhythm.*

(a) Much of the stress and rhythm is very close to that of British English.

(b) The "push" on the vowels for emphasis (see § 375 a, p. 214) is noticeable.

(c) Strong forms are used frequently: *does, not, to,* generally have the forms dʌz, nɒt, tʊ, or tu, *and* is usually ænd (or æn) whenever it follows a pause, but in closely related phrases it is ən: e.g. əkrɒs ðə pəsɪfɪk ən bæ·k; *a* in two places occurs as eɪ. In the word *legislators*, the last syllable is pronounced tɔːz; *November* is noʊvɛmbə.

(d) A number of unimportant words are given importance by a high pitch: e.g. *I* and *and* at the beginning of sentences.

(e) Where the rhythm differs from that of many British English speakers, it is due to

    (i) The use of strong forms as described under (c) together with the spacing out of and slight

stressing of short and what might be considered unimportant words: e.g. ˈðɪs ˈdʌz
ˈnɒt ˈmiːn. This is not, of course, an in-
variable characteristic of American speech :
the record is much more deliberate than
conversation would be.

(ii) The use of longer forms of individual words :
e.g. *immediately* is pronounced əmiˈdɪətlɪ,
whereas in British English it would probably
be ɪmiˈdjətlɪ ; *January* is ʤænjuərɪ as
against djænjʊrɪ ; *temporarily* is tɛmpəˈrærɪlɪ
as against ˈtɛmpərərəlɪ ; and *resources* is
risɔːsɪz as compared with rɪsɔːsɪz.

385. *Intonation.*

(1) The groupings and distribution of Tunes I and II
are very similar to those of normal British English.
(2) Many of the intonation patterns are the same.
(3) The typical fall on a number of stressed syllables
in one group is frequent (see § 375, p. 213).
(4) Note the rise-fall or rise-level intonation for
emphasis (see *Handbook of English Intonation*).

FROM *Pygmalion*, ACT II, p. 119, BY G. BERNARD SHAW.
386. NOTES ON THE PRONUNCIATION OF COCKNEY.

In one type of Cockney, the *t*'s and *d*'s in stressed
positions would probably be affricated, i.e. pronounced
as tˢ and dˣ: this is marked in one case only where
there is extra stress. The diphthong in the word *pay*
(normal peɪ) is represented here by aɪ: the first element
should be pronounced somewhat retracted and centralised, i.e. between cardinal No. 4 and ʌ.

387. *Mrs. Pearce.* ə ˈjʌŋ ˈwʊmən wɒnts tə ˈsiː jʊ, sɜˈ.

Higgins. ə ˈjʌŋ ˈwʊmən ! ˈwɒt dəz ʃɪ ˈwɒnt?

Mrs. Pearce. ˈwɛl, sɜˈ, ʃɪ ˈsez juˈl bɪ ˈɡlæd tə ˈsiː hɜ wɛn
jʊ ˈnoʊ wɒt ʃɪˈ z ˈkʌm əbaʊt. ʃɪˈz ˈkwaɪt ə ˈkɒmən
ɡɜːl, sɜˈ, ˈvɛrɪ kɒmən ɪnˈdiːd. aɪ ʃʊd əv ˈsɛnt hɜr
əˈweɪ, oʊnlɪ aɪ ˈθɔˈt pəhæps jʊ ˈwɒntɪd hɜ tə ˈtɔˈk
ɪntə ˈwʌn ə jɔə məˈʃiːnz. aɪ ˈhoʊp aɪ v ˈnɒt dʌn
ˈrɒŋ ; bət ˈrɪəlɪ jʊ ˈsiˈ sʌʧ ˈkwɪə ˈpiˈpl̩ səmˈtaɪmz—
juˈl ɪksˈkjuːz mi, aɪ m ˈʃʊə, sɜˈ—

Higgins. oʊ ˈðæts ɔˈl raɪt, mɪsɪz pɪəs. ˈhæz ʃɪ ən
ˈɪntrəstɪŋ ˈæksnt?

Mrs. Pearce. ˈoʊ, ˈsʌmθɪŋ ˈdredfʊl, sɜˈ, ˈrɪəlɪ. aɪ
ˈdoʊnt ˈnoʊ haʊ jʊ kən ˈteɪk ən ˈɪntrəst ɪn ɪt.

Higgins. ˈlɛts hæv ər ˈʌp. ˈʃoʊ ər ˈʌp, mɪsɪz pɪəs.

Mrs. Pearce. ˈvɛrɪ ˈwɛl, sɜˈ, ɪts fə ˈjuː tə ˈseɪ.

Higgins. ðɪs ɪz ˈrɑˈðər ə ˈbɪt əv ˈlʌk. aɪ l ˈʃoʊ jʊ haʊ
aɪ ˈmeɪk ˈrɛkɔˈdz. wiːl ˈsɛt hɜ ˈtɔˈkɪŋ ; ˈaɪl teɪk ɪt
ˈdaʊn ˈfɜˈst ɪn ˈbɛlz ˈvɪzɪbl̩ ˈspiˈʧ ; ˈðɛn ɪn ˈbrɔːd
ˈroʊmɪk ; ən ˈðɛn wiːl ˈɡɛt hɜr ɒn ðə ˈfoʊnəɡrɑˈf
soʊ ðət jʊ kən ˈtɜːn hɜr ˈɒn əz ˈɒfn̩ əz jʊ ˈlaɪk wɪð
ðə ˈrɪtn̩ ˈtrɑˈnskrɪpt bɪˈfɔˈ jʊ.

Mrs. Pearce. ˈðɪs ɪz ðə jʌŋ wʊmən, sɜˈ.

Higgins. ˈwaɪ, ˈðɪs ɪz ðə ˈɡɜːl aɪ ˈʤɒtɪd ˈdaʊn ˈlɑˈs ˈnaɪt.
ˈʃiːz noʊ juˈs : aɪv ˈɡɒt ɔˈl ðə ˈrɛkɔˈdz aɪ ˈwɒnt əv
ðə ˈlɪsn̩ ˈɡroʊv lɪŋɡoʊ ; ənd aɪm ˈnɒt ɡoɪŋ tə ˈweɪst
əˈnʌðə ˈsɪlɪndər ɒn ɪt. bɪ ˈɒf wɪð jʊ : aɪ ˈdoʊnt
ˈwɒnt jʊ.

The Flower Girl. ˈdãũʔ ˈjiꜰ ˈbəi ˈsʌʊ ˈsɔːsəi. jiꜰ ˈʔĩa
ˈɜˈd wɒʔ aɪ ˈkam fɔː ˈjɪʔ. dɪʤə ˈtel ɪm aɪ ˈkam ɪn
ə ˈtɛksəi?

Mrs. Pearce. 'nɒnsns, gɜ·l ‖ 'wɒt djʊ 'θɪŋk ə 'gɛntlmən laɪk 'mɪstə 'hɪgɪnz 'kɛəz 'wɒt jʊ keɪm ɪn?

The Flower Girl. 'ʌʊ, wɪ 'ɑː 'prɑːd ! 'ãĩ? ə'bʌv 'gɪvɪn 'lesnz 'nɒ? 'ɪm: aɪ 'ɜ·d ɪm 'saɪ sʌʊ. 'weɔ, aɪ 'ãĩ? kam 'ijə tʊ 'ɑ·s fər enɪ 'kɒmplɪmən? ; ən ɪf 'maːɪ 'manɪz 'nɒ? 'gʊd ɪnaf, aɪ kŋ 'gʌʊ eɔs'weə.

Higgins. 'gʊd ɪnʌf fə 'wɒt?

The Flower Girl. 'gʊd ɪnaf fə 'jiːʉ: "naː jə 'nʌʊ, 'dʌ̃ʊ̃ntʃə? aɪ m 'kam tə ɛv 'lesnz 'ɑːɪ ɛm, ən 'paɪ fər əm "tˢiʉ ; 'maɪ? nʌʊ mɪs'taɪ?.

Higgins. 'wɛl ‖ 'wɒt djʊ ɪk'spɛkt mɪ tə 'seɪ tə jʊ?

The Flower Girl. 'weɔ, ɪf jə wəz ə 'dʒẽ?ɔmən. jə mãĩ? 'ɑ·s mɪ tə 'sɪ 'daːn, 'aɪ θĩ?. 'dʌʊn aɪ 'tel jə aɪ m 'brɪŋɪn jə 'bɪznɪs?.

Higgins. 'pɪkərɪŋ, 'ʃæl wɪ 'ɑ·sk ðɪs 'bægɪdʒ tə 'sɪt 'daʊn, ɔ 'ʃæl wɪ 'θrʊʊ ər 'aʊt əv ðə 'wɪndʊʊ?

The Flower Girl. "ʌʌʌ ... ʊʊʊ ... aɪ' wʌ̃ʊ̃?bɪ 'kɔːd ə 'bɛgɪdʒ wen aɪ v 'ɒfəd tə 'paɪ laɪk 'enɪ 'laɪdɪ.

Pickering. 'wɒt ɪz ɪt jʊ 'wɒnt, maɪ gɜːl?

The Flower Girl. aɪ 'wõ? tə bəi ə 'laɪdɪ ɪn ə 'flɑːʃɒp 'sted ə 'selɪn ə? ðə 'ko·nər ə 'tɒ?nəm 'ko·? 'rʌʊd, bət ðɛɪ 'wʌ̃ʊ̃? 'taɪ? mɪ an'les aɪ kŋ 'to·k mo· dʒen'tɪɔ. 'əi sed ɪ kʊd 'təitʃ məi. 'weɔ, 'ijər aɪ 'ɛm 'redɪ tə 'paɪ ɪm—'nɒ? 'ɑ·stɪn enɪ 'faɪvə—ən ɪ 'trəi?s mɪ əz ɪf ɑ wəz 'dɜ·?.

Mrs. Pearce. 'haʊ kən jʊ bi sʌtʃ ə 'fuˑlɪʃ 'ɪgnərənt 'gɜːl əz tə 'θɪŋk jʊ kʊd ə'fɔːd tə 'peɪ mɪstə 'hɪgɪnz?

The Flower Girl. waɪ 'ʃʊdn aɪ? aɪ 'nʌʊ wɒ? 'lesnz 'kɔːst əz 'wel əz 'jiʉ diʉ ; ən aɪm 'redɪ tə 'paɪ.

Higgins. ˈhaʊ ˈmʌtʃ.

The Flower Girl. ˈnaː jə ˈtoːkɪn. ɑɪ ˈθoˈʔ jəd kam ˈɔːf ɪʔ wen jə ˈsoˈr ə ˈtʃɑːns ə ˈgeʔɪn ˈbɛʔ ə ˈbɪʔ ə ˈwɒʔ jə ˈtʃaʔt əʔ məi ˈlɑˈs ˈnãĩʔ. jəd ˈɛd ə ˈdrɒp ˈɪn, ˈɛntʃəʔ

Higgins. ˈsɪt ˈdaʊn.

The Flower Girl. ˈʌʊ, ɪf jə ˈgʌɪnə maɪʔ ə ˈkɒmplɪmənʔ ɒv ɪʔ—

Higgins. ˈsɪt ˈdaʊn.

Mrs. Pearce. ˈsɪt ˈdaʊn, gɜːl, ˈduː əz jʊə ˈtoʊld.

The Flower Girl. ˈʌʌʌ . . . ʊʊʊ . . .

Pickering. ˈwoʊnt jʊ sɪt ˈdaʊn?

The Flower Girl. ˈdãʊ̃ʔ ˈmãĩn ɪf ɑɪ ˈdɨʉ.

Higgins. ˈwɒts jɔ ˈneɪm?

The Flower Girl. ˈlaɪzə ˈdɨʉlɪʔɔ.

FROM *The Good Companions,* BY J. B. PRIESTLEY, p. 32.

388. NOTE ON THE PRONUNCIATION OF YORKSHIRE.

The transcriber has endeavoured to represent a type of Yorkshire (Bruddersford) pronunciation which would be used by a man like Jess Oakroyd, but it is not the only possible pronunciation: it is probably one degree removed from the broadest dialect of that part of Yorkshire both in pronunciation and vocabulary.

389. ðə ˈnɛkst ˈmoʊmənt hi ˈwɒz ðɛə, ə ˈgraɪmɪ, ˈhɒt ənd ˈæŋgrɪ ˈmæn hu ˈflʌŋ hɪz ˈkæp ənd hɪz ˈbæg əv ˈdʒɔɪnəz ˈtuːlz ˈdaʊn ɒn ðə ˈsoʊfə, ˈðɛn ˈkloʊzd ɔɪ ˈaʊtə ˈdɔə wɪð ə ˈbæŋ. " ˈwiər ɪ ðə ˈneːm ə ˈgʊdnəs av jə ˈbɪin? " hɪz ˈwaɪf dɪˈmɑˈndɪd. " ən jə ˈtɪi ˈweːtɪn ˈiər ə ˈfʊl ˈaːr ən ə ˈaːf ! "

" ˈbɹiːn ɒn tə t ˈɹuːnɪən ɒfɪs," hi ˈɑˑnsəd ˈʃɔˑtlɪ. ʃi
ˈglɑˑnst ət hɪz ˈfeɪs ən ˈðɛn ˈmɒdəreɪtɪd hə ˈtoʊn. " ˈwɒ?
djə wɒnt tə goˑ ˈðiə fɒr ət ˈðɪs taɪm? "

" kɒz av bɹiːn ˈstɒpt." hi ˈbɛnt ˈdaʊn ən bɪˈgæn tu
ˈʌnˈleɪs hɪz ˈhɛvɪ ˈwɜˑkɪŋ ˈbuˑts.

" jəv bɹiːn ˈwɒt?" hɪz ˈwaɪf ˈʃɹiˑkt.

" ˈstɒpt, ˈsakt, ˈpeɪd ˈɒf, wɒˈtɪvə jə ˈwɒnt tə ˈkɔːl ɪt."
hi ˈstreɪtnd hɪmsɛlf ən ˈθruː ən ɪnˈʃʊərəns kɑːd ən səm
ˈmʌnɪ ɒn ðə ˈteɪbl. " am ˈnɒt ɹiˑvn ʊndə ˈnoˑtɪs. ˈɪgdɪnz
əz ˈfɪnɪʃt wɪ mə, ən ˈaːv ˈfɪnɪʃt wɪ ˈðɛm. ðəz ə ˈwiːks
ˈmʊnɪ ˈðiə." hi bɪˈgæn tu ʌnˈleɪs ðɪ ˈʌðə buˑt.

" ˈwɛl a ˈnɪvə ˈdɪd l" ˈkɹaɪd mɪsɪz ˈoʊkrɔɪd. ʃi ˈflɒpt
ˈdaʊn ɪntʊ ə ˈtʃɛə ənd rɪˈgɑˑdɪd hɪm wɪð ðɪ ˈʌtmoʊst
əsˈtɒnɪʃmənt. " ˈwɒt a jə bɹiːn ˈdʊʊɪn?"

" aɪ ˈtɛl jə ɔːl əˈbaːt ɪt ɪn ə ˈmɪnɪt. a ˈwɒnt ə ˈwɛʃ
ən ˈsʊmət tə ˈɛɪt." hi ˈmatʃt ɪn hɪz ˈstɒkɪŋd ˈfiˑt tɔːdz
ðə ˈskʌlərɪ. " ˈgɛ? mɪ ˈtɹi rɛdɪ ən ðɛn jəl ˈsʊɪn ˈnɔː wɒt
av bɹiːn dʊʊɪn," hi ˈædɪd ˈgrɪmlɪ.

ɪn ˈbrʌdəsfəd ˈwaɪvz ˈdoʊnt ˈstænd ɒn ˈsɛrɪmənɪ ət
sʌtʃ ˈmoʊmənts əv ˈkraɪsɪs, ən ˈmɪsɪz ˈoʊkrɔɪd, wɪðaʊt ə
ˈwɜˑd əv ˈproʊtest, ˈmeɪd ðə ˑuː ənd rɪˈliˑst ðə ˈkɪpə frəm
ɪts ˈlɒŋ ɔˑˈdiəl.

" ɪf ˈðɪs iə ˈfɪʃ əd ə bɹiːn bɪ t ˈfaɪər ə ˈmɪnɪt ˈlɒŋə," sɛd
ˈmɪstər ˈoʊkrɔɪd, ˈnaʊ ˈsiˑtɪd ət ðə ˈteɪbl, " ɪt əd ə ˈstaˑtɪd
ˈwaˑpɪn. ɪts ˈlaɪk ə ˈbɪt ə ˈbʌrn? ˈwʊd."

" ˈapm ɪts ˈlast jəl ˈsɪi fər ə bɪt," hɪz ˈwaɪf rɪˈtɔˑtɪd,
hæviŋ biˑn ˈraʊzd baɪ ðɪs grəˈtjuɪtəs ˈsælɪ. " ˈnɛvə
ˈmaɪnd əbaˑ? ˈðaʔ. ˈwɒt av jə ˈgɒ?n ˈstɒpt fɒ?"

" fə ˈnɔʊt, ˈdʒʊs ˈnɔʊt," hi bɪgæn, " ər ɪf jə ˈlaˑɪk fə
ˈbɹiːn ə ˈman ən ˈnʊt ə ˈdamd ˈmʊŋkɪ." hi ˈstɒpt tə
ˌteɪk ə ˈdrɪŋk əv ˈtiː, ˈðɛn, ˈpɔɪntɪŋ hɪz ˈfɔˑk ət mɪsɪz
oʊkrɔɪd, hi rɪˈzjuːmd : " ˈðɪs ˈmɔˑnɪn a ˈadnt ə ˈwagən

ɪn, ən soː wə ˈdʊʊɪn nɔʊt fər ə bɪt.   ˈsɪmsn̩, t ˈʊndə-
manɪʤə, ˈkʊmz ˈʊp ən ˈsɛz, ʻ ˈwɒt ə jə ˈɒn wɪð, oˈkrɔɪd?ʼ
ən a ˈtɛlz ɪm ʻ ˈnɔʊ? ʤʊs ˈnaː.ʼ   ðəˑ ˈpʊtɪn ʊp ə ˈtɛmpərɪ
ˈʃɛd fə? t ˈwagənz, ən so ˈsɪmsn̩ ˈsɛz ʻ ˈwɛl, ˈɛlp wɪ t ˈʃɛd.
jə kŋ ˈstaˑt bɪ ˈgɛtɪn ˈðɪs ɪntə ʃɛːp.ʼ   ən ɪ ˈpɔɪnts tʊ ə
ˈbiəm ðe ˈpʊld aˑt ət t ˈɔʊd ʃɛd, ən ɪ ˈfɪnz t ˈmɛʒəments
fɒ mɪ.   so a ˈbɒrəz ə ˈaks, ən ə ˈbɪg ˈkrɒs kʊt ˈsɔː ən
ˈgɛ?s tə ˈwɜːk ə ˈðɪs iə ˈbiəm.   a ˈavnt briːn ˈat ɪt mʊə
nə ˈtɛn ˈmɪnɪts wɛn ə ˈtʃap ˈtaps mə ɒnt ˈbak.   a ˈdoˑnt
ˈnɔː ɪm bʊd a ˈnɔː ɪz ˈwʊn ə t ˈʃɒp-strɪuədz.   ˈən ˈwɛn
dɪd ˈjʊuː ʤɔɪn t ˈkaˑpɪntəz ˈɪunɪən, ˈkʊmreːd?ʼ ɪ sɛz,
ˈvərɪ ˈnastɪ.   ʻ ˈwɒ? djə ˈmiən,ʼ a sɛz ðo a ˈnɪu wɒ? wəz
ˈkʊmɪn.   ɪ ˈpɔɪntɪd tə t ˈbiəm :   ˈˈðats ə ˈkaˑpɪntəz ʤɒb l̩ʼ
ɪ sɛz, ʻ ən ˈjʊu krɪp ˈɒf ɪt, ˈkʊmreːd.ʼ   a ˈgɪv ɪm ə ˈlʊuk.
ʻ ˈkʊmreːd l̩ʼ a sɛz, ˈˈmaˑɪ ˈgɒd l̩ʼ ʻ av ˈnoˑtɪst ˈjɪu ˈwʊns
ə ˈtwaɪs,ʼ ɪ sɛz, ʻ ən ɪts ˈstrʊk mɪ jəv gɒ? t ˈmɛkɪnz əv ə
ˈblaklɛg,ʼ ɪ sɛz.   ʻ ən ˈsʊmət ˈɛls l̩ straɪk jə ɪn ə ˈmɪnɪt,
meːt, ɪf jə ˈsteː ˈiə ˈkɔˑlɪn ˈmiː ˈneːmz, a sɛz.   ʻ wɛl ˈlɪiv
ˈða? ˈʤɒb əˈloːn,ʼ ɪ sɛz, ən ˈwɔˑks ˈɒf.   ən əv ˈkʊəs a
ˈad tʊu.ˈˈ

hi ˈpɔːzd fə rɪˈfrɛʃmənt, ənd hɪz ˈwaɪf ˈstɛəd ət hɪm
ən ˈsɛd ðət ʃi ˈdɪdnt ˈnʊʊ wɒtˈɛvə ˈθɪŋz wə ˈkʌmɪŋ tuː.

ʻʻ ˈwɛl, ˈlɛ? mə ˈfɪnɪʃ,ʼʼ sɛd mɪstər ʊʊkrɔɪd, əz ɪf ʃi əd
biːn prɪvɛntɪŋ hɪm.   ʻʻ so ad ˈnʊʊt tə ˈdʊʊ əgiən.   ˈbaɪ
ən ˈbaɪ ˈsɪmsn̩ kʊmz ˈraːnd əgiən, ˈðɪs taɪm wɪ? t ˈmanɪʤə
ɪsˈsɛn, ˈʊʊd bʊc ˈɪˑclɪ.   ðe ˈtakɪn ə ˈkwɪk ˈlɪʊk ˈraːnd ən
ˈsɪɪm ə ˈbɪt ˈflʊstəd.   ˈθɔˑlɪ ˈsɪiz ˈmiː.   ʻ ˈwɒ?s ˈðɪs man
ˈdʊʊɪn,ʼ ɪ asks.   ʻ ˈɛɪ, oˈkrɔɪd,ʼ ˈsɪmsn̩ ˈʃaːts əˈkrɒs,
ˈgɛr ɒn wɪ ˈða? ʤɒb ən ˈʃaˑp əˈbaːt ɪt.ʼ   ʻ a ˈkãˑk gɛr ɒn
wɪ ɪt,ʼ a ʃaˑts bak, ən ˈmʊuvz əˈkrɒs tə ˈtɛl əm.   ʻ ˈgo
ˈɒn, man ˈgo ˈɒn, man, ˈgo ˈɒn l̩ʼ sɛz ʊʊd θɔˑlɪ, ˈweˑvɪn
ɪz ˈand at mɪ, ən ˈaɪt ðe ˈgoːz.   ət ˈdɪnə taˑɪm, a ˈiəz

ðat t ˈɡreːt ˈman ɪsˈsɛlf, ˈsɜː ˈdʒɔːzɪf ˈɪɡdɪn, baːt,—ən ɪz
ˈfaðə wə ˈnɒbət ə ˈwɛɪvɪn ˈɔʊəlʊukə laɪk ˈmaːɪn—ɪz ˈɒn
t ˈprɛmɪsɪz. a ˈnɪu ˈnaː waɪ t ˈmanɪdʒəz wə sə ˈflʊstəd.
ʻ aɪ ˈbɛʔ ðə ˈkʊtɪn ˈsʊmət ˈdaːn,ʼ a sɛz. əbaˑʔ ˈθrɪi əˈtɪŋk
ðe ˈlanz ɪ ˈaː dɪpaˑtmɛnt, ˈsɜː ˈdʒɔˑzɪf ən ˈθɔˑlɪ, wɪ ˈsɪmsn
brˈaɪnd. a ˈsɪi ˈsɜː ˈdʒɔˑsɪf ˈwɛˑv ɪz ˈand. ðɛn ˈθɔˑlɪ
ˈlʊuks ˈraːnd, ən a ˈsɪi ɪm ˈlʊuk əʔ ˈmɪi ən ðɛn ˈseˑ sʊmət
tə ˈsɪmsn. ɪn ə ˈmɪnɪt ə tʊu, ˈsɪmsn ˈkʊmz ˈʊp ən ˈsez,
ʻ am ˈsɒrɪ oˑkrɔɪd, bʊt jəl ˈɛ tə ˈtak ə ˈwɪiks ˈnoˑtɪs.ʼ
ʻ ˈwɒʔ ˈfɒʔʼ a sɛz, ʻ ˈwɒt av a ˈdʊnʔʼ ʻ ɪts jər ˈɔːn ˈfɒlt,ʼ
ɪ sɛz, ʻ ðəz ˈsoː mɒnɪ tə bɪ ˈstɒpt, ən jə ˈsʊdnt ə ˈlɛʔ mɪstə
ˈθɔˑlɪ ˈsɪi jə ðɪs ˈmɔˑnɪn.ʼ ʻ ɪʔ wə ˈnoˑ ˈfɒlt ə ˈmaːɪn,ʼ
a sɛz, ʻ ən aˑm ˈɡoɪn tə av ə ˈwɜːd wɪ mɪstə θɔˑlɪ.ʼ ən
a ˈdɪd av ə wɜːd wɪ ɪm, ən ə ˈfaʔ ˈlɒt ə ˈɡʊd ɪʔ ˈdɪd mə.
a brˈɡɪnz tə ˈtɛl ɪm ˈaː ˈlɒŋ ad ˈbɪin ðiə, ən ɪ ˈkʊts mɪ
ˈʃɔˑt ən sɛz ˈsʊm əv ʊz ˈɔʊdə ˈmɛn ɪz əz ˈaɪdl əz t ˈjʊŋ
ənz ɪsˈtɛd ə ˈsɛtɪn ə ɛɡˈzampl. ˈðaʔ wər ɪˈnʊf fə ˈmɪi,
ən a ˈsɛz sʊmət a ˈsʊdnt ə sɛd. ʻ ˈpeː ɪm ˈɒf ən ˈɡɪv ɪm
ɪz ˈkaːd,ʼ ɪ sɛz. ˈðɪs ˈman z ˈfɪnɪʃt wɪ ˈɪɡdɪnz fə ˈɡʊd
ən ˈɔːl.ʼ ˮ

Appendix I

SUGGESTED COURSE OF SPEECH TRAINING IN COLLEGES OF EDUCATION

This scheme is drawn up on the basis of sixty hours work spread over two years, the amount recommended in the Report on the Teaching of English in England. It is possible to give lectures and ear-training to a fairly large number of students at once, but the practical work should be done in groups of not more than fifteen.

The work should consist of:

(*a*) VOICE TRAINING, particularly for those who need it. The simplest outline only of the vocal mechanism is necessary. Exercises on breath control, on relaxation, on the cultivation of clear and pleasing tone, on the avoidance of a high-pitched voice.

(*b*) PHONETIC THEORY. An outline of the formation of English sounds and their distribution in ordinary speech: chief dialectal sounds; how to teach normal sounds, clear articulation, etc., how to get rid of particular defects of speech. If time is to be economised, some parts of the theory can be studied by the students from books.

(*c*) EAR TRAINING. This is most important: each student should have a short ear-training class a week, in which, at first, ordinary English sounds only are used, in meaningless words (such as those given in Appendix II). Later dialectal variants can be introduced, and non-English sounds.

(*d*) PRACTICAL WORK. Exercises for the control of the organs of speech, the making of sounds by the students themselves, sounds of all kinds, those of standard English, of the modified standards, of dialects, of foreign languages. Exercises in usual and unusual combinations of consonants.

Analysis and comparison of the pronunciation of the students; this is again a most valuable form of ear-training, and if approached in the right spirit, is not likely to be misunderstood or resented by the students themselves.[1]

Discussions of questions of theory and methods of teaching: what is to be taught in different parts of the country, and corrected in individuals.

The students should do regular exercises—which need not be long—in transcribing phonetically their own pronunciation, particularly in colloquial speech.

SUGGESTED ARRANGEMENT OF THE WORK.

[The original edition gave a timetable here.
It is omitted in view of the changes in
curricular balance in present-day
Colleges of Education.]

[1] Note to 3rd Edition.   It will be realised that broadcast speech provides an excellent field for the study and comparison of variant pronunciations, and for ear training.

Appendix II

EAR-TRAINING EXERCISES

I. Containing English Sounds only.

(a) Simple.

ˈbɑˈɡʌnət	ˈθuɡlnaɪt	ˈfloʊzˈdʒʌɡpæt
ˈteɪbloʊˈnæp	ˈnoʊmˈbɛtl	ˈvwɔɡˈjʌn
blɛtʃk	ˈbeɪˈnɪdʒnɔ	ˈblætlɛtˈjɔɡ
ˈfrudʒˈdɜvz	ˈbʌdɪˈðændaɪɡ	ˈlɔɪˈvɜnɪ
ˈfkuðɔ	ˈflaɪtˈsɪtʃkri	ˈpeɪˈmoʊθ
ʌbˈlɪtkɑ	ˈɡloʊnɪəˈlaɪkɜ	ˈbaɪɡŋpʌtʃ
ˈætʃˈɡɔvɪɡ	ˈθeɪˈnɒp	ˈsifθɡlɜə
ˈvroəˈtsɛk	ˈfuɡrɒʃʌð	ˈʃteɪklˈpoʊtʃ
ˈpɒŋkˈtɪədaɪb	θrɔtsk	ˈbɜlɪˈfʊstə
ˈɪŋɡaɪθˈbɔɪtn	ʃkʊtʃˈtlɪə	ˈʃtɛɡliˈɡɒtʃ
ˈplɑɡənaɪf	ˈfɒzˈbɔnɪ	ˈkɔdʌntˈblæɡz
ˈfɑˈnʌtpaɪð	ˈjɪdˈnoʊv	ˈnaɪˈðɛtɪpɜ
pʊˈbaɪtl	ˈdʒɔɪˈflʌndə	ˈpænˈɡrɒmɪtʊs
ˈfɑθˈtrɔɪb		

(b) More difficult.

ʃpʃæsps	ˈlaɪprˈðɛəɡʌn	ˈθsnɪpɪtθs
ˈpfɛtˈɡɑvɪɡʌdʒ	ɡŋaɪŋɡ	ˈsɜndoʊˈvɔkɒk
ˈjɛntsɪˈpæʃndɔf	ˈnɛvɪˈpaʊðəˈdʊə	ˈʃkrudɜˈnɪbtʊ
ˈrɔtˈmɑɡənæŋ	ˈtsvaʊbʃɪə	ˈdʒæfkˈsoʊɡæ
ˈtɛpɑkˈnaʊb	ˈflætɪˈŋaʊˈfɛðz	ʃfeɪðpi
ˈpætɪˈŋɔvmʊ	ˈflɛɡɪˈbætəpʊl	ˈdɒnɪˈaɪkə

ˈidnˈkeɪtəʃk	ˈθkɛksˈtʃaʊndʒ	ˈtnærɪpm
ˈgrglˈðaɪvz	ˈfklaɪpsˈplʊdʒ	kʃˈpɒðəˈvɪə
ˈbounɪˈɒtˈgaɪðə	ˈzɔlʌŋˈbourɪəˈgæt	ˈæθɪˈðɛəvətɒf
ˈpʊθˈklɛəbətɒfk	ˈknaɪˈpfɛkʃɪə	ˈθɛstsˈpʌ
ˈblounɪˈaʊvɪˈɔɪ	fɪsθs	ˈθpɪdˈvɛstθs
ˈʒnɪlˈmeɪŋəsouf	ˈgrouglˈpʃɒk	ˈaʃpˈdreɪbzku
pʃguf	ˈdlɪəˈʃɛksʌz	ˈklɪəgɛəˈvraɪbm
ˈtɔˈpaʊəfl	ˈgɒdnˈfɪəʒ	ˈpʃkætʃˈkɔflkaug
ˈsθpɪkəlɛt	ˈbɒkəˈnɔtʃɛə	ˈθraʊfˈrɪəp
ˈkrɪkˈtæθɪdɔp	ˈŋɪdlʌtˈfɛəθbru	ˈprʌtˈθɑˈðɔkl

(c)   *Still more difficult, including some dialectal diphthongs.*

ˈneɪlpʃɛtʃˈkʃaɪv	ˈdzɔʊvɒdʒʌdz	ˈgŋɔvnˈpæʔudʒ
ˈʒnaʊglˈmɜgŋ	ˈʃuʒˈpʌskʃəi	ˈʃklɛʔəpɪkənɪb
pʊθˈklɛəbəˈtɒfkʃ	ˈŋgaɪnˈdɒʔinbʌ	ɜʒˈŋɛkfθ
ˈwɛlɪouˈjaɪnə	ststaɪŋs	ˈdlʌʔˈnɪəgəmeɪʔ
ˈʒlɛɪgŋˈbavɪdɛk	fʃɛˈkatʃɪˈkɒpf	gŋɔgŋ
ˈoʊlɪˈɒdʒɪˈnaɪʃn	ˈkhuriˈʃəupskŋ	kŋɪlˈjɛbɪtʃkʃ
ˈmæntriuklɔr	əbˈsʌnvɪg	ˈbzmjaɪˈfʌʃl
ˈɛəðpʌkˈŋɪlɛɪ	ˈtnɛɪzˈtʃatrʌnst	ɬʊbʃˈkraʊŋɛʃ
ˈpjuʃmækˈwaʊðg	ˈŋɒlˈpmaɪðŋ	ˈzgʊntˈnɔʊljəˈraɪ
ˈtʌnɪˈlætəfˈlatnbaʊə	ˈŋguˈphinɑθˈliə	ˈðɪθwɜðˈpðɪθ
ˈtnɔufˈkleəˈbouʒ	ɬɛɪbʌtɪθæŋ	ˈblʌɪfʊtnoi
ˈæɪdʌˈnɔu	ˈʒɪθɪksˈpɔɪ	ˈskiuˈgɛtəməi

II.   CONTAINING A FEW NON-ENGLISH CONSONANTS AND
        CARDINAL VOWELS, IN ADDITION TO ENGLISH
        SOUNDS.

[*For the values of the non-English symbols, see List of
        Symbols.*]

ǰɪknaɪfθ	ŋaɪçpɔrɪvʒnɛk	ŋaɪpm̩kakʄ
eglpɒtʃkɛ	ɬepɛɪtɛʃkæ	lɔvɛʒapoç

njuzvatʃjɛklɑ   noblfʃɛkspʃ   zgyntwoʊbm
ʃnuglfɛədlnɒt   tjuneçabux   l̥ybiteçop
goxəçaɪl̥u   nobkapm̥pʌŋk   ŋgaɪgŋfaɪç
ŋoʊvpeʔlda   bøniflygatʃ   ŋopmɔʊθ
çɛəbɪktibøʔ   ʃaθɛspɪç   aheogəʔut
lɔxkɧpat   axalepotʃ   zmaɪtəpeɪpsjun
flaʊnɛl̥y   laɲipʊtlbʌʔ   dnʌtlɛətn̥
anfijɛx   nʃærɛmpm̥   ŋgəriaʃexi
dɪɪbõʌʔlbzwaʊn   faʔʊllibetax   mlytʃvrki

BIBLIOGRAPHY

GENERAL PHONETICS AND PHONOLOGY

Abercrombie, D., *Elements of General Phonetics*, Edinburgh University Press, 1967.

Brosnahan, L. F., and Malmberg, B., *Introduction to Phonetics*, Heffer, Cambridge, 1970.

Firth, J. R., *The Tongues of Men* together with *Speech*, Oxford University Press, London, 1964.

Jones, D., *The Phoneme: its Nature and Use*, 3rd ed., Heffer, Cambridge, 1967.

Pike, K. L., *Phonetics*, University of Michigan Press, Ann Arbor, 1943.

————— *Phonemics*, University of Michigan Press, Ann Arbor, 1947.

Principles of the International Phonetic Association, London, 1949.

Westermann, D., and Ward, I. C., *Practical Phonetics for Students of African Languages*, Oxford University Press, London, 1933, reprinted 1964.

ENGLISH PHONETICS

Cohen, A., *The Phonemes of English*, Martinus Nijhoff, The Hague, 1962.

Gimson, A. C., *An Introduction to the Pronunciation of English*, 2nd ed., Edward Arnold, London, 1970.

Jones, Daniel, *An Outline of English Phonetics*, 9th ed., Heffer, Cambridge, 1960, reprinted 1969.

————— *The Pronunciation of English*, 4th ed., Cambridge University Press, 1956; paperback 1966.

————— *An English Pronouncing Dictionary* (ed. A. C. Gimson), 13th ed., Dent, London, 1967.

Kenyon, J. S., *American Pronunciation*, 10th ed., Wahr, Ann Arbor, Michigan, 1950.

————— and Knott, T. A., *A Pronouncing Dictionary of American English*, Merriam, Springfield, Mass., 1953.

Lewis, J. W., *A Guide to English Pronunciation*, Oslo University Press, 1969.

MacCarthy, P. A. D., *English Pronunciation*, 4th ed., Heffer, Cambridge, 1959, reprinted 1967.

Miller, G. M., *BBC Pronouncing Dictionary of British Names*, Oxford University Press, 1971.

O'Connor, J. D., *Better English Pronunciation*, Cambridge University Press, 1967, paperback 1971.

Orton, H., and Dieth, E., *Survey of English Dialects*, E. J. Arnold, Leeds, 1962.

Pitman, J., and St John, J., *Alphabets and Reading: the Initial Teaching Alphabet*, Pitman, 1969.

Pring, J. T., *Colloquial English Pronunciation*, Longmans, London, 1959, reprinted 1970.

Quirk, R., *The Use of English*, 2nd ed., Longmans, London, 1968.

Silvertsen, E., *Cockney Phonology*, Oslo University Press, 1960.

Strevens, P. D., *Spoken Language*, Longmans, London, 1956.

Thomas, C. K., *Introduction to the Phonetics of American English*, 2nd ed., Ronald Press, New York, 1958.

ENGLISH STRESS AND INTONATION

Armstrong, L. E., and Ward, I. C., *A Handbook of English Intonation*, 2nd ed., Heffer, Cambridge, 1931, last reprint 1967.

Crystal, D., *Prosodic Systems and Intonation in English*, Cambridge University Press, 1969.

Halliday, M. A. K., *Intonation and Grammar in British English*, Mouton, The Hague, 1967.

Hill, L. A., *Stress and Intonation Step by Step*, Oxford University Press, London, 1965.

Kingdon, R., *The Groundwork of English Intonation*, Longmans, London, 1958.

—— *The Groundwork of English Stress*, Longmans, London, 1958.

Lee, W. R., *An English Intonation Reader*, Macmillan, London, 1960.

MacCarthy, P. A. D., *English Intonation Reader*, Longmans, London, 1956.

O'Connor, J. D., and Arnold, G. F., *Intonation of Colloquial English*, Longmans, London, 1961.

Schubiger, M., *English Intonation: its Form and Function*, Niemeyer, Tübingen, 1958.

ENGLISH PHONETIC READERS

Abercrombie, D., *English Phonetic Texts*, Faber, London, 1964.

Arnold, G. F., and Gimson, A. C., *English Pronunciation Practice*, University of London Press, 1965.

Jones, Daniel, *Phonetic Readings in English*, Winter, Heidelberg, 1956.

O'Connor, J. D., *New Phonetic Readings from Modern English Literature*, Francke, Bern, 1948.

Scott, N. C., *English Conversations*, Heffer, Cambridge, 2nd ed., 1965, reprinted 1969.

Tibbitts, E. L., *Practice Material for the English Sounds*, Heffer, Cambridge, 1963.

JOURNALS

Journal of the International Phonetic Association (formerly *Le Maître Phonétique*), London.

English Language Teaching, Oxford University Press, London.

British Journal of Disorders of Communication, College of Speech Therapists, London.

Transactions of the Scottish Dialect Committee.

Transactions of the Yorkshire Dialect Society.

Transactions of the Philological Society. Certain papers on English Dialects.

INDEX

The Index is in two parts, (*a*) subjects, (*b*) phonetic. The phonetic symbols are given in the order shown in the list of symbols at the beginning of the book.

The numbers indicate paragraphs.

Accent, 5, 286, **321**

"Africa" script, note on, p. 35.

Affricative Consonants: formation, 252–3; diagrams of, 252; English, 254

Analogy: false, **41**

Assimilation: 66; modern tendencies in, 66, 69, 329; definition, 330; illustrations of, 338–48; affecting vocal chords, 339; affecting soft palate, 340; affecting tongue, 341; diagram illustrating, 343; affecting lips, 346; in phrases, 348; historical, 331; juxtapositional, **331–3**

Bi-labial *f* and *v*, 84(*c*)

Bilingualism, 13

Breath, **74, 75**

Broadcasting: influence of, 14; Committee on Pron., 33; intonation in, 364.

Broadcast Speech Lessons, 31; in Scotland, 31

Cardinal Vowels, 93; gramophone records of, 93; figure in common use, 94n; tongue positions of, 95; diagram of, 95; use of, 97;
and English vowels, 98; numbers of, 99.

Class distinctions, 10; dialect, 4

Clear l (and dark), 107, 109, 262–4, 268, 367

Cockney Speech, 294, p. 194n; *see also* Consonants and Vowels

Colleges of Education, 12; Appendix I

Consonants: insertion of, 65; dropping of, 65, 355–6; definition of, 89; English consonants in detail, 236–85; classification of, 236; diagram of, 238; voiced and voiceless, 238; voiced cons. in initial and final positions, 239; plosive, 240–51; affricative, 252–4; nasal, 255–9; lateral, 261–8; rolled, 269, 271–2; fricative, 275–8; American, 367–70, 383

Correction: of pronunciation, 12; method of, 115–16; principles of, 115–16

Dark l: 107, 109; 262–4; **268**

Dialect: local, 4, 11; class, 4; pronunciation (see under headings of each sound), 24–5

Diphthongs: definition, 191; falling, 192; representation of, 192; English diphthongs numbered, 193; on Cardinal figure, 194; drawling of, 226
Dissimilation, 66, 69, 345
Drawling, 226, 294; cure of, 295
Dropping one's g's, 260
Dropping one's h's, 65, 278 (vii)

Ear Training: use of, 44–5; exercises in, Appendixes I(c) and II
Eighteenth Century Grammarians, 63–5
Elphinston: *Inglish Orthoggraphy Epittomized*, 65
Emphasis: 288, 298, 310–16.
English Language: prestige of, 9

Faucal or Nasal Plosion, 247–8
Fricative Consonants: formation, 275–6; English, 277; notes on, 278

Glottal stop: drawing of, 75; use of, 250(d); in dialectal speech, 250(d); to avoid, 251
Glottis, 72
Grant: *Pronunciation of English in Scotland*, 151n, 159, 163
Gullet, 72

h: dropping of, 65, 278(vii)
His Majesty King George V, 28, 317; Broadcast Message to the Empire, 379–80

Intelligibility: mutual, 7; limit of, 8, 20
Intonation: 301–21; definition; 301; varieties of, 302–3, 319–20; "Tunes," 304; Tune I, 304–7, Tune II, 304, 308–10; Emphatic, 311–15; for Intensity, 312; of King George V, 317; American, 374, 375–8; of President Roosevelt, 385; changes in, 364; Northern and Southern compared, 319

Jespersen: *Modern English Grammar*, 163n
Jones, Daniel: pronunciation cone 7; cardinal vowels, 93
Jones: *Expert Orthographer*, 65

Labio-dental nasal, 353
Language: auxiliary, 4
Larynx, 72, 75
Lateral Consonants: formation, 261; English, 262–3; syllabic, 265; voiceless, 266, 334
Lateral Plosion, 249
Laxness, 102
Length: of sounds, 293; rules of, 293; of American vowels, 372; modern tendencies, 361(vi), 362
Lips, 72; use in formation of speech sounds, 84,85; exercises for control of, 86; use of in formation of vowels, 100–1; photographs of, 100

Microphone Technique, 26

Nasal Consonants: formation, 255–6; voiceless, 257; syllabic, 258

Nasal, or Faucal Plosion, 247–8

Nasal sounds, 78

Nasal vowels, 231–2; cure of, 233–4; in American speech, 373, 382

Nasalised sounds, 78

Nasality: cure of 233–5

Northern speech: ɑ and æ in N. speech, 142; strong forms in, 327–8

Northern and Southern Speech: summary of main differences, 283–5

Organs of speech: training of, 46; use in formation of sounds, 71; movable, 73

Palate: hard, 72; soft, 72, 78–9

Pharynx, 72; nasal, 72

Phoneme: 103; definition of, 103; illustration of, 104; existence of, 108; importance of knowledge of, 108.

Phonetician: work of, 57

Phonetics: use of, in teaching of English, 57; in teaching of elocution and singing, 57; in curing speech defects, 58; in teaching the deaf, 59; in teaching of reading, 59; in study of Philology, 60

Phonetic Alphabet, 51; use of, 52; use of in study of dialects, 54; use of for ear-training, 55

Phonetic Dictionary: use of, 51; limitations of, 51

Phonetic Theory: use of, 47; limitations of, 50; App. I (b)

Phonetic Transcription: use of, 51; interpretation of, 53; criticism of, 53

Pitch: 289, 290, 301

Plosive consonants: formation, 240; voiceless, 241; aspiration of, voiceless plosives, 241; over-aspiration of, 242; cure of over-aspiration, 243; incomplete, 245–6; notes on, 250

Practical work: App. I (d)

President Roosevelt: Broadcast speech, 381–5

Prominence: 286–7, 290–1; special, 288; and intonation, 289–90; and neutral vowels, 289 (5), 290

Pronunciation: standard, 1, 20–1, 30; slovenly, 5; cone, 7; educated, 8; Received, 8, 11; correction of, 12; B.B.C. committee on, 14, 33; spelling, 61–70; changes in, 61, 358ff.; variant, 105 (see also under headings of each sound); American, 365ff.; of announcers, 21, 23

r sounds: 269–74; different kinds of, 271; rolled r, 269, 271–2; semi-rolled r, 271 (ii); fricative r, 271 (iii); inverted r, 271 (iv); uvular r, 271 (v); linking r, 273; intrusive r, 274, 360

Rhythm: 28; 285; 296, 298; 328; American, 374, 376–8

Rolled consonants: formation of, 269; lingual rolled r, 271; uvular r, 271 (v); teaching of rolled r, 272

Semi-vowels: 279–82

Semi-weak vowels: 186–8

Sense-group, 28, 322

Similitude: 334, 337; examples of, 349–54

Soft palate: two positions of, 78; functions of, 78; exercises for control of, 79

Sonority, 87

Sound attributes, 286ff.

Sounds and letters, 19

Sounds: use of sounds not found in educated speech, 34; insertion of, 34; omission of, 34; use of wrongly formed, 36; use of normal sounds in wrong places, 37; classification of, 87–90

Speech: differences of, 34; organs of, 71ff.; unit of, 322

Speech sounds, formation of, 74; classification of, 87–90; definition of, 103

Speech Training: suggested course of, 12; App. I

Spelling Pronunciations, 61–70; modern tendencies in, 69

Spoken word, 18, 19, 30

Standard: Pronunciation, 1; English, 2, 5, 15

Stress: 286, 289–91; word stress 296–7; sentence stress, 296–300; meaning, 297; of compound words, 299–300; and rhythm, 298(e); influence of, 324–5

Strong forms: 325–7; misuse of, 326; in Northern speech, 327–8

Strong and weak forms, 42, 184–6, 289 (5), 324–6

Teacher: work of, 38; the phonetically trained, 40

Teaching of English in England: Committee on, 2; Report on, 2

Teeth: 72; ridge, 72

Tenseness, 102

Tongue: blade of, 72; front of, 72; back of, 72; root of, 72; use in formation of speech sounds, 80; exercises for control of, 81, 82; spreading and contraction of, 81; tenseness and laxness of, 82, 102

Triphthongs, 227 ff

Unvoiced vowels, 278 (vi)

Uvula, 72

Uvular r, 271 (v)

Vocal cords: 72; description of, 75; drawings of, 75; exercises for control of, 76

Voice: 75; training, App. I (a)

Voiced consonants: in initial and final positions, 239

Voiced and voiceless consonants, 76, 238

Voiceless l, m, n, ŋ, r: 76, 77, 238; w, 281

Vowel quality, 91, 289 (5)

Vowels: change of pronunciation due to spelling, 67; nasal, 79; definition of, 88; classification of 91; front, 91; back, 91; central, 91; close, 91; half-close, 91; half-open, 91; open, 91; cardinal 93–101; comparison of, 94; English vowels in detail, 113–90

Vowels: English vowels numbered, 113; English vowels placed on Cardinal figure, 117; semi-weak, 186–8; nasalisation of, 231–35; neutral, 181–6, 324–6

Whisper, 75

Windpipe, 72

Written word, 18, 19

Wyld: *History of Modern Colloquial English*, 64; *Studies in English Rhymes*, 64; on spelling pron., 64; on weak vowels, 327

Yorkshire speech: illustration of, 388 ff; *see also* description of vowels and consonants.

PHONETIC INDEX

i: phoneme, 118–19; variant pron. of, 120; teaching of, 121; in unstressed positions, 122

ɪ: phoneme, 124–5, 131; final, 126–7; in final closed syllable, 128; alternative pron. of unstressed ɪ; teaching of, 132

ɛ: phoneme, 133–4; variant pron. 135; teaching of, 136–7

æ: phoneme, 138-40; variant pron. of, 141; teaching of, 142

ɑ: phoneme, 141–2; variant pron. of, 143; teaching of, 144; ɑ-æ is N and S pron., 145

ɒ: phoneme, 149-50; variant pron. of, 151; teaching of, 152; ɒ and ɔ, alternative pron. of, 153–4

ɔ: phoneme, 157–8; variant pron. 159–164; teaching of, 160; in *or, ore, oar, oor, our* words, 161; variants of these, 162–3

ʊ: phoneme, 165–6; variant pron. of, 167–8

u: phoneme, 169–70; variant pron. of, 171; teaching of, 172

ʌ: phoneme 173–4; variant pron. of, 175; northern pron. of 175 (note); teaching of, 176

ɜ: phoneme, 177–8; variant pron. of, 179; teaching of, 180

ə: phoneme, 181–2; variant pron. of, 183; in weak forms, 184–6

eɪ: phoneme, 195; variant pron. of, 196; teaching of, 197

oʊ: phoneme, 199; variant pron. of, 200; teaching of, 201; unstressed, alternative pron. 202

aɪ: phoneme, 203; variant pron. of, 204; teaching of, 207

aʊ: phoneme, 208; variant pron. of, 209–10, teaching of, 211

ɔɪ: phoneme, 212; variant pron. of, 213; teaching of, 214

ɪə: phoneme, 215; variant pron. of, 216; teaching of, 217

ɛə: phoneme, 218; variant pron. of, 219; teaching of, 220

ɔə: phoneme, 221; variant pron. of, 161–2

ʊə: phoneme, 223; variant pron. of, 224; teaching of, 225–6

aɪə: 227–8

aʊə: 227–8

p: formation, 240–42; aspiration of, 241–3; unexploded, 245

b: formation, 240–4; unexploded, 245

t: formation, 240; aspiration of, 241–3; unexploded, 245; dental, 250 (a); dropping of, 65 (b); used instead of k, 336

d: formation, 240; unexploded, 245; dental, 250 (a); substitution for t, 250 (b); dropping of 65 (b); used instead of g, 336

k: formation, 240; aspiration of, 241–2; unexploded 245; dropping of, 65 (a).

g: formation, 240.

tʃ: formation, 252; 254

dʒ: formation, 252; 254

m: formation, 255; voiceless, 76; 77 (d); 257; syllabic, 258

n: formation, 255; voiceless, 76, 77 (d); syllabic, 258

ŋ, formation, 255; syllabic, 258; substitution of ŋg in Midland pronunciation, 260

l: clear, 107; formation of, 261–64; 268; dark, 107; overdark l, 267; influence of, 268; correction of overdark l, 268, voiceless, 76, 77, 266; with other vowel resonances, 264; syllabic, 265

r: rolled, 269; semi-rolled, 271 (ii); fricative, 271 (iii); inverted, 271 (iv); uvular, 271 (v); linking, 273; intrusive, 274

f: formation, 275; replaced by v, 278(i).

v: formation, 275

θ: formation, 275, replaced by f, 278(iv); dropping of, 278(v)

ð: formation, 275; replaced by v 278(iv); dropping of, 278(v)

s: formation, 275

z: formation, 275

ʃ: formation, 275

ʒ: formative, 275

h: insertion of, 65(g); dropping of, 65, 278(vii); formation, 278(vi); voiced, 278(vi)

w: formation, 280; voiceless, 281

ʍ: use of, 65 (i), 281

j: formation, 282; voiceless, 282

ʔ: diagram, 75; use of, 250(d); in dialectal speech, 250(e); to avoid, 251